ADOBE® DREAMWEAVER® CS5
CLASSROOM IN A BOOK®

The official training workbook from Adobe Systems

www.adobepress.com

Adobe

Writer: James J. Maivald
Project Editor: Nancy Peterson
Production Editor: Cory Borman
Development Editor: Robyn G. Thomas
Technical Editors: Lynn Grillo, Clint Funk
Copyeditors: Darren Meiss and Scout Festa
Compositor: WolfsonDesign
Indexer: Jack Lewis
Media Producer: Eric Geoffroy
Cover Design: Eddie Yuen
Interior Design: Mimi Heft

Printed and bound in the United States of America

ISBN-13:   978-0-321-70177-0

ISBN-10:   0-321-70177-1

9 8 7 6 5 4 3 2 1

WHAT'S ON THE DISC

Here is an overview of the contents of the Classroom in a Book disc

The *Adobe Dreamweaver CS5 Classroom in a Book* disc includes the lesson files that you'll need to complete the exercises in this book, as well as other content to help you learn more about Adobe Dreamweaver CS5 and use it with greater efficiency and ease. The diagram below represents the contents of the disc, which should help you locate the files you need.

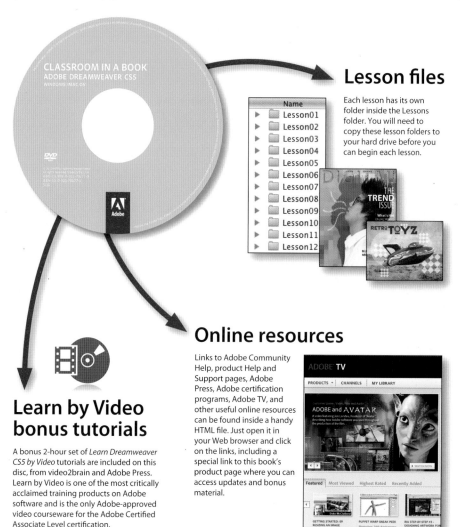

Lesson files

Each lesson has its own folder inside the Lessons folder. You will need to copy these lesson folders to your hard drive before you can begin each lesson.

Name
▶ 📁 Lesson01
▶ 📁 Lesson02
▶ 📁 Lesson03
▶ 📁 Lesson04
▶ 📁 Lesson05
▶ 📁 Lesson06
▶ 📁 Lesson07
▶ 📁 Lesson08
▶ 📁 Lesson09
▶ 📁 Lesson10
▶ 📁 Lesson11
▶ 📁 Lesson12

CLASSROOM IN A BOOK
ADOBE DREAMWEAVER CS5
WINDOWS/MAC OS

Online resources

Links to Adobe Community Help, product Help and Support pages, Adobe Press, Adobe certification programs, Adobe TV, and other useful online resources can be found inside a handy HTML file. Just open it in your Web browser and click on the links, including a special link to this book's product page where you can access updates and bonus material.

Learn by Video bonus tutorials

A bonus 2-hour set of *Learn Dreamweaver CS5 by Video* tutorials are included on this disc, from video2brain and Adobe Press. Learn by Video is one of the most critically acclaimed training products on Adobe software and is the only Adobe-approved video courseware for the Adobe Certified Associate Level certification.

CONTENTS

GETTING STARTED

Adobe® Dreamweaver® CS5 is the industry-leading web authoring program. Whether you create websites for a living or plan to create one for your own business, Dreamweaver offers all the tools you need to get professional-quality results.

About Classroom in a Book

Adobe Dreamweaver CS5 Classroom in a Book® is part of the official training series for graphics and publishing software developed with the support of Adobe product experts.

The lessons are designed so that you can learn at your own pace. If you're new to Dreamweaver, you'll learn the fundamentals of putting the program to work. If you are an experienced user, you'll find that *Classroom in a Book* teaches many advanced features, including tips and techniques for using the latest version of Dreamweaver.

Although each lesson includes step-by-step instructions for creating a specific project, you'll have room for exploration and experimentation. You can follow the book from start to finish, or complete only those lessons that correspond to your interests and needs. Each lesson concludes with a Review section containing questions and answers on the subjects you've covered.

Prerequisites

Before using *Adobe Dreamweaver CS5 Classroom in a Book*, you should have a working knowledge of your computer and its operating system. Be sure you know how to use the mouse, standard menus, and commands, and also how to open, save, and close files. If you need to review these techniques, see the printed or online documentation that was included with your Microsoft Windows or Apple Macintosh operating system.

Installing the program

Before you perform any exercises in this book, verify that your computer system meets the hardware requirements for Dreamweaver CS5, that it's correctly configured, and that all required software is installed.

Adobe Dreamweaver CS5 software is not included on the disc; you must purchase it separately as a stand-alone product or as part of one of the Creative Suite editions. For complete instructions on installing the software, see the "How to Install" file on the Adobe Dreamweaver CD.

Copying the Classroom in a Book files

The *Classroom in a Book* CD includes folders containing all the files necessary for the lessons. Each lesson has a folder that contains the files and assets needed to complete the lesson. You must install these folders on your hard disk to perform the exercises in each lesson. It is recommended that you copy all lesson folders to your hard drive at once but, to conserve space on your hard disk, you can install individual folders for each lesson as you need them. It is vitally important that you store all lesson folders within a single folder on your hard drive. If you follow the recommended lesson order, this master folder will serve as the local site root folder, as described more fully in Lesson 4.

To install the *Classroom in a Book* files:

1   Insert the *Adobe Dreamweaver CS5 Classroom in a Book* CD into your computer's optical disc drive.

2   Navigate to the CD/DVD drive on your computer.

3   If you intend to complete all lessons in the book in order, drag the Lessons folder to your computer hard drive. Otherwise, skip to step 5.

    The *Lessons* folder contains all the individual lesson folders and other assets needed for the training.

4   Rename the *Lessons* folder **DW-CIB**.

    This folder will be the local site root folder.

5   If you desire to perform one or more lessons individually, copy each lesson folder to your hard drive as separate folders, as needed. Then, proceed to the "Jumpstart" section for more instructions.

    The files and folders for each lesson cannot be used interchangeably.

Recommended lesson order

The training herein is designed to take you from A to Z in basic to intermediate website design, development, and production. Each new lesson builds on previous exercises, using the files and assets you create to develop an entire website. It is recommended that you perform each lesson in sequential order to achieve a successful result and the most complete understanding of all aspects of web design.

The ideal training scenario will start in Lesson 1 and proceed through the entire book to Lesson 17. Since each lesson builds essential files and content for the next, once you start this scenario you shouldn't skip any lessons, or even individual exercises. While ideal, this method may not be a practicable scenario for every user. So, if desired, individual lessons can be accomplished using the jumpstart method described in the next section.

Jumpstart

For users who don't have the time or inclination to perform each lesson in the book in order, or who are having difficulty with a particular lesson, a jumpstart method is included to facilitate the performance of individual lessons in or out of sequence. Once you start using the jumpstart method, you will have to use this method for all subsequent lessons. For example, if you want to jumpstart Lesson 6, you will have to jumpstart Lesson 7, too. In many instances, essential files needed for subsequent exercises were built in earlier lessons and exercises and may not be present in a jumpstart environment.

Each lesson folder includes all the files and assets needed to complete the exercises contained within that lesson. Each folder contains finished files, staged files, and customized Template and Library files. You may think these folders contain seemingly duplicative materials. But these duplicate files and assets, in most cases, cannot be used interchangeably in other lessons and exercises. Doing so will probably cause you to fail to achieve the goal of the exercise.

The jumpstart method for completing individual lessons treats each folder as a stand-alone website. To jumpstart a lesson, copy the lesson folder to your hard drive and create a new site for that lesson using the Site Setup dialog box. Keep your jumpstart sites and assets in their original folders to avoid conflicts. One suggestion is to organize the lesson folders, as well as your own site folders, in a single *webs* or *sites* master folder near the root of your hard drive. But avoid using the Dreamweaver application folder or any folders that contain a web server, like Apache, ColdFusion, or Internet Information Services (IIS).

Feel free to use the jumpstart method for all lessons if you prefer.

To set up a jumpstart site, do the following:

1 Choose Site > New Site.

  The Site Setup dialog box appears.

2 In the Site Name field, enter the name of the lesson, such as **lesson06**.

3 Next to the Local Site Folder field, click the Browse (📁) icon. Navigate to the lesson folder you copied from the *Adobe Dreamweaver CS5 Classroom in a Book* CD and click Select/Choose.

4 Click the arrow (▶) next to the Advanced Settings category to reveal the tabs listed there. Select the Local Info category.

5 Next to the Default Images Folder field, click the Browse icon. When the dialog box opens, navigate to the Images folder contained within the lesson folder and click Select/Choose.

6 In the Site Setup dialog box, click Save.

7 The name of the currently active website will appear in the Files panel Show pop-up menu. If necessary, press Ctrl-Shift-F/Cmd-Shift-F to display the Files panel and select the desired website from the Show menu.

These steps will have to be repeated for each lesson you wish to jumpstart. For a more complete description of how to set up a site in Dreamweaver, see Lesson 4, "Getting a Quick Start."

Setting up the workspace

Dreamweaver includes a number of workspaces to accommodate various computer configurations and individual workflows. For this book, the Designer workspace is recommended.

1 In Dreamweaver CS5, locate the Application bar. If necessary, choose Window > Application Bar to display it.

2 The default workspace is called Designer. If it is not displayed, use the pop-up menu in the Application bar to choose it.

Most of the book's images show the Designer workspace. When you finish the lessons in this book, experiment using various workspaces to find the one that you prefer.

For a more complete description of the Dreamweaver workspaces, see Lesson 1, "Customizing Your Workspace."

Windows vs. Macintosh instructions

In most cases, Dreamweaver performs identically in both Windows and Mac OS X. Minor differences exist between the two versions, mostly due to platform-specific issues out of the control of the program. Most of these are simply differences in keyboard shortcuts, how dialog boxes are displayed, and how buttons are named. Screen shots alternate between platforms throughout the book. Where specific commands differ, they are noted within the text. Windows commands are listed first, followed by the Macintosh equivalent, such as Ctrl-C/Cmd-C. Common abbreviations are used for all commands whenever possible, as follows:

WINDOWS	MACINTOSH
Control = Ctrl	Command = Cmd
Alternate = Alt	Option = Opt

Finding Dreamweaver information

For complete, up-to-date information about Dreamweaver panels, tools, and other application features, visit the Adobe website. Choose Help > Dreamweaver Help. The Adobe Help application opens and downloads the latest Help files from the Adobe Community Help website. These files are cached locally so you can access them even when you are not connected to the Internet. You can also download a PDF version of the Dreamweaver Help files from the Adobe Help application

For additional information resources, such as tips, techniques, and the latest product information, visit www.adobe.com/support/dreamweaver to access the Adobe Community Help page.

Checking for updates

Adobe periodically provides software updates. You can obtain these updates using Adobe Updater if you have an active Internet connection.

1 In Dreamweaver, choose Help > Updates. The Adobe Updater automatically checks for updates for your Adobe software.

2 In the Adobe Updater dialog box, select the updates you want to install and then click Download And Install Updates to install them.

Note: If Dreamweaver detects that you are not connected to the Internet when you open the application, choose Help > Dreamweaver Help to open the Help HTML pages that are installed with Dreamweaver. For more up-to-date information, view the online Help files or download the current Dreamweaver Help PDF.

Note: To choose preferences for future updates, click Preferences. You can choose how often Adobe Updater should check for updates, identify applications to be updated, and choose whether to download updates automatically. Click OK to accept the new settings.

Additional resources

Adobe Dreamweaver CS5 Classroom in a Book is not meant to replace documentation that comes with the program or to be a comprehensive reference for every feature. Only the commands and options used in the lessons are explained in this book. For comprehensive information about program features and tutorials, refer to these resources:

Adobe Community Help: Community Help brings together active Adobe product users, Adobe product team members, authors, and experts to give you the most useful, relevant, and up-to-date information about Adobe products. Whether you're looking for a code sample or an answer to a problem, have a question about the software, or want to share a useful tip or recipe, you'll benefit from Community Help. Search results will show you not only content from Adobe, but also from the community.

With Adobe Community Help you can:

- Access up-to-date definitive reference content online and offline
- Find the most relevant content contributed by experts from the Adobe community, on and off Adobe.com
- Comment on, rate, and contribute to content in the Adobe community
- Download Help content directly to your desktop for offline use
- Find related content with dynamic search and navigation tools

To access Community Help: If you have any Adobe CS5 product, then you already have the Community Help application. To invoke Help, choose Help > Dreamweaver Help. This companion application lets you search and browse Adobe and community content, plus you can comment on and rate any article just like you would in the browser. However, you can also download Adobe Help and language reference content for use offline. You can also subscribe to new content updates (which can be automatically downloaded) so that you'll always have the most up-to-date content for your Adobe product at all times. You can download the application from www.adobe.com/support/chc/index.html.

Adobe content is updated based on community feedback and contributions. You can contribute in several ways: add comments to content or forums, including links to web content; publish your own content using Community Publishing; or contribute Cookbook Recipes. Find out how to contribute: www.adobe.com/community/publishing/download.html.

See http://community.adobe.com/help/profile/faq.html for answers to frequently asked questions about Community Help.

Adobe Dreamweaver Help and Support: www.adobe.com/support/dreamweaver is where you can find and browse Help and Support content on adobe.com.

Adobe TV: http://tv.adobe.com is an online video resource for expert instruction and inspiration about Adobe products, including a How To channel to get you started with your product.

Adobe Design Center: www.adobe.com/designcenter offers thoughtful articles on design and design issues, a gallery showcasing the work of top-notch designers, tutorials, and more.

Adobe Developer Connection: www.adobe.com/devnet is your source for technical articles, code samples, and how-to videos that cover Adobe developer products and technologies.

Resources for educators: www.adobe.com/education includes three free curriculums that use an integrated approach to teaching Adobe software and can be used to prepare for the Adobe Certified Associate exams.

Also check out these useful links:

Adobe Forums: http://forums.adobe.com lets you tap into peer-to-peer discussions, questions, and answers on Adobe products.

Adobe Marketplace & Exchange: www.adobe.com/cfusion/exchange is a central resource for finding tools, services, extensions, code samples, and more to supplement and extend your Adobe products.

Adobe Dreamweaver CS5 product home page: www.adobe.com/products/dreamweaver

Adobe Labs: http://labs.adobe.com gives you access to early builds of cutting-edge technology, as well as forums where you can interact with both the Adobe development teams building that technology and other like-minded members of the community.

Adobe certification

The Adobe training and certification programs are designed to help Adobe customers improve and promote their product-proficiency skills. There are four levels of certification:

- Adobe Certified Associate (ACA)
- Adobe Certified Expert (ACE)
- Adobe Certified Instructor (ACI)
- Adobe Authorized Training Center (AATC)

The Adobe Certified Associate (ACA) credential certifies that individuals have the entry-level skills to plan, design, build, and maintain effective communications using different forms of digital media.

The Adobe Certified Expert program is a way for expert users to upgrade their credentials. You can use Adobe certification as a catalyst for getting a raise, finding a job, or promoting your expertise.

If you are an ACE-level instructor, the Adobe Certified Instructor program takes your skills to the next level and gives you access to a wide range of Adobe resources.

Adobe Authorized Training Centers offer instructor-led courses and training on Adobe products, employing only Adobe Certified Instructors. Check out http://partners.adobe.com/public/partnerfinder/tp/show_find.do for a directory of AATCs.

For information on the Adobe Certified programs, visit www.adobe.com/support/certification/.

Accelerate your workflow with Adobe CS Live

Adobe CS Live is a set of online services that harness the connectivity of the web and integrate with Adobe Creative Suite 5 to simplify the creative review process, speed up website compatibility testing, deliver important web user intelligence, and more, allowing you to focus on creating your most impactful work. CS Live services are complimentary for a limited time* and can be accessed online or from within Creative Suite 5 applications.

Adobe BrowserLab is for web designers and developers who need to preview and test their web pages on multiple browsers and operating systems. Unlike other browser compatibility solutions, BrowserLab renders screenshots virtually on demand with multiple viewing and diagnostic tools, and can be used with Dreamweaver CS5 to preview local content and different states of interactive pages. Being an online service, BrowserLab has fast development cycles, with greater flexibility for expanded browser support and updated functionality.

Adobe CS Review is for creative professionals who want a new level of efficiency in the creative review process. Unlike other services that offer online review of creative content, only CS Review lets you publish a review to the web directly from within InDesign, Photoshop, Photoshop Extended, and Illustrator and view reviewer comments back in the originating Creative Suite application.

Acrobat.com is for creative professionals who need to work with a cast of colleagues and clients in order to get a creative project from creative brief to final product. Acrobat.com is a set of online services that includes web conferencing, online file sharing, and workspaces. Unlike collaborating via e-mail and attending time-consuming in-person meetings, Acrobat.com brings people to your work instead of sending files to people, so you can get the business side of the creative process done faster, together, from any location.

Adobe Story is for creative professionals, producers, and writers working on or with scripts. Story is a collaborative script development tool that turns scripts into metadata that can be used with the Adobe CS5 Production Premium tools to streamline workflows and create video assets.

SiteCatalyst NetAverages is for web and mobile professionals who want to optimize their projects for wider audiences. NetAverages provides intelligence on how users are accessing the web, which helps reduce guesswork early in the creative process. You can access aggregate user data such as browser type, operating system, mobile device profile, screen resolution, and more, which can be shown over time. The data is derived from visitor activity to participating Omniture SiteCatalyst customer sites. Unlike other web intelligence solutions, NetAverages innovatively displays data using Flash, creating an engaging experience that is robust yet easy to follow.

You can access CS Live three different ways:

1 Set up access when you register your Creative Suite 5 products and get complimentary access that includes all of the features and workflow benefits of using CS Live with CS5.

2 Sign up online and get complimentary access to CS Live services for a limited time. Note, this option does not give you access to the services from within your products.

3 Desktop product trials include a 30-day trial of CS Live services.

CS Live services are complimentary for a limited time. See www.adobe.com/go/cslive for details.

1 CUSTOMIZING YOUR WORKSPACE

Lesson Overview

In this lesson, you'll familiarize yourself with the Dreamweaver CS5 (Creative Suite 5) program interface and learn how to:

- Switch views
- Work with panels
- Adjust toolbars
- Select a workspace layout
- Personalize preferences
- Use the Property inspector

 This lesson will take about 40 minutes to complete. Before beginning, make sure you have copied the files for Lesson 4 to your hard drive as described in the "Getting Started" section at the beginning of the book.

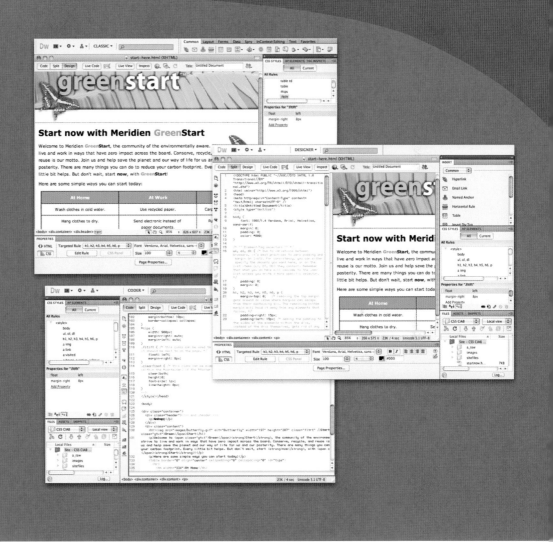

Dreamweaver offers a customizable and easy-to-use WYSIWYG HTML editor that doesn't compromise when it comes to power and flexibility. You'd probably need a dozen programs to perform all the tasks that Dreamweaver can do and none of them would be as fun to use.

Touring the workspace

Dreamweaver is the industry leading Hypertext Markup Language (HTML) editor, with good reasons for its popularity. The program offers an incredible array of design and code-editing tools. Dreamweaver offers something for everyone.

Coders love the variety of enhancements built into the Code view environment, and developers enjoy the program's support for ASP, PHP, ColdFusion, and JavaScript, among other programming languages. Designers marvel at seeing their text and graphics appear in an accurate What You See Is What You Get (WYSIWYG) depiction as they work, saving hours of time previewing pages in browsers. Novices certainly appreciate the program's simple-to-use and power-packed interface. No matter what type of user you are, if you use Dreamweaver you don't have to compromise.

The Dreamweaver interface features a vast array of user-configurable panels and toolbars. Take a moment to familiarize yourself with the names of these components.

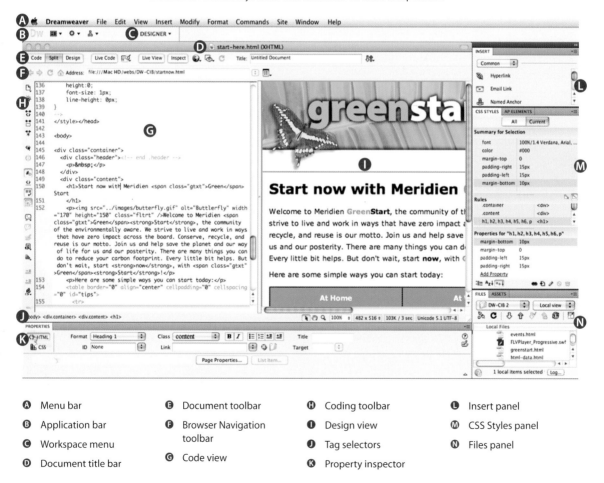

A Menu bar	**E** Document toolbar	**H** Coding toolbar	**L** Insert panel
B Application bar	**F** Browser Navigation toolbar	**I** Design view	**M** CSS Styles panel
C Workspace menu		**J** Tag selectors	**N** Files panel
D Document title bar	**G** Code view	**K** Property inspector	

You'd think a program with this much to offer would be dense, slow, and unwieldy, but you'd be wrong. Dreamweaver provides much of its power via dockable panels and toolbars you can display or hide and arrange in innumerable combinations to create your ideal workspace.

This lesson introduces you to the Dreamweaver interface and gets you in touch with some of the power hiding under the hood. If you want to follow along on the tour, choose File > Open. Navigate to the lesson01 folder and choose **start-here.html**. Click Open.

Switching and splitting views

Dreamweaver offers dedicated environments for coders and designers as well as a composite option that blends both together.

Design view

Design view focuses the Dreamweaver workspace on its WYSIWYG editor, which provides a close, but not perfect, depiction of the web page as it would appear in a browser. To activate Design view, click the Design view button in the Document toolbar.

Design view

Code view

Code view focuses the Dreamweaver workspace exclusively on the HTML code and a variety of code-editing productivity tools. To access Code view, click the Code view button in the Document toolbar.

Code view

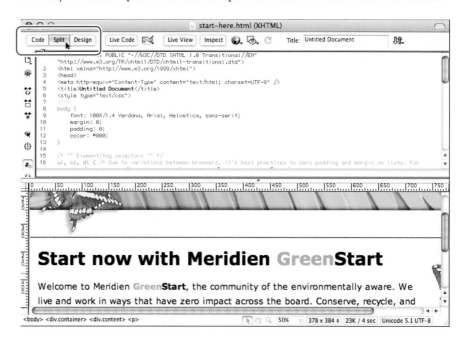

Split view

Split view provides a composite workspace that gives you access to both the design and code simultaneously. Changes made in either window update in the other instantly. To access Split view, click the Split view button in the Document toolbar.

Split view

To take advantage of the expanded width of the new flat-panel displays, Dreamweaver offers the means to split the workspace vertically, as well. To access this feature, choose View > Split Vertically.

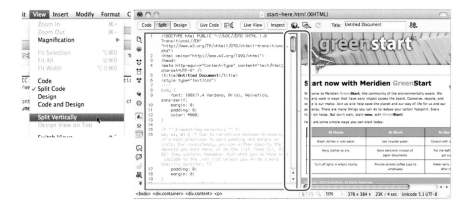

Split view vertically

Working with panels

Although you can access most commands from the menus, Dreamweaver scatters much of its power in user-selectable panels and toolbars. You can display, hide, arrange, and dock panels at will around the screen. You can even move them to a second or third video display if you desire.

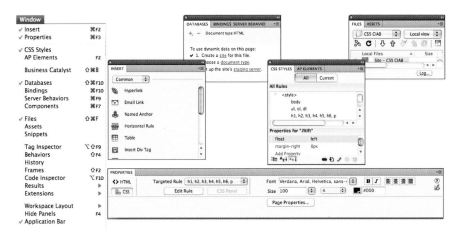

Standard panel grouping

The Window menu lists all the available panels. If you do not see a specific panel on the screen, choose it from the Window menu. A check mark appears in the menu to indicate that the panel is open. Occasionally, one panel may lie behind another on the screen and be difficult to locate. In such situations, simply choose the desired panel in the Window menu and it will rise to the top of the stack.

Minimizing

To create room for other panels or to access obscured areas of the workspace, you can minimize or expand individual panels in place. To minimize a panel, double-click the tab containing the panel name. To expand the panel, double-click the tab again.

Minimizing floating panel by double-clicking the tab

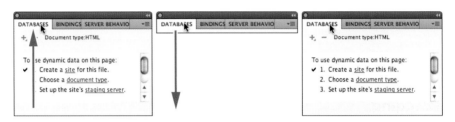

You can also minimize or expand one panel within a stack of panels individually by double-clicking its tab.

Minimizing one panel in a stack using its tab

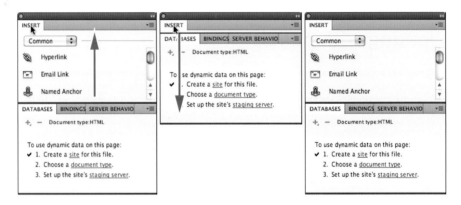

To recover more screen real estate, you can minimize panel groups or stacks down to icons by double-clicking the title bar. When minimized to an icon, you access any of the individual panels by clicking its icon or button. The selected panel will appear on the left or right of your layout wherever room permits.

Minimizing sequence to icons

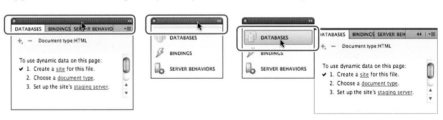

Floating

A panel grouped with other panels can be floated separately. To float a panel, click and drag it from the group by its tab.

Pulling a panel out by its tab

Dragging

You can reorder a panel tab by dragging it to the desired position within the group.

Dragging a tab to change its position

To reposition panels, groups, and stacks in the workspace, simply drag them by the title bar.

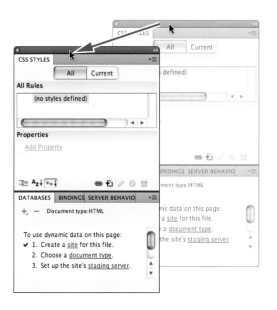

Dragging a whole panel group or stack to a new position

Grouping, stacking, and docking

You can create custom groups by dragging one panel into another. When you've moved the panel to the correct position, Dreamweaver highlights the area, called the drop zone, in blue (as shown in the following figure). Release the mouse button to create the new group.

Creating new groups

In some cases, you may want to keep both panels visible simultaneously. To stack panels, drag the desired tab to the bottom of another panel. When you see the blue drop zone appear, release the mouse button.

Creating panel stacks

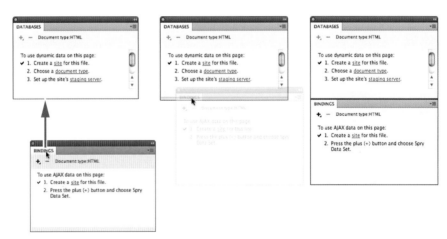

Floating panels can be docked to the right, left, or bottom of the Dreamweaver workspace. To dock a panel, group, or stack, drag its title bar to the edge on which you wish to dock. When you see the blue drop zone appear, release the mouse button.

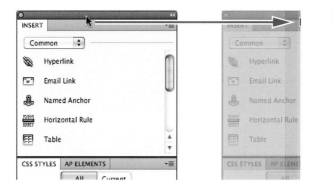

Docking panels

Selecting a workspace layout

A quick way to customize the program environment is to use one of the prebuilt workspaces in Dreamweaver. These workspaces have been optimized by experts to put the tools you need at your fingertips.

Dreamweaver CS5 includes eight prebuilt workspaces. To access these workspaces, choose them from the Workspace menu located in the Application bar.

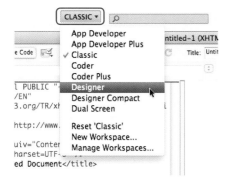

Workspace menu

Long-time users of Dreamweaver may choose the Classic workspace, which displays the panels and toolbars they're accustomed to seeing and using in previous Dreamweaver versions.

Classic workspace

The Coder workspace produces a workspace that focuses Dreamweaver on the HTML code and its code-editing tools.

Coder workspace

The Designer workspace provides the optimum environment for visual designers.

Adjusting toolbars

Some program features are so handy you may want them available all the time in the form of a toolbar. Four of the toolbars—Style Rendering, Document, Standard, and Browser Navigation—appear horizontally at the top of the document window. The Coding toolbar, however, appears vertically, but only in the Code view window. You will explore the capabilities of these toolbars in later exercises.

Display the desired toolbar by selecting it from the View menu.

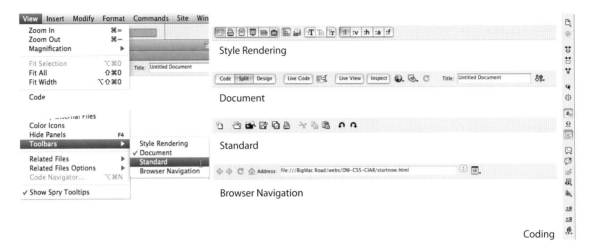

Personalizing preferences

As you continue to work with Dreamweaver, you will devise your own optimal workspace of panels and toolbars for each activity. You can store these configurations in a custom workspace of your own naming.

To save a custom workspace, choose New Workspace from the Workspace menu in the Application bar.

Saving a custom workspace

Creating custom keyboard shortcuts

Another power feature of Dreamweaver is the capability of creating your own keyboard shortcuts and changing existing ones. Keyboard shortcuts are loaded and preserved independent of custom workspaces.

Is there a command you can't live without that doesn't have a keyboard shortcut? Create it yourself. Try this:

1 Choose Dreamweaver > Keyboard Shortcuts.

2 Click the Duplicate Set button to create a new set of shortcuts.

3 Enter a name in the Name of Duplicate Set field. Click OK.

4 Choose Menu commands from the Commands menu.

5 Select Save All from the File command list.

Note that the Save All command does not have an existing shortcut, although you will use the command frequently in Dreamweaver.

6 Insert the cursor in the Press Key field. Press Cmd-Option-S/Ctrl-Alt-S.

Note the error message indicating that the keyboard combination you chose is already assigned to a command. Although we could reassign the combination, let's choose a different one.

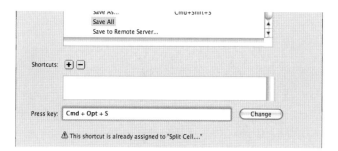

7 Press Ctrl-Cmd-S/Ctrl-Alt-Shift-S.

This combination is not currently being used, so let's assign it to the Save All command.

8 Click the Change button.

The new shortcut is now assigned to the Save All command.

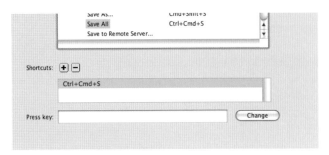

9 Click OK to save the change.

You have created your own keyboard shortcut, and you'll use this shortcut in upcoming lessons.

Using the Property inspector

One tool that is vital to your workflow is the Property inspector. This panel typically appears at the bottom of the workspace. The Property inspector is context driven and adapts to the type of element you select.

Using the HTML tab

Insert the cursor into any text content on your page, and the Property inspector provides a means to quickly assign some basic HTML codes and formatting. When the HTML button is selected, you can apply heading or paragraph tags, as well as bold, italics, bullets, numbers, and indenting, among other formatting and attributes.

HTML Property inspector

Using the CSS tab

Click the CSS (cascading style sheet) button to quickly access commands to assign or edit CSS formatting.

CSS Property inspector

Image properties

Select an image in a web page to access the image-based attributes and formatting control of the Property inspector.

Image Property inspector

Table properties

To access table properties, insert your cursor into a table and then click the table tag selector at the bottom of the document window.

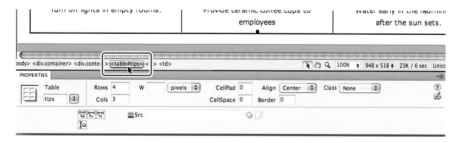

Table Property inspector

Review questions

1 Where can you access the command to display or hide any panel?

2 Where can you find the Code, Design, and Split view buttons?

3 What can be saved in a workspace?

4 Do workspaces also load keyboard shortcuts?

5 What happens in the Property inspector when you insert the cursor into various elements on the web page?

Review answers

1 All panels are listed in the Window menu.

2 These buttons are components of the Document toolbar.

3 Workspaces can save the configuration of the document window, selected panels, size, and their location on the screen.

4 No, keyboard shortcuts are loaded and preserved independently of a workspace.

5 The Property inspector adapts to the selected element, displaying pertinent information and formatting commands.

2 HTML BASICS

Lesson Overview

In this lesson, you'll familiarize yourself with HTML and learn how to:

- Write HTML code by hand

- Understand HTML syntax

- Insert code elements

- Format text

- Add HTML structure

- Create HTML with Dreamweaver

 This lesson will take about 45 minutes to complete. There are no support files for this lesson.

HTML is the backbone of the web, the skeleton of your web page. Like the bones in your body, it is the structure and substance of the Internet, although it is usually unseen except by the web designer. Without it, the web would not exist. Dreamweaver has many features that help you access, create, and edit HTML code quickly and effectively.

21

What is HTML?

"What other programs can open a Dreamweaver file?"

This question was asked by a student in a recent class; although it might seem obvious to an experienced developer, it illustrates a basic problem in teaching and learning web design. Most people confuse the program with the technology. They assume that the extension .htm or .html belongs to Dreamweaver or Adobe. For example, designers are used to working with files ending with .ai, .psd, .indd, and so on. These are proprietary file formats created by programs that have specific capabilities and limitations. The goal in most cases is to create a final printed piece. The program in which the file was created provides the power to interpret the code that produces the printed page. Designers have learned over time that opening these file formats in a different program may produce unacceptable results.

On the other hand, the goal of the web designer is to create a web page for display in a browser. The power and/or functionality of the originating program has little bearing on the resulting browser display, because the display is all contingent on the HTML code and how the browser interprets it. Although a program may write good or bad code, it's the browser that does all the hard work.

The web is based on Hypertext Markup Language (HTML). The language and the file format don't belong to any individual program or company. In fact, it is a non-proprietary, plain-text language that can be edited in any text editor, in any operating system, on any computer. Dreamweaver is an HTML editor at its core, although it is much more than this. But to maximize the potential of Dreamweaver, you first need to have a good understanding of what HTML is and what it can and can't do. This chapter is intended as a concise primer for HTML and its capabilities and as a foundation for understanding Dreamweaver.

Where did HTML begin?

HTML and the first browser were invented in the early 1990s by Tim Berners-Lee, a scientist working at the CERN (Conseil Européen pour la Recherche Nucléaire, which is French for European Council for Nuclear Research) particle physics laboratory in Geneva, Switzerland. He intended the technology as a means for sharing technical papers and information via the fledgling Internet that existed at the time. He shared his HTML and browser inventions openly as an attempt to get the scientific community at large and others to adopt it and engage in the development themselves. The fact that he did not copyright or try to sell his work started a trend for openness and camaraderie on the web that continues today.

The language that Berners-Lee created almost 20 years ago was a much simpler construct of what we use now, but HTML is still surprisingly easy to learn and master. Basically, HTML consists of less than 100 code elements, such as html, head, body, h1, p and so on. These elements are used to enclose, or mark up, text and graphics to enable a browser to display them in a specified way. Some elements are used to create page structures, others to format text, and yet others enable interactivity and programmability. Even though Dreamweaver obviates the need for manually writing most of the code for any particular web page or project, the ability to read and interpret HTML code is still a recommended skill for any burgeoning web designer.

Basic HTML Code Structure

Properly structured, or balanced, HTML markup consists of an opening and a closing tag. Tags are enclosed within the lesser-than (<) and greater-than (>) brackets. You create a closing tag by repeating the original tag and typing a slash (/) after the opening bracket. Empty tags, like the horizontal rule, can be written in an abbreviated fashion, as shown.

Writing your own HTML code

The idea of writing code may sound difficult, but creating a web page is actually much easier than you think. In the next few exercises, you will learn how HTML works by creating a basic web page and adding and formatting some simple text content:

1 Launch Notepad (Windows) or TextEdit (Mac).

2 Enter the following code in the empty document window:

```
<html>

<body>

Welcome to my first web page

</body>

</html>
```

Note: In TextEdit, you may need to choose Format > Format As Plain Text before you can save the file as .html.

Note: Some text editors may try to change the .html extension or prompt you to confirm the choice.

3 Save the file to the desktop as **firstpage.html**.

4 Launch Internet Explorer, Safari, Firefox, or another installed web browser.

5 Choose File > Open. Navigate to the desktop and select **firstpage.html**, and then click OK/Open.

Congratulations, you just created your first web page. It doesn't take much code to create a serviceable web page.

Text editor   Browser

Understanding HTML syntax

By adding content to your new web page, you will learn some important aspects of HTML code syntax:

1 Switch back to the text editor without closing the browser.

2 Insert your cursor at the end of the text "Welcome to my first page" and press Enter/Return to insert a paragraph return.

3 Type **Making web pages is fun**, and then press the spacebar five times to insert five spaces. Finish by typing **and easy!** on the same line.

4 Save the file.

5 Switch to the browser and refresh the window to load the updated page.

As you can see, the browser is displaying the new text, but it's ignoring the paragraph return between the two lines and the extra spaces. In fact, you could add hundreds of paragraph returns between the lines and dozens of spaces between each word and the browser display would be no different. That's because the browser is programmed to ignore extra white space and honor only HTML code elements. By inserting a tag here and there, you can easily correct the text display.

Inserting HTML code

In this exercise you will insert HTML tags to correct the text display:

1   Switch back to the text editor.

2   Add the bold tags to the text as follows:

    <p>Making web pages is fun   and easy!**</p>**

    To add letter spacing, or other special characters, within a line of text, HTML provides code elements called *entities*. Entities are entered into the code differently than tags. For example, the method for inserting a nonbreaking space is by typing the entity:

3   Replace the five spaces in the text with nonbreaking spaces, so that the text looks like the following sample:

    <p>Making web pages is fun**   **and easy!</p>

4   Save the file. Switch to the browser and reload or refresh the page display.

The browser is now showing the paragraph return and desired spacing.

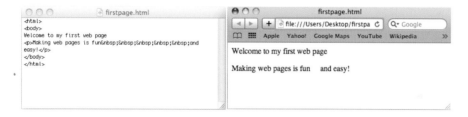

Formatting text with HTML

Tags often serve multiple purposes. Besides creating paragraph structures as demonstrated earlier, they can impart basic text formatting, as well as identify the relative importance of the page content. For example, HTML provides six heading tags (<h1> to <h6>) you can use to set off headings from normal paragraphs. The <h1> tag identifies the heading as being the highest in importance but also automatically formats the enclosed text in bold and at the largest relative size. In this exercise, you will add a heading tag to the first line:

1   Switch back to the text editor.

2   Add the bold tags to the text as follows:

    <h1>Welcome to my first web page**</h1>**

3   Save the file. Switch to the browser and reload or refresh the page display.

Note how the text changed. It is now larger and bold in format.

Web designers use the heading tags to identify the importance of specific content to improve their site rankings on Google, Yahoo, and other search engines.

Applying inline formatting

So far, all the tags you have used work as paragraph or stand-alone elements. These are referred to as *block* elements. HTML also provides the ability to apply formatting and structure to content that's contained within another tag, or *inline*. A typical use of inline code would be to apply bold or italic styling to a portion of a paragraph. In this exercise, you will apply inline formatting:

1   Switch back to the text editor.

2   Add the bold tags to the text as follows:

```
<p>Making web pages is fun     <strong>
<em>and easy!</em></strong></p>
```

3   Save the file. Switch to the browser and reload or refresh the page display.

Most formatting, both inline and otherwise, is properly applied using cascading style sheets (CSS). The <strong> and <em> tags are among the few still acceptable ways to apply inline formatting using strictly HTML code elements. Overall there is an industry-supported move to separate the content and its presentation, or formatting. See Chapter 3, "CSS Basics," for a full explanation of the strategy and application of CSS in standards-based web design.

Adding structure

Most web pages feature at least three fundamental elements: a root (typically <html>), body, and head. These elements create the essential underlying structure of the web page. The root element contains all the code and content for the web page. It is used to declare to the browser, and any browser applications, what types of code elements to expect within the page. The <body> element holds all the visible content, such as text, tables, images, movies, and so on. The <head> element holds code that performs vital background tasks, including styling, links, and other information.

The sample page you created doesn't have a <head> element. A web page can exist without this section, but adding any advanced functionality to this page without one would be difficult. In this exercise, you will add <head> and <title> elements to your web page:

1 Switch back to the text editor.

2 Add the bold tags and content to the text as follows:

    <html>

    <head>

    <title>HTML Basics for Fun and Profit</title>

    </head>

    <body>

3 Save the file. Switch to the browser and reload or refresh the page display.

Did you notice what changed? It may not be obvious at first. Look at the title bar of the browser window. The words "HTML Basics for Fun and Profit" now magically appear above your web page. By adding the <title> element, you have created this display. But, it's not just a cool trick; it's good for your business, too. Google, Yahoo, and the other search engines catalog the <title> element of each page and use it, among other criteria, to rank web pages. The content of the title is one of the items typically displayed within the results of a search. A well-titled page could be ranked higher than one with a bad title or one with none at all.

Writing HTML in Dreamweaver

So, the inevitable question is "If I can write HTML in any text editor, why do I need to use Dreamweaver?" Although a complete answer awaits you in the following 15 chapters, the question begs for a quick demonstration. In this exercise, you will re-create the same web page using Dreamweaver:

1   Launch Dreamweaver CS5.

2   Choose File > New.

3   In the New Document window, select **Blank Page** from the first column.

4   Select **HTML** from the Page Type column and **<none>** from the Layout column. Click Create.

  A new document window opens in Dreamweaver. The window may default to one of three displays: Code view, Design view, or Split view.

5   If it's not already selected, click the Code view button in the upper left of the document window.

The first thing you should notice in the Code view window is that Dreamweaver has provided a huge head start over using the text editor. The basic structure of the page is already in place, including the root, head, body, and even title tags, among others. The only thing Dreamweaver makes you do is add the content itself.

6 Insert the cursor after the opening <body> tag and type **Welcome to my second page** following the tag.

Dreamweaver makes it a simple matter to format the first line as a heading 1.

7 Move the cursor to the beginning of the text "Welcome to my second page." Type **<** to open the code hinting feature.

Note how Dreamweaver automatically opens a drop-down list of compatible code elements. This is Dreamweaver's code hinting feature. When activated, code hinting provides a drop-down list of applicable HTML, CSS, and JavaScript elements.

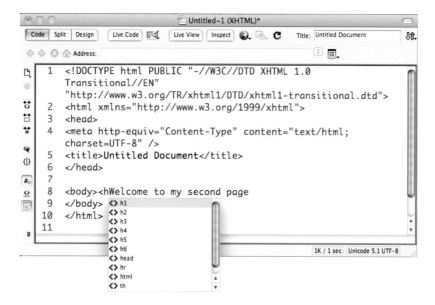

8 Double-click h1 from the list to insert it in the code. Type **>** to close the element.

9 Move the cursor to the end of the text. Type **</** at the end of the sentence.

Note how Dreamweaver closes the <h1> tag automatically. But most coders add the tags as they write, in the following way:

10 Press Enter/Return to insert a line break. Type **<**.

11 Type **p** and press Enter/Return to insert the element. Type **>** to close the element.

12 Type **Making web pages in Dreamweaver is even more fun!**, and then type **</** to close the <p> element.

Tired of hand-coding yet? Dreamweaver offers multiple ways for formatting your content.

13 Select the word "more." In the Property inspector, click the **B** and the **I** buttons to apply the `<strong>` and `<em>` tags to the text. These tags produce the appearance of bold and italic formatting on the selected text.

Something missing?

When you reached for the B and I buttons in step 13 were they missing? When you make changes in Code view, the Property inspector occasionally needs to be refreshed before you can access the formatting commands featured there. Simply click the Refresh button and the formatting commands will reappear.

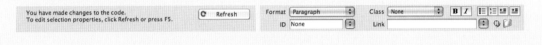

Only two more tasks remain before your new page is complete. Note that Dreamweaver created the `<title>` element and inserted the text "Untitled Document" within it. You could select the text within the code window and enter a new title, or you could change it using another built-in feature.

14 Locate the Title field at the top of the document window and select the "Untitled Document" text.

15 Type **HTML Basics, Page 2** in the Title field.

16 Press Enter/Return to complete the title.

The Title field enables you to change the content of the `<title>` element without having to work in the HTML code.

Note that the new title text appears in the code replacing the original content. It's time to save the file and preview it in the browser.

17 Choose File > Save. Navigate to the desktop. Name the file **secondpage**. Click Save.

Dreamweaver adds the proper extension (html) automatically.

18 Choose File > Preview in Browser.

The completed page appears in the browser window.

Using Dreamweaver you completed the task in a fraction of the time it took you to do it manually.

You have just completed two web pages—one by hand and the other using Dreamweaver. In both cases, you can see how HTML played a central role in the whole process. To learn more about this technology, go to the website of the W3 Consortium at www.w3.org, or check out any of the books in the following section.

Recommended books on HTML

HTML, XHTML, and CSS: Visual QuickStart Guide, 6th Edition,
Elizabeth Castro, (Peachpit Press, 2006), ISBN: 0-321-43084-0

HTML and XHTML Pocket Reference,
Jennifer Niederst Robbins, (O'Reilly, 2006), ISBN: 978-0-596-52727-3

Head First HTML with CSS & XHTML,
Elizabeth and Eric Freeman, (O'Reilly, 2005), ISBN: 978-0-596-10197-8

Frequently used HTML 4 codes

HTML code elements serve specific purposes. Tags can create structures, apply formatting, identify logical content, or generate interactivity. Tags that create stand-alone structures are called *block* elements; the ones that perform their work within the body of another tag are called *inline* elements.

HTML tags

The following table shows some of the most frequently used HTML tags. To get the most out of Dreamweaver and your web pages, it helps to understand the nature of these elements and how they are used. Remember, some tags can serve multiple purposes.

Table 2.1 Frequently used HTML tags

TAG	DESCRIPTION	STRUCTURAL	BLOCK	INLINE
`<!--...-->`	Comment. Add notes within the HTML code.	•		
`<a>`	Anchor. Creates a hyperlink.			•
`<blockquote>`	Quotation. Creates a stand-alone, indented paragraph.		•	
`<body>`	Designates the document body. Contains the entire visible portions of the page content.	•		
` `	Inserts a line break without creating a new paragraph.	•		
`<div>`	Page division. Creates boxes around page content and is used to simulate columnar layouts.		•	
`<em>`	Emphasis. Adds semantic emphasis. Displays as italics by default.			•
`<form>`	Designates an HTML form.	•		
`<h1>` to `<h6>`	Headings. Creates bold headings. Adds semantic emphasis to formatted text.		•	
`<head>`	Designates the document head. Contains code that performs background functions, such as meta tags, scripts, styling, links, and other information.	•		
`<hr />`	Horizontal rule. Empty element that generates a horizontal line.	•	•	
`<html>`	Root element of most web pages. Contains an entire web page, except in certain cases where server-based code must load before the opening `<html>` tag.	•		
`<iframe>`	Inline frame. A structural element that can contain another document.	•	•	
`<img />`	Image.	•		•
`<input />`	Input element for a form.	•		•
`<li>`	List item.		•	
`<link />`	Designates the relationship between a document and an external resource.	•		
`<meta />`	Metadata.	•		
`<ol>`	Ordered list. Creates a numbered list.	•	•	
`<p>`	Paragraph. Creates a stand-alone paragraph.		•	

Table 2.1 Frequently used HTML tags (continued)

TAG	DESCRIPTION	STRUCTURAL	BLOCK	INLINE
`<script>`	Script. Contains scripting elements or points to an external script.	•		
`<span>`	Designates a document section. Provides a means to apply formatting to a portion of a document.			•
`<strong>`	Strong. Adds semantic emphasis. Displays as bold by default.			•
`<style>`	Calls CSS style rules.	•		
`<table>`	Designates a table.	•		
`<td>`	Table cell.	•		
`<textarea>`	Multi-line text input element for a form.	•		•
`<th>`	Table header cell.	•		
`<title>`	Title.	•		
`<tr>`	Table row.	•		
`<ul>`	Unordered list. Creates a bulleted list.	•	•	

HTML character entities

Entities exist for every letter and character. If a symbol can't be entered directly from the keyboard, it can be inserted by typing the name or numeric value listed in the following table:

Table 2.2 HTML character entries

CHARACTER	DESCRIPTION	NAME	NUMBER
©	Copyright	&copy;	&#169;
®	Registered trademark	&reg;	&#174;
™	Trademark		&#153;
•	Bullet		&#149;
–	En dash		&#150;
—	Em dash		&#151;
	Nonbreaking space		

Where Is HTML Going?

The current version of HTML has been around for over 10 years and has not kept pace with many of the advances in technology, such as the iPhone. The World Wide Web Consortium (W3C), the standards organization responsible for maintaining and updating HTML and other web standards, has been working diligently on updating the language and released a working draft of HTML 5 in October, 2009. A final version is not scheduled to be ready for several years, so what does that mean for current or up-and-coming web designers? Not much—yet.

Websites and their developers change and adapt to current technologies and market realities quickly, but the underlying technologies progress at a more glacial pace. Browser manufacturers are certain to add support for HTML 5 in the next few years. Early adopters will attract developers and users interested in the latest and greatest. Some say the full transition won't happen until 2020 or later. In any case, backward-compatibility to HTML 4.01 will be certain well into the future, so your old pages and sites won't suddenly explode or disappear.

To learn more about HTML 5, check out www.w3.org/TR/2009/WD-html5-20090825.

To learn more about W3C, check out www.w3.org.

Review questions

1 What programs can open HTML files?

2 What does a markup language do?

3 HTML is comprised of how many code elements?

4 What are the three main parts of most web pages?

5 What's the difference between a block and inline element?

Review answers

1 HTML is a plain-text language that can be opened and edited in any text editor and viewed in any web browser.

2 It places tags contained within brackets < > around plain-text content to pass information concerning structure and formatting from one application to another.

3 Less than 100 codes are defined in the HTML specifications.

4 Most web pages are composed of three sections: a root, head, and body.

5 A block element creates a stand-alone element. An inline element can exist within another element.

3 CSS BASICS

Lesson Overview

In this lesson, you'll familiarize yourself with CSS and learn:

- CSS (cascading style sheets) terms and terminology

- The difference between HTML and CSS formatting

- How cascade, inheritance, descendant, and specificity theories affect how browsers apply CSS formatting

- How CSS can format objects

 This lesson should take 30 minutes to complete. Before beginning, make sure you have copied the files for Lesson 3 to your hard drive as described in the "Getting Started" section at the beginning of the book. If you are starting from scratch in this lesson, use the method described in the "Jumpstart" section of "Getting Started."

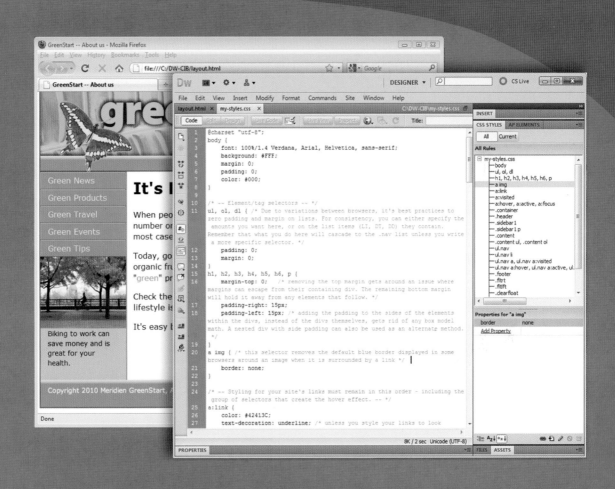

Cascading style sheets control the look and feel of a web page. The language and syntax is complex and powerful, and endlessly adaptable. It takes time and dedication to learn and years to master. A modern web designer can't live without them.

What is CSS?

HTML was never intended to be a design medium. Other than bold and italic, version 1 lacked a standardized way to load fonts or format text. Formatting commands were added along the way up to version 3 of HTML to address these limitations, but these changes weren't enough. Designers resorted to various tricks to produce desired results. For example, they used the `<table>` tag to simulate multicolumn layouts, and they used images when they wanted typefaces other than Times or Helvetica.

Using the expanded table mode in Dreamweaver (top) you can see how this web page relies on tables and images to produce the final design (bottom).

HTML-based formatting was so misguided a concept it was deprecated from the language less than a year after it was formally adopted in favor of cascading style sheets. CSS avoids all the problems of HTML formatting, while saving time and money, too. Using CSS lets you strip the HTML code down to its essential content and structure and then apply the formatting separately, so you can more easily tailor the web page to specific applications.

HTML vs. CSS formatting

When comparing HTML-based formatting to CSS-based formatting, it's easy to see how CSS produces vast efficiencies in time and effort. In the following exercise, you'll explore CSS power and efficacy by editing two web pages, one formatted by HTML, the other by CSS:

1   Launch Dreamweaver, if it is not currently running.

2   Choose File > Open.

3   Navigate to the lesson03 folder and open **HTML_formatting.html**.

4   Click the Split view button.

Each element of the content is formatted individually using the deprecated `<font>` tag. Note the attribute `color="blue"` in each `<h1>` and `<p>` element.

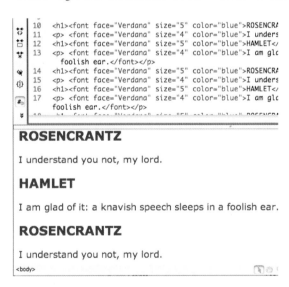

5   Replace the word `blue` with **green** in each line in which it appears. Click in the Design view window to update the display.

The text displays in green now. As you can see, formatting using the obsolete `<font>` tag is not only slow, it's prone to error, too. Type **greeen** or **geen** and the browser ignores the formatting altogether.

6   Open **CSS_formatting.html** from the lesson03 folder.

7   If it's not currently selected, click the Split view button.

The content of the file is identical to the previous document, except that it's formatted by CSS. The code that formats the HTML elements are called *rules* and appears in the `<head>` section of this file. Note the code contains two `color: blue;` attributes.

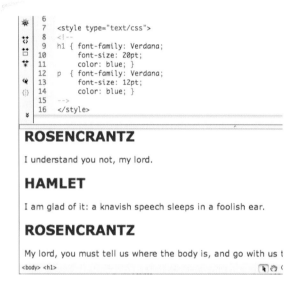

```
 6
 7   <style type="text/css">
 8   <!--
 9   h1 { font-family: Verdana;
10        font-size: 20pt;
11        color: blue; }
12   p  { font-family: Verdana;
13        font-size: 12pt;
14        color: blue; }
15   -->
16   </style>
```

ROSENCRANTZ

I understand you not, my lord.

HAMLET

I am glad of it: a knavish speech sleeps in a foolish ear.

ROSENCRANTZ

My lord, you must tell us where the body is, and go with us t

`<body> <h1>`

8   Select the word `blue` in the h1 rule and type **green** to replace it. Click in the Design view window to update the display.

In Design view, all the heading elements display in green. The paragraph elements remain blue.

9   Select the word `blue` in the p rule and type **green** to replace it. Click in the Design view window to update the display.

In Design view, the heading and the paragraph elements are green.

In this exercise CSS accomplished the color change with two simple edits, whereas the HTML `<font>` tag required you to edit *every* line. Has it dawned on you why the W3C deprecated the `<font>` tag and developed cascading style sheets? This exercise highlights just a small sampling of the formatting power and productivity enhancements offered by CSS that can't be matched by HTML alone.

CSS box model

The browser normally reads the HTML code, interprets its structure and formatting, and then displays the web page. CSS does its work by stepping between HTML and the browser, redefining how each element should be rendered. It imposes an imaginary *box* around each element and then enables you to format almost every aspect of how that box and its contents are displayed.

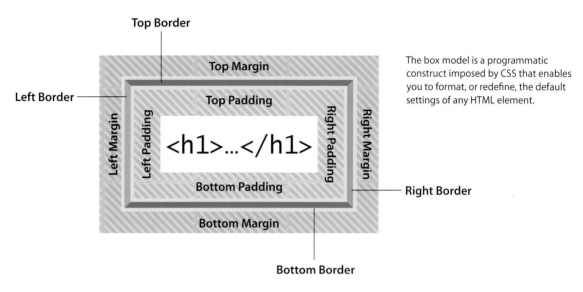

The box model is a programmatic construct imposed by CSS that enables you to format, or redefine, the default settings of any HTML element.

CSS permits you to specify fonts, line spacing, colors, borders, background shading and graphics, and margins and padding, among other things. These boxes are usually invisible, by default. In fact, CSS does not require you to specify any formats for the boxes at all.

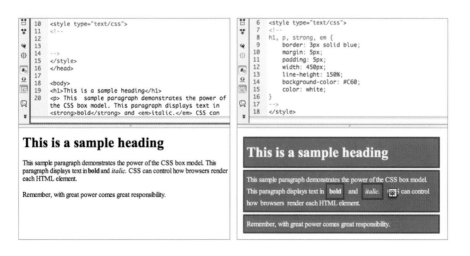

Here is the same text, side-by-side. The text on the left displays the HTML default settings; the text on the right has been formatted by CSS to show color, borders, background shading, margins, and padding for every element.

HTML defaults

Each of the nearly 100 HTML tags comes right out of the box with one or more default formats, characteristics, and/or behaviors. So if you don't do anything, the text will already be formatted in a certain way. One of the essential tasks in mastering CSS is learning and understanding these defaults.

Even without declaring a single style, HTML elements display a raft of formatting by default.

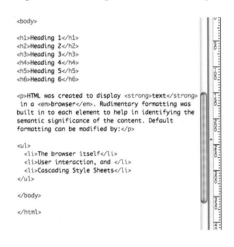

So, what are these settings? What point size does an <h1> tag generate? How much space is added between <p> tags or to <blockquote> indents? It *depends*. HTML elements draw characteristics from multiple sources. First, look to the W3C, the web standards organization, which establishes Internet specifications and protocols. You can find a default style sheet at www.w3.org/TR/CSS21/sample.html that describes the typical formatting and behaviors of all HTML 4 elements.

You can find the specifications at www.w3.org/TR/css3-box that describe how the box model is supposed to render documents in various media.

To save time and give you a bit of a head start, the following table pulls together some of the most common defaults:

Table 3.1 Common HTML defaults

ITEM	DESCRIPTION
Background	In most browsers, the page background color is white. The background of <div>, <table>, <td>, <th>, and most other tags is transparent.
Headings	Headings <h1> through <h6> are bolded. The six heading tags apply differing font size attributes.
Body text	Outside of a table cell, text aligns to the left and to the top of the page.
Table cell text	Text within table cells <td> aligns horizontally to the left and vertically to the center.

Table 3.1 Common HTML defaults *(continued)*

ITEM	DESCRIPTION
Table header	Text within header cells <th> aligns horizontally and vertically to the center.
Fonts	Text color is black. Default typeface and font is specified and supplied by the browser (or by any browser preferences specified by the user).
Margins	External spacing. Many HTML elements feature margin spacing.
Padding	Internal spacing. No element features default padding.

Another important task is identifying the browser that is currently displaying the HTML, *and* its version. That's because browsers frequently differ—and have since the very beginning of the web—in the way they interpret, or display, HTML elements and, today, CSS formatting. Even versions of the same browser can produce wide variations from identical code.

The best practice is to build and test your web pages to make sure that they work properly in the browser(s) that most of your visitors use, or at least the one(s) used by the majority of web users. As of November 2009, the W3C published the following statistics identifying the most popular browsers:

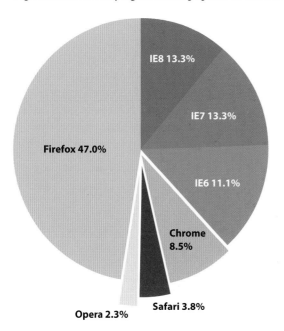

Although it's nice to know which browsers are the most popular among the general public, it's crucial that before you build and test your pages you identify the browser(s) that your target audience uses.

While these statistics are valid for the Internet overall, the statistics for your own site may vary.

Formatting text

You can apply CSS formatting in three ways: inline, embedded in an internal style sheet, or via an external style sheet. A CSS formatting instruction is called a *rule*. A rule consists of two parts—a *selector* and one or more *declarations*. The selector identifies what element or combination of elements are to be formatted, while the declaration contains the formatting specifications. CSS rules can redefine any existing HTML element, as well as define two custom selector modifiers called "class" and "id." If this wasn't enough power and flexibility, a rule can also combine selectors to target the formatting to specific instances within a page where elements appear in unique ways, such as when one element is nested within another.

These sample rules demonstrate some typical constructions used in selectors and declarations. As explained, the way the selector is written determines how the styling is applied.

CSS Rule Construction

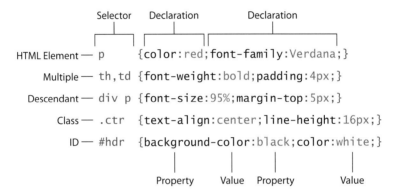

Applying a CSS rule is not a simple matter of selecting some text and applying a paragraph or character style as in InDesign or Illustrator. CSS rules can affect single words, paragraphs of text, or combinations of text and objects. A single rule can affect an entire page. A rule can be specified to begin and end abruptly, or to format content continuously until changed by a subsequent rule.

There are many factors that come into play in how a CSS rule performs its job. To help you better understand how it all works, the following sections illustrate four CSS theories: cascade, inheritance, descendant, and specificity.

Cascade theory

The cascade theory describes how the order and placement of rules in the style sheet or on the page affects the application of styling. In other words, if two rules conflict, which format wins out?

For example, both the following rules change the color of the <h1> element, but which one is honored by the browser?

```
h1 { color: blue; }
h1 { color: red; }
```

When rules collide which one wins?

In this case, the second rule wins because it is the last rule declared, or the closest one to the actual content. Switch the rules and the text displays in blue. *Proximity* is a powerful factor in how CSS is applied. When you try to determine which CSS rule will be honored, remember that browsers typically use the following order of hierarchy, with 4 being the highest:

1 Browser defaults

2 External style sheet

3 Internal style sheet (in the head section)

4 Inline style (inside an HTML element)

Inheritance theory

The inheritance theory describes how one rule can be affected by one or more previously declared rules. Inheritance can affect rules of the same name and rules that format parent elements or elements that nest one inside another.

Examine the following rules:

```
h1 { color: blue; }
h1 { font-family: Verdana; }
```

Some rules play nicely together.

This may look like two separate rules (and that's true), but because the second rule doesn't contradict the first, or reset the `color` attribute, both rules will be honored. In other words, all paragraph text will be formatted as blue, Verdana.

Take a look at these rules:

```
h1 { color: blue; font-family: Verdana; }
div h1 { color: red; }
```

I stand alone.

Hi, I'm in a div tag.

In this situation, all `<h1>` elements will be formatted as: blue, Verdana. However, `<h1>` elements contained, or *nested*, within a `<div>` element will *inherit* the Verdana font but be displayed in red.

In this example:

```
p { color: blue; font-family: Verdana; }
```

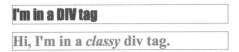

you can see that the `<em>` and `<strong>` tags are not mentioned at all in the CSS rule. However, the text formatted by them in HTML inherits the font *and* color applied to the entire paragraph while still applying bold and italic as expected.

Descendant theory

The descendant theory describes how formatting can target a particular element based on its position in relationship to other elements. By building the selector of multiple elements, as well as `id` and `class` attributes, you can target the formatting to specific instances of text within your web page. Can you interpret the following rules correctly?

```
h1 { font-family: Verdana; color: blue; }
div h1 { font-family: Impact; color: red; }
div.product h1 { font-family: Times; color: green; }
```

I stand alone.

I'm in a DIV tag

Hi, I'm in a *classy* div tag.

The first rule formats all `<h1>` elements everywhere in the page as blue, Verdana. The second rule resets the font and color to red, Impact for `<h1>` elements, but only when they appear within a `<div>` element. The third rule further narrows the target to `<h1>` elements within `<div>` elements that are formatted with a class of `product`, resetting the font and color again, this time to green, Times.

Specificity theory

Specificity describes the concept of how browsers determine what formatting to apply when rules conflict. Some refer to this as *weight*—giving certain rules more weight based on proximity, inheritance, and descendant relationships. These conflicts are the bane of most web designers' existence and can waste hours of time in troubleshooting CSS formatting errors. Can you determine—based on the following rules—what formatting should apply to the sample text as shown?

```
h1 { font-family: Verdana; color: blue; }

div h1 { font-family: Impact; color: red; }

div.product h1 { font-family: Times; color: green; }
```

```
30   <div class="product">
31     <h1 style="color:orange">Can you guess how I will be displayed?</h1>
32   </div>
33
```

Can you guess how I will be displayed?

If you identified the inline style, you are ahead of the game. Remember, an inline style trumps any other formatting. But in most cases, the answer will not be so straightforward.

Formatting objects

The last concept you'll explore in this lesson is also the most complex and prone to error: object formatting. Consider object formatting as the specifications directed at modifying an element's positioning, size, borders and shading, and margins and padding. Since CSS can redefine any HTML element, object formatting basically can be applied to any tag, although it's most commonly directed at the `<div>` element.

Positioning

By default, all elements start at the top of the browser screen and appear consecutively one after the other from left to right, top to bottom. Block elements generate their own line, or paragraph, breaks; inline elements appear at the position of insertion.

CSS breaks all these default constraints and lets you place elements almost anywhere you want them to be. Positioning can be specified in *relative* terms (such as left, right, center, and so on) or by *absolute* coordinates measured in pixels, inches, centimeters, or other standard measurement system. Using CSS you can even place one element on top of or below another in a stack to create amazing graphical effects.

By using positioning commands carefully, you can create a variety of web layouts, including popular multicolumn designs.

As in this example, multiple positioning methods can be combined on one page to create a variety of special effects and designs.

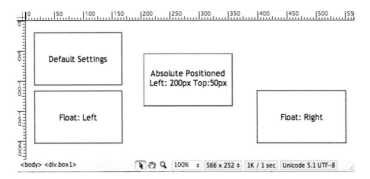

The examples shown in the figure demonstrate some of the possible positioning alternatives offered by CSS. Unfortunately, as powerful as this functionality seems to be, it is the one feature of CSS that is most prone to misinterpretation by the various browsers in use today. Commands and formatting that work fine in one browser can be ignored with tragic results in another. In fact, formatting that works fine on one page of your website can fail on another page containing a different mix of code elements.

Size

You can specify the width and height of an element's box in CSS. You can express measurements in relative terms (percentages or ems or exs) or in absolute terms (pixels, inches, points, centimeters, and so on).

By default, most block elements occupy 100 percent of the width of the browser window. Otherwise, CSS can define element measurements in absolute or relative terms.

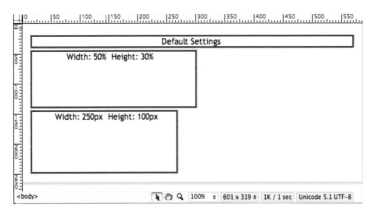

The examples shown in the figure demonstrate some of the size options available in CSS. Older browsers frequently fail to honor width commands and especially height commands.

Borders and shading

Each element can feature four individually formatted borders (top, bottom, left, and right). These are not only handy for creating boxed elements, but you can place them at the top and/or bottom of paragraphs in place of <hr/> (horizontal rule) elements to separate text areas.

Borders can be used for more than boxes. Here you see them as graphical accessories to paragraphs and to simulate a three dimensional button.

Backgrounds are transparent, by default. But CSS enables you to add colors and/or graphics to the background. If both are added, the color will appear behind the graphic if the image has a transparent background. If the graphic has a background that fills all the visible space or is set to repeat, you may not see the color at all.

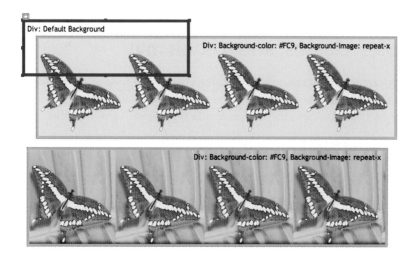

The top div is transparent by default. The middle div features an image with a transparent background that permits the background color to appear in the open space. The bottom div uses an image that obscures the background color.

Margins and padding

Margins create space outside an element—between one element and another; padding adds spacing between the content of an element and its border, whether it's visible or not.

The headings, paragraph, and bulleted list on the left display default margins. The margins on the right have been reset to zero.

Heading 1

Heading 2

Heading 3

Heading 4

Heading 5

Heading 6

HTML was created to display **text** in a *browser*. Rudimentary formatting was built in to each element to help in identifying the semantic significance of the content. Default formatting can be modified by:

- The browser itself
- User interaction, and
- Cascading Style Sheets

Heading 1
Heading 2
Heading 3
Heading 4
Heading 5
Heading 6

HTML was created to display **text** in a *browser*. Rudimentary formatting was built in to each element to help in identifying the semantic significance of the content. Default formatting can be modified by:
- The browser itself
- User interaction, and
- Cascading Style Sheets

As you can see in the figure, many familiar elements, such as `<p>`, `<h1>` through `<h6>`, `<ol>`, and `<ul>`, feature default margins, which many designers find unsightly. A popular practice today is to set all margins and padding, among other settings, to zero before starting a new design. This technique is called *normalization*.

Multiples, classes, and IDs, oh my!

By taking advantage of cascade, inheritance, descendant, and specificity theories you can target formatting to almost any element anywhere on a web page. But CSS offers a few more ways to optimize and customize the formatting even further.

Applying formatting to multiple elements

To speed things up, CSS allows you to apply formatting to multiple elements at once by listing each in the selector separated by commas. For example, the formatting in the following rules:

```
h1 { font-family: Verdana; color: blue; }

h2 { font-family: Verdana; color: blue; }

h3 { font-family: Verdana; color: blue; }
```

can also be expressed like this:

```
h1, h2, h3 { font-family: Verdana; color: blue; }
```

Creating CSS class selectors

Frequently, you will want to create unique formatting to apply to objects, paragraphs, phrases, words, or even characters appearing within a web page. To accomplish this, CSS allows you make your own selectors called classes and ids.

A class can be applied to any number of elements on a page, while an id may only appear once per page. For print designers, classes are similar to Adobe InDesign's paragraph, character, and object styles combined. Class and id names can be any combination of letters and numbers, a single word, abbreviation, almost anything, but may not start with a number or contain spaces. While it's not strictly prohibited, you should avoid using HTML tag and attribute names.

To declare a CSS class selector, insert a period before the name within the style sheet, like this:

```
.ctr { text-align: center; }
.blue { color: blue; }
```

Then, you apply the CSS class to an entire HTML element as an attribute, like this:

```
<h1 class="ctr">Type heading here</h1>
```

or to a block of characters or words inline, this way:

```
Here is <span class="blue">some text</span> formatted
differently.
```

Creating CSS ID selectors

An id is supposed to be a unique selector. It should appear only once per page. Most web designers use the id to point at specific components within the page, like the elements that contain the header, footer, or main content. But don't stop there. An id can also target images, tables, and specific content to assist you in building powerful hypertext navigation within your page and site. You will learn more about using ids this way in Lesson 10, "Working with Navigation."

To declare a CSS id selector, insert a number sign, or hash mark, before the name within the style sheet, like this:

```
#header { width: 80%; float: left; }
#footer { width: 80%; clear: both; }
```

You apply the CSS id to an entire HTML element as an attribute, like this:

```
<div id="header"></div>
<div id="footer"></div>
```

CSS formatting is so complex and powerful that this short lesson can't cover all aspects of the subject. For a full examination of CSS check out the following books:

- *Bulletproof Web Design: Improving flexibility and protecting against worst-case scenarios with XHTML and CSS* (2nd Edition), Dan Cederholm, (New Riders Press, 2007) ISBN: 978-0321509024

- *CSS Web Site Design Hands-On Training*, Eric Meyer, (Peachpit Press, 2006), ISBN: 978-0321293916

- *CSS: The Missing Manual*, David Sawyer McFarland, (O'Reilly Media, 2009) ISBN: 978-0596802448

- *Stylin' with CSS: A Designer's Guide* (2nd Edition), Charles Wyke-Smith (New Riders Press, 2007) ISBN: 978-0321525567

- *The Art & Science of CSS*, Jonathan Snook, Steve Smith, Jina Bolton, Cameron Adams, and David Johnson, (SitePoint, 2007), ISBN: 978-0975841976

Review questions

1 Should you still use HTML-based formatting?

2 What does CSS impose on each HTML element?

3 True or false? If you do nothing, HTML elements will feature no formatting or structure.

4 What four theories affect the application of CSS formatting?

5 What is the difference between block and inline elements?

Review answers

1 No. HTML-based formatting was deprecated in 1997 when HTML 4 was adopted. Industry best practices recommends using CSS-based formatting instead.

2 CSS imposes an imaginary box on each element that can then be formatted with fonts, borders and shading, and margins and padding.

3 False. Even if you do nothing, many elements feature built-in formatting.

4 The four theories that affect CSS formatting are cascade, inheritance, descendant, and specificity.

5 Block elements create stand-alone structures; inline elements appear at the insertion point.

4 GETTING A QUICK START

Lesson Overview

In this lesson, you'll be introduced to the Dreamweaver web page building features while learning how to work within its workspace. You'll learn how to do the following:

- Set up a site in Dreamweaver

- Create a new page using a CSS layout

- Save a document

- Modify the page title and change text headings

- Insert text from an external document

- Add foreground and background images

- Create, modify, and select CSS styles

- Preview your page in Live view and a browser

 This lesson will take about 1 hour and 15 minutes to complete. Before beginning, make sure you have copied the files for Lesson 4 to your hard drive as described in the "Getting Started" section at the beginning of the book. If you are starting from scratch in this lesson, use the method described in the "Jumpstart" section of "Getting Started."

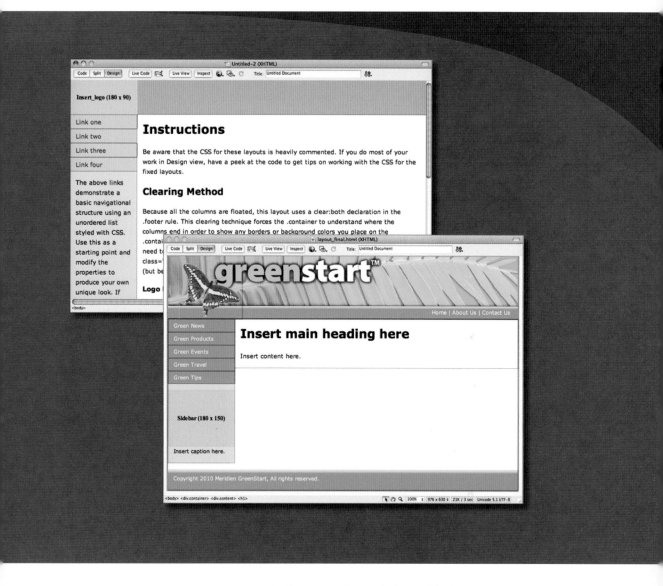

Use Dreamweaver's expertly designed CSS layouts to quickly create a standards-based web page, ready for your personalized content.

Defining a Dreamweaver site

The lessons in this book function within a Dreamweaver site. In Dreamweaver, you work with a *local* site stored in a folder on your hard drive. When you are ready to publish your site (see Lesson 17, "Publishing to the Web"), you upload your completed files to a *remote* site, stored on your web host's server. The folder structures and files of the local and remote sites are usually mirrors of each other.

First, set up your local site:

1 Launch Adobe Dreamweaver CS5, if necessary.

2 Choose Site > New Site, and the Site Setup dialog box appears.

 If you've used any previous version of Dreamweaver, you will notice that the Site Setup dialog box has been redesigned and simplified. Gone are the Basic and Advanced views. Now to create a website in Dreamweaver CS5 you need only to name it and select the local site folder:

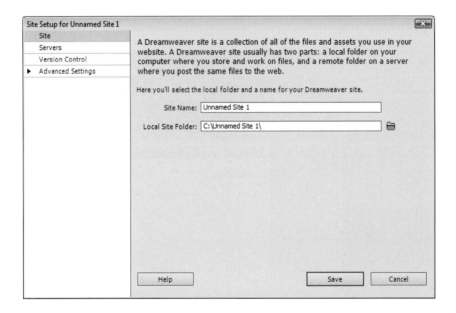

3 In the Site Name field, type **DW-CIB**.

Site names typically relate to a specific project or client and will appear in the Files panel.

4 Next to the Local Site Folder field, click the folder (📁) icon. When the Choose Root Folder dialog box opens, navigate to the DW-CIB folder containing the files you copied from the *Adobe Dreamweaver CS5 Classroom in a Book* CD and click Select/Choose.

You could click Save at this time and begin working on your new website, but we'll add one more piece of handy information.

5 Click the arrow (▶) next to the Advanced Settings category to reveal the tabs listed there. Select the Local Info category.

Although it's not required, a good policy for site management is to store different file types in separate folders. For example, many websites provide individual folders for images, PDFs, video, and so on. Dreamweaver assists in this endeavor by including an option for a *default images* folder. Later, as you insert images from other places on your computer, Dreamweaver will use this setting to automatically move the images into the site structure.

6 Next to the Default Images Folder field, click the folder (📁) icon. When the dialog box opens, navigate to the DW-CIB > images folder containing the files you copied from the *Adobe Dreamweaver CS5 Classroom in a Book* CD and click Select/Choose.

You've entered all the information required to begin your new site. In subsequent lessons you'll add more information to enable you to upload files to your remote site and to be able to test dynamic web pages.

7 In the Site Setup dialog box, click Save.

Setting up a site is a crucial first step in beginning any project in Dreamweaver. Knowing where the site root folder is located determines link pathways and enables many site-wide options in Dreamweaver such as Find and Replace.

Using the Welcome screen

The Dreamweaver Welcome screen provides quick access to recent pages, easy creation of a range of page types, and a direct connection to several key help topics. The Welcome screen appears when you first start the program or when no other documents are open. Let's use the Welcome screen to explore ways to create and open documents:

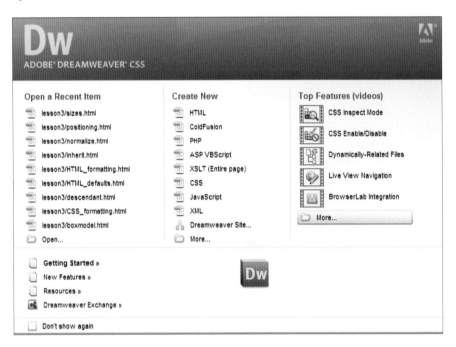

1   In the Create New column of the Welcome screen, click HTML to create a new, blank HTML page.

2   Choose File > Close.

   The Welcome screen reappears.

3   In the Open A Recent Item section of the Welcome screen, click the Open button. This allows you browse for files to open in Dreamweaver. Click Cancel.

The Welcome screen shows you a list of up to nine of your recently used files. Recently used files are shown in the sample figure; however, your installation may not display any used files at this point. Choosing a file from this list is a quick alternative to choosing File > Open when you want to edit an existing page you have recently opened or created.

You will use the Welcome screen several times in this book. When you've completed the lessons in this book, you may prefer not to use the Welcome screen. If so, you can disable it by selecting the Don't Show Again option in the lower left of the window. You can re-enable the Welcome screen in the General category of preferences.

Selecting a CSS layout

Adobe Dreamweaver CS5 provides 16 different CSS layouts. In this exercise, you'll select and modify one. The CSS layouts are carefully built and tested to comply with web standards and to work cross-platform in all major browsers with no additional changes to the layout. Popular one-, two-, and three-column choices are included, specified either in fixed-width dimensions set in pixels or in relative measurements set in percentages:

1   Choose File > New.

2   In the New Document dialog box, from the first column, select Blank Page.

3   In the Page Type column, select HTML.

Dreamweaver allows you to create a wide range of page types. HTML is the page type most commonly used for building basic web pages.

4   In the Layout column, select "1 Column Fixed, Centered, Header And Footer."

The preview for this layout displays a padlock (🔒) symbol to indicate that the width is fixed at a set number of pixels. Other layouts display a spring (QQ) symbol to indicate that the width will expand or contract with the browser window.

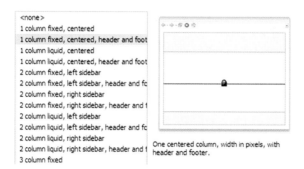

One centered column, width in pixels, with header and footer.

5   Leave all other options at their default settings and click Create.

Your new page appears in Dreamweaver as a document with filler text and default coloring. This is the document window where you add your own content and customize the appearance of the page.

Saving a page

After you've created a page, it's a good practice to save it immediately:

1   Choose File > Save. Alternatively, you could press Ctrl-S/Cmd-S.

2   When the Save As dialog box appears, navigate to the DW-CIB folder.
    Type **greenstart.htm** or **greenstart.html** in the Filename field.

    It's a matter of personal preference whether you use three- or four-letter
    extensions in your filenames; either will work fine on the web. Just remember
    to be consistent. (This book will use .html.)

3   Click Save.

Modifying the page title

As described in Lesson 2, "HTML Basics," the title of a web page is displayed in
the browser's title bar. Page titles are one of the elements used by search engines
to index and rank websites. It's important to always change Dreamweaver's default
page title of "Untitled Document" to a phrase that describes your specific web page:

1   If necessary, choose File > Open Recent > **greenstart.html**.

2   Click the Design button to view the page in Design view.

3   In the Title field of the document toolbar, select the placeholder text, *Untitled
    Document*.

4   Type **Get a green start with Meridien GreenStart** and press Enter/Return.

Changing headings

Dreamweaver's CSS layouts are populated by sample headings, body text, and
colors. Placeholder headings and text help you visualize the layout as it will appear
when your final content is placed on the page. Changing the placeholders is a
simple process:

1   Double-click the placeholder text, *Instructions*, to select it. Then type **It's Easy
    Being Green with GreenStart** to replace it.

Note that the new text remains formatted as an `<h1>` element.

Instructions

It's Easy Being Green with Green**S**|

2   Choose File > Save.

Note: Dreamweaver provides a number of methods for selecting text that operate similar to word processing software, such as dragging the mouse to highlight text, double-clicking a single word, or triple-clicking to select an entire paragraph.

Inserting text

You can change paragraph text as easily as you changed the heading. You can enter text manually, but Dreamweaver also allows you to insert text from other sources, such as Microsoft Office:

1   Click the Design button to view the page in Design view.

2   Choose Window > Files to display the Files panel, if it isn't visible.

3   Display the lesson04 folder. Click the triangle (▶) to the left of the folder name to reveal its contents. Double-click **easygreen.rtf** to open it.

Although Dreamweaver can't open an RTF file, your computer will select a compatible application, such as Word, WordPad, TextEdit, or so on, and open the RTF file.

4 When the file opens, select all the text and press Ctrl-C/Cmd-C to copy the text to the clipboard. Do not close the application displaying **easygreen.rtf**.

Note how the text is formatted in Times New Roman, with indentation, bolding, and green highlighting.

5 Switch to Dreamweaver and position the mouse pointer below the header, "It's Easy Being Green with GreenStart." With the mouse pointer at the beginning of the first paragraph element immediately following this heading, click and drag to the end of the text in the main content area—so that all the placeholder headings and paragraphs are selected—but don't select the text in the footer.

6 Press Ctrl-V/Cmd-V to paste the text from the clipboard.

Note: Results may differ when pasting text into Dreamweaver, depending on the originating program. Most types of font-based formatting are ignored, but the application of bold and italics may be honored. For example, Word will pass bold and italic formatting to Dreamweaver; WordPad and TextEdit will not.

Before proceeding to the next step, it's important to examine what just happened. You probably noticed that the pasted text replaced the selection and was automatically formatted as a paragraph <p> element. However, although the text itself came over successfully, the paragraph indents and font formatting didn't. Besides ignoring the fonts and color, Dreamweaver missed something more important: the paragraph breaks.

7 Insert your cursor at the end of the third paragraph "…only a click away." Click the Code view button. Observe the code element that appears at the end of the paragraph.

```
    Today, going green is easier than ever before. Recycled paper, organic fruits
and vegetables, solar products and hundreds of other &quot;green&quot; products and
services are available in most urban centers  <br />
    Check the GreenStart bulletin board for products and services near you. Your
green lifestyle is only a click away.<br />
    It's easy being green, with GreenStart.</p>
```

It turns out that Dreamweaver didn't completely ignore the paragraph returns, but instead of </p> tags it inserted <br /> line break elements. It's important to know that Dreamweaver translates single paragraph returns copied from other programs into break codes. The trick for producing true HTML <p> elements is to insert additional returns between each of the original paragraphs.

8 Switch back to the application displaying **easygreen.rtf**.

9 Insert the cursor at the end of each paragraph and press Enter/Return to insert a second paragraph return.

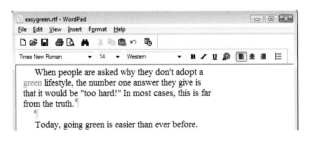

In Word and other programs, you can automate the process of inserting extra returns for longer documents by using the Find/Change command to replace single paragraph returns with two in a row.

10 Select and copy all the text in **easygreen.rtf**.

11 Switch to Dreamweaver. Click the Design view button.

12 Select the improperly formatted text in the main content area. Press Ctrl-V/ Cmd-V to paste from the clipboard.

The difference between the new and the old text is dramatic. The new text clearly displays extra space delineating each paragraph.

13 Select any of the newly pasted paragraphs. Click the Code view button. Observe the code elements at the beginning and end of each paragraph.

The newly pasted text is now properly structured with <p>...</p> tags.

```
    <p>When people are asked why they don't adopt a green lifestyle, the number one
answer they give is that it would be &quot;too hard!&quot; In most cases, this is far
from the truth. </p>
    <p>Today, going green is easier than ever before. Recycled paper, organic fruits
and vegetables, solar products and hundreds of other &quot;green&quot; products and
services are available in most urban centers. </p>
    <p>Check the GreenStart bulletin board for products and services near you. Your
green lifestyle is only a click away.</p>
    <p>It's easy being green, with GreenStart!</p>
```

14 Place the cursor in the footer area. Select the placeholder text and type **Copyright 2010 Meridien GreenStart, All rights reserved** to replace it.

The placeholder copy is replaced as you type.

15 Press Ctrl-S/Cmd-S to save.

Inserting images

Inserting images and graphics in Dreamweaver is straightforward. Once an image has been placed on a page, its image properties, such as alignment, can be adjusted using the Property inspector or within the CSS. In this exercise, you will replace the image placeholder with a banner graphic and insert an inline image into the site content:

1 If necessary, choose File > Open Recent > **greenstart.html** and click the Design button to view the page in Design view.

2 Select the image placeholder in the header section of the page. Although its dimensions are displayed in the placeholder itself, note its width and height in the Property inspector. If the Property inspector is not visible, choose Window > Properties.

The placeholder is 180 pixels by 90 pixels in size.

3 Double-click the placeholder.

The Select Image Source dialog box appears.

4 Navigate to the DW-CIB > images folder and select **banner.jpg**. Note the dimensions of the image displayed in the dialog box.

The banner image is 950 pixels by 200 pixels in size—quite a bit larger than the placeholder.

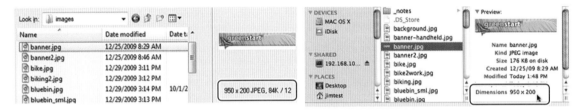

5 Click OK/Choose.

The banner image appears in the layout.

It is a recommended practice for web designers to enter a brief alternate description of images. The alternate text, or alt text, is seen when the image is not visible. The alt text will also appear for users with certain mobile devices, screen readers, or other browsing devices that may not see images. You can add the alt text using the Property inspector.

6 In the Property inspector Alt field, select the text *Add logo here,* type **GreenStart banner** in the Alternate Text field. Click OK.

Note the size of the banner in the Property inspector. Although the placeholder was only 180 by 90 pixels in size, Dreamweaver ignored these dimensions. That's because the size of the placeholder doesn't determine the size of the inserted image; Dreamweaver always honors an image's actual size.

Note that the banner is not as wide as the predefined website structure. You'll adjust this width in an upcoming exercise. Let's insert an image within the page's main content area.

7 Insert the cursor at the beginning of the paragraph "When people are asked...." Choose Insert > Image.

8 In the Select Image Source dialog box, navigate to the DW-CIB > images folder and choose **butterfly.gif**. Click OK/Choose.

9 In the Image Tag Accessibility Attributes dialog box, choose <empty> from the Alternate Text menu.

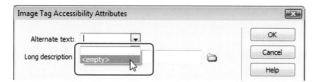

Web standards recommend that the <empty> attribute should be assigned to any graphics used for decorative or spacing purposes, and ones that add no specific information or semantic meaning to the page content. Assistive readers and other devices will ignore images with such a designation.

10 Click OK.

The butterfly appears in the first line of the paragraph and displaces the text in an unappealing way.

It's Easy Being Green with GreenStart

When people are asked why they don't adopt a green lifestyle, th would be "too hard!" In most cases, this is far from the truth.

You could adjust the image position using the HTML `align` attribute accessible from the Property inspector. But this attribute is deprecated in HTML 4.01 and was removed from the HTML 5 specification. Instead, you'll use a method already included with the layout, powered by CSS.

11 With the newly inserted image selected, choose **fltrt** from the Class pop-up menu in the Property inspector.

The class `fltlft` (abbreviation for *float left*) aligns the image to the left side of its container with text wrapping around it to the right. The class `fltrt` (abbreviation for *float right*) aligns the image to the right of its container and forces the text to flow around the left side of the image. All 16 CSS sample layouts include .fltrt and .flt1ft in their default style sheet.

Float is a CSS relative property that moves an element to the left or right of the element containing it. (In this exercise, the container is div.content.) When one element floats, any subsequent element in the same container will flow or wrap around it. The float attribute essentially overrides, or resets, an element's block attribute (if any), essentially making it perform as an inline element. Check out Lesson 3, "CSS Basics," to learn more about CSS positioning.

The page now contains both text and images. In the next exercise, you will improve on the appearance by modifying the CSS styles.

12 Choose File > Save.

Selecting and modifying CSS styles

CSS styles are the current standard for all web styling and layout. In this exercise, you'll adjust the width of the page, modify the background colors, add a background graphic to a page section, and adjust several text attributes. All these changes are accomplished using Dreamweaver's CSS Styles panel.

Changing the page width

You probably noticed that the image inserted in the header section is slightly narrower than the predefined page width. The width attribute of a web page is typically applied either to the <body> element or to a *parent* <div> element that contains the main content. The first step to changing the width is to identify the CSS rule that is controlling it, which will take some CSS detective work:

1 If necessary, choose File > Open Recent > **greenstart.html** and click the Design button to view the page in Design view.

2 Insert the cursor anywhere in the page content. Observe the name and order of the tag selectors at the bottom of the document window.

The tag selector display order directly correlates to the page's code structure. Elements appearing to the left are parents, or containers, of all elements to the right. The element farthest to the left is the highest in the page structure. As you can see, the `<body>` element is highest and `<div.container>` is second. No matter where you click the page, this relationship doesn't change, so by simple deduction you can be certain that one or the other of these two suspects probably contains the width attribute you're looking for.

3   Choose Window > CSS Styles, if the panel is not visible and open.

Minimize or close any panels as necessary to give maximum access to the CSS Styles panel.

4   In the CSS Styles panel, click the All button to switch from Current view, if necessary.

The All view displays the entire style sheet associated with the current page. The Current view displays only the styles that affect a selected element. A document must be open to see any styles in the CSS Styles panel.

5   Expand the `<style>` entry in the CSS Styles panel by clicking the plus symbol (➕) / disclosure triangle (▶).

6   In the CSS Styles panel, click the body rule. Examine its properties. You may have to drag down the bottom border of the CSS Styles panel to see them all.

As displayed, the body rule has attributes for background, color, font, margins, and padding, but not for the width. Time to check the other suspect.

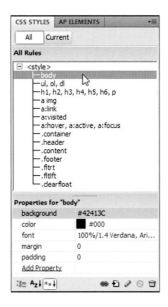

> **Note:** In this page, the style rules are in the document head section. Dreamweaver indicates that styles are internal to the document with brackets: `<style>`. In later lessons you will work with styles stored in an external style sheet. Dreamweaver will list these style sheets by their filenames (for example, mystyles.css) in the CSS styles panel.

7   Click the .container rule. Observe its properties.

This rule features a width attribute of 960 pixels. Since the banner was 950 pixels in width, it seems clearly to be the culprit we're looking for. Rules can be modified directly in the Properties section of the panel.

8 In the Properties section, click the number 960. Type **950** and press Enter/Return.

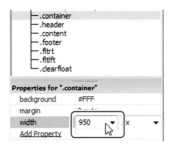

The web page collapses to the width of the banner graphic.

Changing the page background colors

As you learned in Lesson 3, a CSS rule can alter the properties and behavior of any HTML element, such as <body>. In this exercise you'll modify the background color of the entire page.

1 Click the Design button to view the page in Design view.

2 In the CSS Styles panel, click the body rule, and then click the Edit Rule (✏) button.

3 When the "CSS Rule Definition For *body*" dialog box appears, select the Background category. Click the Background-color color box to display the color picker.

● **Note:** Hexadecimal colors are typically written in six characters, two characters for each color channel: red, green, and blue. When both characters in a pair match, it can be abbreviated; for example, #003366 can be written as #036.

4 In the color picker, use the eyedropper to click the white color chip.

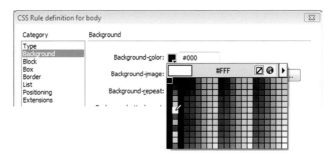

Dreamweaver automatically inserts the hexadecimal value for white, #FFF, in the Background-color field.

5 Click OK to complete the change.

Dreamweaver displays the new color in the Properties section of the CSS Styles panel—the body rule background color has now changed from dark gray to white. The header and footer background colors have not changed. Let's assign a background color to the footer section.

6 Insert the cursor into the footer section. Observe the tag selectors.

The tag `<div.footer>` appears at the bottom of the document window. Although it seemed obvious, don't assume how an element is styled. Always rely on your tag selectors a foolproof way to identify the page structure.

7 In the CSS Styles panel, double-click the `.footer` rule.

8 Change the Background-color to **#060**. Click OK.

The footer background changes from gray to dark green.

9 Choose File > Save.

Inserting a graphic background into the footer

Using one solid color over large sections of a page can make for a dull design. But intelligent use of gradient images can add a multidimensional flourish without unduly burdening Internet bandwidth. By combining background colors and background images, you can achieve amazing results. While foreground images are inserted directly onto the page, background images are placed using CSS. As with many other formatting commands, the support of background images using HTML-based attributes was deprecated in HTML 4.01. In this exercise, you will add a background graphic to the footer using CSS to create a three-dimensional effect:

1 Click the Design button to view the page in Design view, if necessary.

2 In the CSS Styles panel, double-click the `.footer` rule.

3 Select the Background category. Click the Browse button next to the Background-image field.

The Select Image Source dialog box appears.

4 Navigate to DW-CIB > images and select **background.jpg**. Observe the image dimensions and preview.

The image is 5 pixels by 30 pixels and 2 kilobytes in size. Since the page is 950 pixels, this graphic could never fill the footer unless it was copied and pasted hundreds of times. But, such antics are unnecessary with background images; they have a special capability called *repeat*.

5 Click OK/Choose. Click Apply.

The background image repeats automatically—both vertically and horizontally —to fill the entire footer. In some cases, a background is not designed to repeat in both directions. This graphic, for example, was intended to create a rounded 3D effect for the top edge of a `<div>` element. CSS allows you to control the repeat function, such as limiting it to either the vertical or horizontal axis among other settings.

6 Choose repeat-x from the Background-repeat field menu. Click Apply.

The graphic repeats only horizontally now; it aligns to the top of the `<div>` element by default. But the background color selected earlier doesn't match the graphic; it's too dark.

7 Select the Background-color color box to access the Eyedropper tool. Click the Eyedropper tool on the lighter of the two shades of green in the footer, which enters #090 into the Background-color field.

8 Click OK.

The background color now matches the background image perfectly. The result is the effect of a green container with a 3D rounded top edge. We'll experiment with more dramatic effects in later lessons.

9 Choose File > Save.

Adjusting text fonts, colors, and sizes

CSS gives you tremendous control over page appearance. For example, it's easy to change a page's overall font formatting and appearance by changing a single rule.

Let's take a look at the font types:

1 Click the Design button to view the page in Design view, if necessary.

2 In the CSS Styles panel, double-click the body rule.

3 When the "CSS Rule Definition for *body*" dialog box opens, observe the entry displayed in the Font-family field: Verdana, Arial, Helvetica, sans serif.

Why *four* typefaces? Can't Dreamweaver make up its mind?

The answer is a simple, but ingenious, solution to a twofold problem. Not all computers have the same fonts installed, and HTML 4.01 can't currently embed fonts in a web page. That means if you chose a single font and it wasn't installed on the visitor's computer, your carefully designed and formatted web page could immediately and tragically appear in Courier or some other equally undesirable font.

Normal browser display

Browser defaulting to Courier

By specifying fonts in groups, the browser is given a second, third, and perhaps fourth (or more) choice to default to before it picks for itself (egads!). Some call this technique "degrading gracefully."

Dreamweaver CS5 offers more than a dozen predefined font groups out of the box. If you don't see a combination you prefer, notice the Edit Font List option at the bottom of the Font-Family field menu that allows you to create new groups of your own.

But before you start building your own group, remember this: Your main consideration is not to pick *your* favorite font, but to figure out what fonts are installed on your *visitors'* computers. You may prefer the font Hoefelter Allgemeine Bold Condensed, but it's unlikely that a majority of web users have it installed on their computers. By all means select Hoefelter as your first choice, just don't forget to slip in some of the more tried-and-true fonts like Arial, Helvetica, Tahoma, Times New Roman, Trebuchet MS, Verdana, and finally serif and sans serif.

Changing font and color

Using different fonts and colors helps to develop visual interest on a web page. You'll use the CSS Styles panel to change the font type and color:

1 If necessary, choose File > Open Recent > **greenstart.html** and click the Design button to view the page in Design view.

2 In the CSS Styles panel, double-click the body rule.

3 From the Font-family menu, choose "Trebuchet MS, Arial, Helvetica, sans-serif." Click OK.

   You have successfully changed the basic font of the entire web page by editing one rule.

   Note that the black footer text is a bit difficult to read against the green back-ground. You can adjust the footer text color this way, too.

4 In the CSS Styles panel, double-click the .footer rule.

5 In the "CSS Rule Definition For *.footer*" dialog box, select the Type category.

6 Enter **#FFF** in the Color field. The footer text displays in white.

7 Click OK.

Altering text size

In addition to changing the font style and color, as in the previous exercise, you can also alter text size with CSS:

1 If necessary, choose File > Open Recent > **greenstart.html** and click the Design button to view the page in Design view.

The font size is set to 100% for this CSS layout in the body rule. All elements on the page will inherit this formatting unless otherwise specified. Let's change the size of the text in the main content area.

2   Insert the cursor in the main content. Observe the tag selectors at the bottom of the document window. Identify the `<div>` element that contains the main content itself.

The main content is contained in `<div.content>`.

3   In the CSS Styles panel, double-click the `.content` rule.

4   In the "CSS Rule Definition For *.content*" dialog box, type **90** in the Font-size field, and choose **%** from the unit of measurement menu. Click OK.

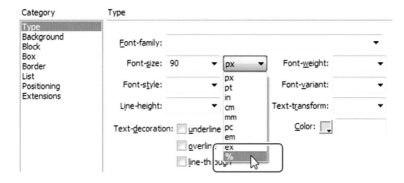

The text in `<div.content>` element now displays at 90 percent of its original size.

5   Choose File > Save.

Using the Property inspector

The Property inspector has traditionally been used to apply quick HTML formatting. It now has the ability to create custom CSS formatting, too:

1   Click the Design button to view the page in Design view, if necessary.

2   If you don't see the Property inspector docked under the Document window, choose Window > Properties.

3   On the left side of the Property inspector, click the HTML button, if necessary, to display the HTML formatting commands.

4   Select the name "GreenStart" wherever it appears in the paragraph copy and click the B button to apply the `<strong>` tag.

The text "GreenStart" is displayed in bold. Let's create a custom CSS rule using the Property inspector.

5   In the Property inspector, click the CSS button.

Note: If you copied and pasted the text from Word in the exercise earlier in this chapter, the text may already be formatted in bold. Clicking the B button in this case will toggle the bold formatting off. Leave the bold formatting in place.

6 In the main heading, select "Green" in the word "GreenStart".

7 Type **#090** in the Color field and press Enter/Return to change the text's color to match the green color used in the footer.

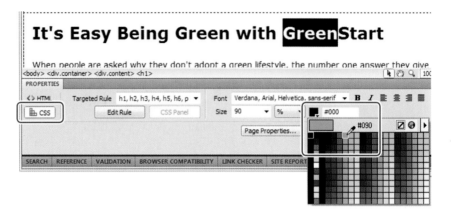

The New CSS Rule dialog box appears.

8 Choose Class from the Selector Type pop-up menu, if it is not displayed. Type **green** in the Selector Name field. Click OK.

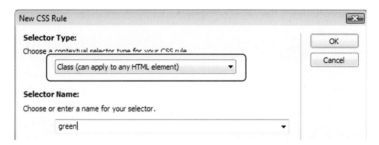

The selected text changes color. Note the `<span.green>` tag selector at the bottom of the document window when you insert the cursor in the formatted text.

9 Click the Code view button and observe the selected code. It should look like this:

```
<span class="green">Green</span>Start
```

Dreamweaver created a CSS class and automatically applied it to the selected text using the `<span>` tag.

10 Click the Design view button.

11 Locate the word "GreenStart" in the paragraph copy. Select "Green" in the word "GreenStart". In the Property inspector, click the HTML button and choose **green** from the Class menu.

The selected text displays in green. Although the text in the <h1> and <p> elements are formatted completely differently, the .green class still works as desired in both cases.

12 Click the Code view button and observe the selected code. It should look like this:

```
<span class="green"><strong>Green</strong></span><strong>
    Start</strong>
```

This time, not only did Dreamweaver apply the .green class to the word "Green", it also restructured the <strong> tag to comply with standard code syntax.

13 Apply the .green class to the words "Green" or "green" wherever they appear on the page.

14 Choose File > Save.

These few examples highlight how useful the Property inspector can be and the reason most web designers leave it open at all times while they work.

Previewing a page in Live view

So far you have been working in Dreamweaver using Code and Design view to build and format most of the page content. However, Code view ignores the graphical display, and Design view doesn't always display page elements and formatting accurately. This requires you to switch back and forth from Dreamweaver to the browser frequently to preview the code as it will actually appear on the Internet. To save time and improve productivity, Dreamweaver has a built-in feature called Live view that does a better job generating the page display and virtually eliminates the need to switch to the browser. Live view has additional features that will be explored in later lessons.

1 If necessary, choose File > Open Recent > **greenstart.html** and click the Design button to view the page in Design view.

2 In the toolbar, click the Live View button. You may also press Alt-F11/Option-F11 to enter Live view.

The standard Dreamweaver document display is replaced by a live, simulated browser display. If the page includes elements such as links, JavaScript, or Flash movies, they will be active in Live view. However, you won't be able to add text or images or modify most types of formatting while Live view is active.

3 To resume editing the document, click the Live view button again, or press Alt-F11/Option-F11 again.

Previewing pages in a browser

Although Dreamweaver does an excellent job of rendering web pages in the Document window and in Live view, it's important to always review your pages in one or more browsers. Dreamweaver can automatically launch the desired browser and load the page, once it has been specified in Dreamweaver's preferences. Browsers installed on your computer when Dreamweaver is installed will automatically be added to this list. Browsers installed later can be added manually.

Can you see the subtle variations between these views? Remember, the only one that matters is the browser.

Design view   Live view   Browser display

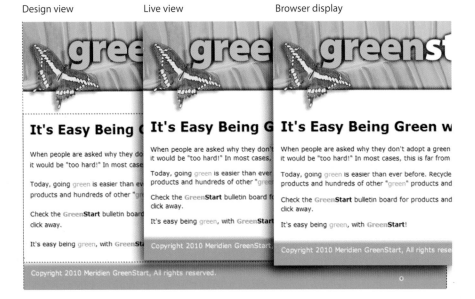

1   Choose File > Preview In Browser > Edit Browser List.

The Preferences dialog box appears, with the Preview In Browser category selected.

2   If your desired browser is not already in the list, click the Add (![+]) button to add it to the list.

3   In the Add Browser dialog box, leave all fields blank and click Browse.

4   When the Select Browser dialog box opens, navigate to the folder containing your preferred browser:

- Windows: All browsers will be installed by default in the Program Files folder.

- Mac: All browsers will be installed by default in the Applications folder.

5   Click Open.

6   In the Add Browser dialog box, in the Name field, type the name you want to appear in the browser list, such as Firefox, Internet Explorer, or Safari, if necessary.

7 Select the Primary Browser option to pick the browser that will open when you preview a page in your preferred browser. Click OK.

Only one browser can be primary. If another browser was designated primary, selecting this option will deselect the previous selection.

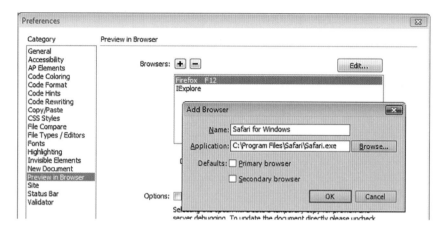

8 In the Preferences dialog box, click OK.

9 Select File > Preview in Browser and choose your primary browser to preview the current page.
If you haven't saved the page, Dreamweaver will remind you to do so.

In the Document window, clicking the Preview/Debug In Browser (⬤) button allows you to manually select the browser that will preview the open page.

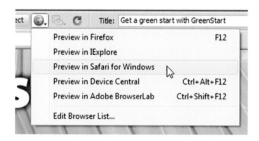

● **Note:** Use the same method to add any additional browsers you may have installed. Viewing your pages in as many browsers as possible is a good testing practice.

10 After you've previewed your new web page, close your browser or simply switch back to Dreamweaver.

Congratulations—you've created your first full-blown web page in Dreamweaver. Using a Dreamweaver CSS layout as a head start, you learned how to modify text, change colors, add images, add and modify CSS rules, and quickly produce a professional-looking web page. You have previewed the page in Live view and in a browser. It's easy to see how Dreamweaver combines substantial power with ease of use.

Review questions

1 What's the advantage in using a CSS layout?

2 How can you use the tag selectors to determine what CSS element to edit?

3 How do you change the background color in a page section?

4 What special capability does a background image have, and how can you use it to create special effects?

5 How can you create custom CSS formatting using the Property inspector?

Review answers

1 The CSS layouts included with Dreamweaver have been carefully built and tested to work trouble-free in all major browsers.

2 When you insert the cursor anywhere in the page content, the names and the order of the elements in the tag selector display directly correlates to the structure of the HTML elements at that position, with the highest parent element farthest to the left.

3 Double-click the CSS rule that formats the element and enter a color into the Background-color field of the CSS Rule Definition dialog box. Click OK.

4 Background images can repeat multiple times, both vertically and horizontally. By combining them with background color, you can create special effects, like 3D.

5 In the Property inspector, click the CSS button. Select text or an object within the web page and then choose any of the formatting commands in the inspector. Dreamweaver will create a custom CSS rule based on the selection and formatting.

5 CREATING A PAGE LAYOUT

Lesson Overview

In this lesson, you'll learn:

- The basics of web page design theory and strategy

- How to create design thumbnails and wireframes

- How to insert and format new components into a predefined CSS layout

- How to use Code Navigator to identify CSS formatting

- How to check for browser compatibility

 This lesson should take 1 hour and 30 minutes to complete. Before beginning, make sure you have copied the files for Lesson 5 to your hard drive as described in the "Getting Started" section at the beginning of the book. If you are starting from scratch in this lesson, use the method described in the "Jumpstart" section of "Getting Started."

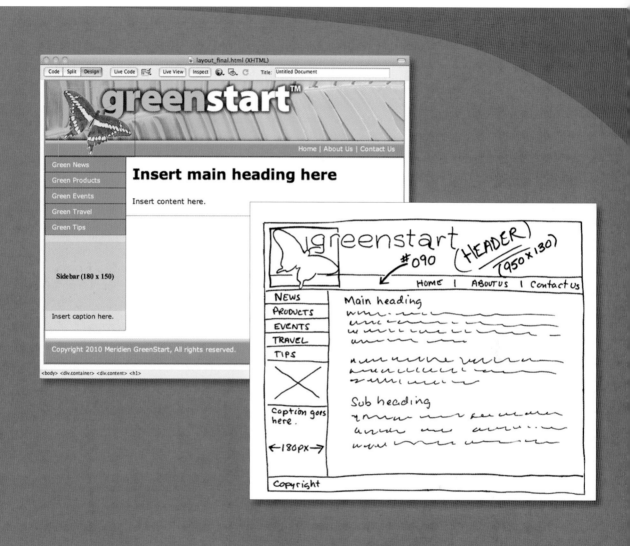

Whether you use thumbnails and wireframes or just a vivid imagination, Dreamweaver can quickly turn design concepts into complete, standards-based CSS layouts.

Web design basics

Before you begin any web design project for yourself, or for a client, there are three important questions you need to answer first:

- What is the purpose of the website?
- Who is the customer?
- How do they get here?

What is the purpose of the website?

Will the website sell or support a product or service? Is your site for entertainment or games? Will you provide information and/or news? Will you need a shopping cart or database? Do you need to accept credit card payments or electronic transfers? Knowing the purpose of the website tells you what type of content you'll be developing and working with, and what types of technologies you'll need to incorporate.

Who is the customer?

Are the customers adults, children, seniors, professionals, hobbyists, men, women, everyone? Knowing *who* your market will be is vital to overall design and functionality. A site intended for children probably needs more animation, interactivity, and bright engaging colors. Adults will want serious content and in-depth analysis. Seniors may need larger type and other accessibility enhancements.

A good first step is to check out the competition. Is there an existing website performing the same service or selling the same product? Are they successful? You don't have to mimic others just because they're doing the same thing. Look at Google and Yahoo. They perform the same basic service but their site designs couldn't be more different from one another.

Can two sites be more different than Google and Yahoo? Yet they both perform the same service.

How do they get here?

This sounds like an odd question when speaking of the Internet. But, like a brick-and-mortar business, your online customers can come to you in a variety of different ways. For example, are they accessing your site on a desktop computer, laptop, PDA, or cell phone? Are they using high-speed Internet or dial-up service? What browser do they most like to use and what is the size and resolution of the display? These answers will tell you a lot about what kind of experience your customers will expect. Dial-up and cell phone users may not want to see a lot of graphics or video, while users with large flat panel displays and high-speed connections may demand as much bang and sizzle as you can send at them.

So, where do you get this information? Some you'll have to get through painstaking research and demographic analysis. Some you'll get from educated guesses based on your own tastes and understanding of your market. But, a lot of it is actually available on the Internet itself. The W3C, for one, keeps track of tons of statistics regarding access and usage, all updated regularly:

- **www.w3schools.com/browsers/browsers_stats.asp**: Provides more information about browser statistics.

- **www.w3schools.com/browsers/browsers_os.asp**: Gives the breakdown on operating systems.

- **www.w3schools.com/browsers/browsers_display.asp**: Lets you find out the latest information on screen resolutions.

If you are redesigning an existing site, your web hosting service itself may provide valuable statistics on historical traffic patterns and even the visitors themselves. If you host your own site, third-party tools are available, like Google Analytics and Adobe Omniture, which you can incorporate into your code to do the tracking for you for free, or for a small fee.

When you boil down all the statistics, this is what you will find: Windows (80 to 90%) dominates the Internet, with most users divided almost equally between Firefox (46%) and various versions of Internet Explorer (37%). The current average browser resolution is set at 1024 pixels by 768 pixels, or *higher*. If it weren't for cell phones and PDAs, these statistics would be great news for most web designers and developers. But the truth is the scope and penetration of cell phone usage on the Internet is an unknown quantity.

Each day more people are using cell phones to access the Internet. Younger users may use them to access the Internet more frequently than they use desktop computers. This presents a nagging problem to web designers. For one thing, cell phone screens are a fraction of the size of even the smallest flat panel display. How do you cram a two- or three-column page design into meager 200 to 300 pixels?

Another problem is that only the high-end smart phones can run web-based Flash content and some other client-based applications available today. Keep this in mind as you go through the process of designing your site.

Many of the concepts of print design are not applicable to the web because you are not in control of the user's experience. A page carefully designed for a typical flat panel is basically useless on a cell phone.

Scenario

For the purposes of this book you have been working on a website for Meridien GreenStart, a fictitious community-based organization dedicated to green investment and action. This website will offer a variety of different products and services and require a broad range of web page types, including dynamic pages using server-based technologies like ASP, ColdFusion, and PHP.

Your customers come from a broad demographic including all ages and education levels. They are people who are concerned about environmental conditions and who are dedicated to conservation, recycling, and reuse of natural and human resources.

Your marketing research indicates that most of your customers use desktop computers or laptops, connecting via high-speed Internet services, but that you can expect 10 to 20 percent of your visitors via cell phone and other mobile devices.

Working with thumbnails and wireframes

The next step after you have nailed down the answers to the three questions about the website purpose, customer, and access method, is to figure out how many pages you'll need, what those pages will do, and finally, what they will look like.

Creating thumbnails

Many web designers start by drawing thumbnails with pencil and paper. Thumbnails are a graphical shopping list of the pages you need to create for the website. Thumbnails can also help you work out the website navigation. Draw lines between the thumbnails showing how your navigation will connect them.

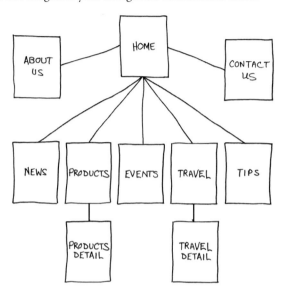

Thumbnails list the pages that need to be built and how they are connected to each other.

Most sites are divided into levels. The first level includes all the pages in your main navigation, the ones a visitor can reach directly from the home page. The second level includes pages you can only reach through specific actions or from specific locations, like a shopping cart or product detail page.

Creating a page design

Once you've figured out what your site needs in terms of pages, products, and services, you can then turn to what those pages will look like. Make a list of components you want on each page, such as headers and footers, navigation, and areas for the main content and sidebars, if any. Put aside any items that won't be needed on every page. What other factors do you need to consider?

1. Header (includes banner and logo)
2. Footer (copyright info)
3. Horizontal navigation (for internal reference, i.e., Home, About Us, Contact Us)
4. Vertical navigation (links to products and services)
5. Main content (one-column with chance of two or more)

Identifying the essential components for each page helps in creating an effective page design that will meet your needs.

Do you have a company logo, business identity, graphic imagery, or color scheme you want to accent? Do you have publications, brochures, or advertising you want to emulate? It helps to gather them all together in one place so you can see everything all at once on a desk or conference table. If you're lucky, a theme will rise organically from this collage.

Once you've created your checklist of the components you'll need on each page, develop several rough layouts that work for these components. Most designers usually settle on one basic page design that compromises between flexibility and sizzle. Minimizing the number of page designs may sound like a major limitation, but it's key to producing a professional-looking site. It's the reason why some professionals, like doctors and airline pilots, wear uniforms. Using a consistent page design lends a sense of professionalism and confidence to your visitor.

Wireframes allow you to experiment with page designs quickly and easily without wasting time with code.

While you figure out what your pages will look like, you'll have to address the size and placement of the basic components. Where you put a component can drastically affect its impact and usefulness. In print, designers know that the upper-left corner of a layout is one of the "power positions," a place where you want to locate important aspects of a design, such as a logo or title. This is because in western culture we read from left to right, top to bottom. The second power position is the lower-right corner because this is the last thing your eyes will see when you're finished reading.

Unfortunately, in web design this theory doesn't work so well because of one simple reason: You can never be certain how the user is seeing your design. Are they on a 20-inch flat panel or a 2-inch cell phone?

That means the only thing you can be certain of is that the user can see the upper-left corner of your page. Do you want to waste this position by slapping the company logo here? Or, make the site more useful by slipping in a navigation menu? This is one of the key dilemmas of the web designer. Do you go for design sizzle, workable utility, or something in between?

Creating wireframes

After you pick the winning design, wireframing is a fast way to work out the structure of each page in the site. A wireframe is like a thumbnail, but bigger, that sketches out each page and fills in more details about the components, such as actual link names and main headings. This step helps to catch or anticipate problems before you discover them when working in the code.

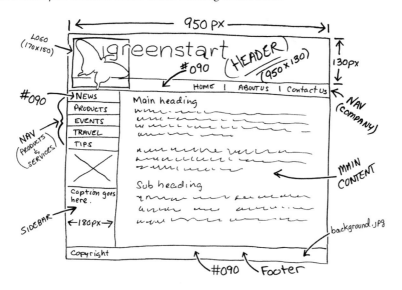

The wireframe for the final design should identify the components and feature markup for content, color, and dimensions.

Once the basic concepts are worked out, many designers take an extra step and create a full-size mockup or proof of concept using a program like Adobe Fireworks, Photoshop, or even Illustrator. It's a handy thing to know because you'll find that some clients just aren't comfortable giving an approval based only on pencil sketches. The advantage here is that all these programs allow you to export the results to a full-size image (JPEG, GIF, or PNG) that can be viewed in a browser. Such mockups are as good as seeing the real thing but may take only a fraction of the time to produce.

▶ **Tip:** For years designers have started the design process in Fireworks, where they can create a fully functional mockup with menus, links, and hotspots that can then be exported to a CSS-based HTML layout and edited in Dreamweaver.

In some cases, creating a mockup in Photoshop or Fireworks can save hours of tedious coding to receive a needed approval.

Previewing your completed file

To understand the layout you will work on in this lesson, preview the completed page in the browser.

1 Open Adobe Dreamweaver CS5.

2 If necessary, press F8 to open the Files panel, and select **DW-CIB** from the site list.

3 In the Files panel, expand the **lesson05** folder.

4 Double-click **layout_final.html** to open it.

This page represents the layout you will create in this lesson. In some ways it is similar to the page you created in Lesson 4, "Getting a Quick Start," but differs in that it has a left sidebar area and two navigation components.

5 Choose File > Close.

Modifying an existing CSS layout

The predefined CSS layouts provided by Dreamweaver are always a good starting point. They are easy to modify and adaptable to most projects. Using a Dreamweaver CSS layout, you will create a proof-of-concept page to match the final wireframe design. This page will then be used to create the main project template in subsequent lessons. Let's find the layout that best matches the wireframe:

1 Choose File > New.

2 Choose Blank Page > HTML in the New Page dialog box. Examine each of the 16 sample CSS layouts to find the one that best fits the needs.

The layout *2 column fixed, left sidebar, header and footer* has the most in common with the target design.

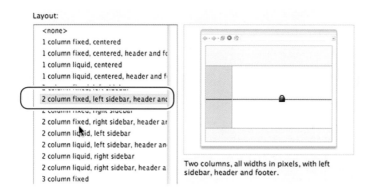

Two columns, all widths in pixels, with left sidebar, header and footer.

3 Select **2 column fixed, left sidebar, header and footer** from the layout list. Click Open/Create.

4 Switch to Design view, if necessary. Click in each content area, and using the tag selector display at the bottom of the document window, note the structure of the page components. Don't be afraid of using Code view, if you desire.

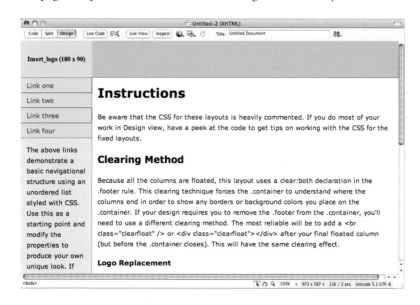

Using the skills you have learned in the last few lessons you should be able to deconstruct this CSS layout easily. The page consists of four content <div> elements (header, footer, sidebar1, and content) and one <div> that wraps around all the others (container). To understand exactly how much this design depends on CSS, it's sometimes a good idea to shut off CSS styling.

5 Choose View > Style Rendering > Display Styles to shut off CSS styling.

Style display is typically on by default (showing a check mark in the menu). By selecting it you'll toggle CSS styling off temporarily.

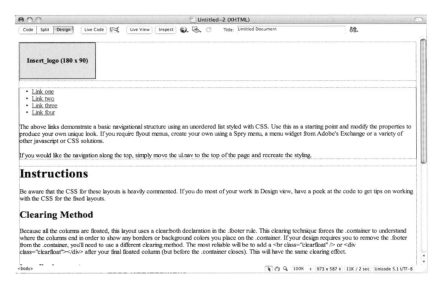

6 Note the identity and order of each page component.

Without CSS, the HTML skeleton is exposed for all to see. It's instructive to know what the page will look like if somehow the cascading style sheet is disabled or not supported by a particular browser. Now it's easier to identify the page components and their structure.

In fact, the order of elements is an important facet of how CSS styling and positioning works (and sometimes doesn't work). Although it is not strictly required, items that display higher on the page, like the header, usually are inserted before other elements that appear lower; items that align to the left should be inserted before elements aligned to the right. Therefore, the order of the elements in this layout—header, sidebar1, content, and footer—conforms to CSS best practices. The div.container holds all the other elements together and helps to make them behave properly in different browsers.

One last important aspect you should notice is the navigation menu. Without the CSS styling, the navigation menu reverted back to a simple bulleted list with hyperlinks. A few years ago this menu would have been built with images and complex rollover animation. When those menus broke, for whatever reason, they usually became a jumbled unusable mess. Although the hyperlinks continued to work, without the images there were no words to tell the user what they were clicking. In this case, even without styling, these hyperlinks will always be usable.

7   Choose View > Style Rendering > Display Styles to turn on CSS styling again.

It's a good idea to get into the habit of saving files before you modify any settings or add content. Dreamweaver doesn't offer a backup or recovered-file feature; if it crashes before you save, all your work in any open, unsaved file will be lost.

8   Choose File > Save. In the Save As dialog box, navigate to the site root folder, if necessary. Name the file **mylayout.html** and click Save.

Dreamweaver normally saves HTML files to the default folder specified in the site definition, but it's a good idea to double-check the destination to make sure your files end up in the right place. All HTML pages created for the final site will be saved in the site root folder.

Adding a background image to the header

The final design features a banner similar to the one used in the previous lesson. You could insert the banner directly into the header, but adding it as a background image has the advantage of leaving the `<div>` open for other content.

1   Choose Window > CSS Styles to display the CSS Styles panel, if necessary.

2   Select the image placeholder *Insert_logo (180x90)* in the header. Press Delete.

The empty header will collapse to a fraction of its former size after deleting the image placeholder because it has no CSS height specification.

3   Double-click the `.header` rule to edit it.

4   In the Background category of the "CSS Rule Definition for *.header*" dialog box, click the Browse button next to the Background-image field.

5   Select **banner2.jpg** and note the dimensions of the image. Click OK/Choose.

Note that this banner doesn't feature the extra white space at the bottom or the butterfly as did the one used in Lesson 4. The new banner will better accommodate the horizontal navigation menu shown in the wireframe design. Eliminating the white portion also protects the overall page appearance in case something causes the header to expand in height exposing that part of the image. However, you're not totally out of the woods; remember that background images repeat both vertically and horizontally by default. To ensure this setting doesn't cause any undesirable effects, you'll need to change the repeat behavior.

6   Choose **no-repeat** from the Background-repeat menu.

7   Click Apply to view the results.

The header is wide enough but not tall enough to display the entire background image. Since background images aren't truly inserted in an element, they have no effect on the size of a container, good or bad. To ensure the <div> is large enough to display the entire image, you need to add a height specification to the .header rule.

8   In the Box category, type **130** in the Height field and choose px from the Unit of measurement menu. Click Apply.

There's no point setting the width attribute here. You learned in Lesson 4 the width of the layout in that example is specified in the .container rule. Chances are the same is true in this layout, too.

Before clicking OK, let's add some finishing touches to the header.

9   In the Background category, type **#090** in the Background-color field. Click OK.

It's important to start anticipating what would happen if things go wrong, say for example if the background image doesn't display. The green specified is part of the site color scheme and will be used throughout the website.

10 Choose File > Save.

Inserting new <div> components

The wireframe design shows two new <div> elements added to the default layout. The first contains the butterfly image, the second the horizontal navigation bar. Did you notice how the butterfly actually overlaps both the header and the horizontal navigation bar? There are several ways to achieve this effect. In this case, an absolutely positioned <div> will work nicely.

1 Insert the cursor into the header, if necessary. Select the <div.header> tag selector. Press the Left Arrow key.

Note: To better understand how this technique works, try this step in Split view.

This procedure should insert the cursor before the opening <div> tag for the header. If you had pressed the Right Arrow key, the cursor would move outside the closing </div> tag for the header instead. Remember this technique—you'll use it frequently in Dreamweaver when you want to insert the cursor in a specific location before or after a code element without resorting to Code view.

2 Choose Insert > Layout Objects > AP Div.

An AP div will appear at the top left of the header. Note the id (#1pDiv1) assigned to the new div in the tag selector. A corresponding rule has been added to the CSS Styles panel.

In previous versions of HTML, an AP div would have been assigned its size and position using inline HTML attributes. In a concession to new CSS-based web standards, these specifications are applied by CSS via a unique id created by Dreamweaver at the moment you insert the element.

3 Click the <div#apDiv1> tag selector.

The Property inspector displays the properties for <div#apDiv1>. Note the width and height specifications displayed in the Property inspector. These values are actually stored in the #apDiv1 rule generated by Dreamweaver.

Note: In previous versions of Dreamweaver, values entered in the Property inspector were added as inline HTML attributes. In CS5, most of these values will be added as custom CSS markup.

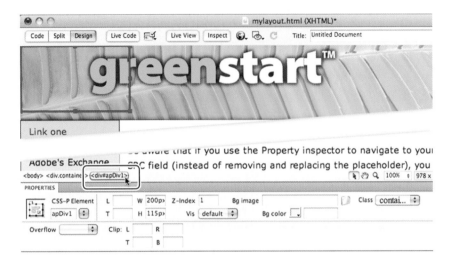

4 Insert the cursor into `<div#apDiv1>`.

5 Choose Insert > Image. Select **butterfly-ovr.gif** from the images folder. Observe the dimensions of the image: 170 pixels by 150 pixels.

6 Click OK/Choose.

The Image Tag Accessibility Attributes dialog box appears.

Note: In most cases, an image that's larger than its container will distort the container. Using images that are too large can destroy a carefully designed CSS layout. Pay close attention to the dimensions of images you use in your site.

7 Type **GreenStart Logo** in the Alternate text field in the Image Tag Accessibility Attributes dialog box. Click OK.

You'll notice that the AP div is slightly wider than the butterfly image. Although the extra space shouldn't cause any trouble, it's a good idea to match the dimensions of the container to the image.

8 Double-click the #apDiv1 rule in the CSS Styles panel.

The "CSS Rule definition for *.container #apDiv1*" dialog box appears.

9 In the Box category, type **170** in the Width field. Type **150** in the Height field.

The `<div>` dimensions now match the height and width of the image.

10 Deselect the Same For All checkboxes for Margins.

11 Type **15 px** in the Top margin field. Type **30 px** in the Left margin field. Click OK.

When the rule definition dialog box vanishes, `<div#apDiv1>` appears floating over the header, 15 pixels from the top and 30 pixels from the left.

An AP div acts like a free agent. It ignores the other page components and can even be positioned above or below other `<div>` elements and content.

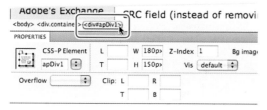

The `<div#apDiv1>` is complete. Let's create the `<div>` for the horizontal navigation bar.

12 Insert the cursor back into the header. Click the `<div.header>` tag selector. Press the Right Arrow key.

The cursor should now appear after the ending `</div>` tag of the header.

13 Choose Window > Insert, if the Insert panel is not visible. Choose Layout from the Category menu. Click Insert Div Tag.

The Insert Div Tag dialog box appears. Note that the Insert menu displays the selection "At insertion point". The new `<div>` will be inserted into the code at that position and not wrap around any other elements.

14 Type **h-navbar** in the ID field. Click the New CSS Rule button.

The New CSS Rule dialog box appears with the ID #h-navbar automatically entered in the Selector Name field. Click OK.

15 In the Type category, type **90** in the Font-size field and select the percentage sign (%) from the pop-up list. Type **#FFC** in the Color field.

16 In the Background category, type **#090** in the Background-color field. Click the Browse button next to the Background-image field.

17 Select **background.jpg** from the images folder. Click OK/Choose.

18 Choose repeat-x from the Background-repeat menu.

19 In the Block category, select Right from the Text-align field.

20 In the Box category, deselect the Same For All check box for Padding.

Type **5 px** in the Top padding field.

Type **20 px** in the Right padding field.

Type **5 px** in the Bottom padding field.

● **Note:** To enter values in the bottom field, remember to deselect the Same For All checkboxes in each section first.

21 In the Border category, enter the following values only in the Bottom border fields: **solid**, **2 px**, **#060**. Click OK in the CSS Rule Definition dialog box. Click OK in the Insert Div Tag dialog box.

The `<div#h-navbar>` appears below the header fully formatted and filled with placeholder text.

22 Delete the placeholder text. Type **Home | About Us | Contact Us** in `<div#h-navbar>` as placeholders for the organizational navigation links. You will convert these to actual hyperlinks in Lesson 10, "Working with Navigation."

23 Press Ctrl-S/Cmd-S to save the file.

Modifying the page width and background color

Before you convert this file into the project template, let's tighten up the formatting and the placeholder content. As you did in the last lesson, the overall width has to be modified to match the banner image.

1 Double-click the `.container` rule in the CSS Styles panel.

2 In the Box category, change the width to **950 px**. Click OK.

The `<div.container>` element now matches the width of the banner image, but you probably noticed there was an unintended consequence when you changed the overall width. The main content area shifted down below the sidebar. To understand what happened, you'll have to do a quick investigation.

3 In the CSS Styles panel, click the `.content` rule and check its properties. Note its width: 780 pixels.

4 Click the `.sidebar1` rule and check its width: 180 pixels.

Combined, the two `<div>` elements total 960 pixels. The elements are too wide to sit side by side in the main container. This type of error is common in web design and easily fixed.

5 Click the `.content` rule in the CSS Styles panel. In the Properties section of the panel, change the width to **770 px**.

The `<div.content>` element moves back to its intended position. This was a good reminder that the size, placement, and specifications of page elements have important interactions that can affect the final design and display.

Let's remove the page background color.

6 Double-click the body rule. In the Background category, change the Background-color to **#FFF**. Click OK.

Notice that the absence of the background color gives the impression that the page's content area drifts off into the wide expanse. You could give `<div.container>` its own background color or simply add a border to give the page a definitive edge.

7 Double-click the `.container` rule. In the Border category, select the Same For All option and enter the following values for all border fields: **solid**, **2px**, and **#060**. Click OK.

8 Save the file.

Modifying existing content and formatting

As you can see, the CSS layout is already equipped with a vertical navigation menu. The generic hyperlinks are simply placeholders, waiting for your final content. Let's change the placeholder text in the menu to match the pages outlined in the thumbnails and modify the colors to match the site color scheme.

1 Select the placeholder text *Link one* in the first menu button.
Type **Green News**.
Change *Link two* to read **Green Products**.
Change *Link three* to read **Green Events**.
Change *Link four* to read **Green Travel**.

One of the advantages of using bulleted lists as navigational menus is that it's easy to insert new links.

2 With the cursor still at the end of the words *Green Travel*, press Enter/Return. Type **Green Tips**.

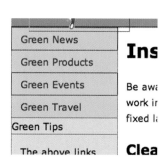

The new text appears in what looks like a button structure, but the background color doesn't match and the text isn't aligned with other menu items. You could probably figure out what's wrong in Design view, but in this case, the problem may be identified faster in Code view.

3   With the cursor still inserted in the menu, select Code view. Observe the menu items and compare the first four with the last. Can you see the difference?

```
164    <div class="sidebar1">
165       <ul class="nav">
166          <li><a href="#">Green News</a></li>
167          <li><a href="#">Green Products</a></li>
168          <li><a href="#">Green Events</a></li>
169          <li><a href="#">Green Travel</a></li>
170          <li>Green Tips</li>
171       </ul>
```

The difference is obvious in Code view. The last item is formatted with the <li> element like the others—as part of the bulleted list—but it doesn't feature the <a href="#"> code that's used as a hyperlink placeholder. For *Green Tips* to look like the other menu items, you have to add a hyperlink, or at least a similar placeholder.

4   Select the text *Green Tips*. In the Link field of the HTML Property inspector, type # and press Enter/Return.

The code in all the items is identical now.

5   Select Design view.

All the menu items are identically formatted now. You'll learn more about how to format text with CSS to create a menu in Lesson 6, "Working with Cascading Style Sheets."

The current menu color doesn't match the site color scheme. To change the color, you'll have to do some investigative work to find which CSS rule controls this formatting. This is a good time to learn how to use the Code Navigator.

6   Insert the cursor into any of the menu items.

After a few seconds the Code Navigator (⬡) icon will appear.

7 Click the Code Navigator icon.

A small window opens displaying a list of 11 CSS rules that affect the targeted element. The list is in order of specificity, with the most powerful rule at the bottom. In some cases, the rules listed may only affect the element in a roundabout way, as in the body rule, which affects *all* HTML elements on the page.

8 Move the cursor over the first CSS rule in the list. Observe the formats displayed.

Another window appears listing all the formats specified in the selected rule. You're looking for a background color that's applied to the menu items. Be careful. There's probably more than one background-color in the listed rules, so if you find one, it's important to determine whether it actually affects the menu or something else.

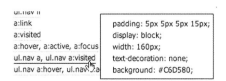

9 Examine each rule until you find the pertinent one.

The .sidebar1 rule specifies a background-color, but it affects the <div> and not the menu. The one you're actually looking for is applied by the rule: ul.nav a, ul.nav a:visited. This rule specifies a background-color for a <ul> (unordered list) element with a class attribute of nav that contains an <a> (hyperlink) element. Sound right?

10 Locate the rule `ul.nav a, ul.nav a:visited` in the CSS Styles panel and select it. In the Properties section of the panel, change the existing background-color to **#090**.

The color of the menu items now matches `<div#h-navbar>`. The black text is difficult to read in the green background color. You can use the Properties section of the CSS Styles panel to add as well as edit element properties.

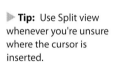

11 Click the Add Property link in the Properties section of the CSS Styles panel.

A new property field appears.

12 Choose Color from the Property field menu. Enter **#FFC** in the Value field. Press Enter/Return to complete the new rule property.

13 Save the file.

Inserting an image placeholder

The sidebar will feature photos, captions, and short blurbs on environmental topics. Let's insert a placeholder image and caption below the vertical menu.

1 Insert the cursor into the text directly below the vertical menu. Click the `<p>` tag selector.

The placeholder image should not be inserted within the `<p>` element. If it were, it would inherit any margins, padding, and other formatting applied to the paragraph, which could cause it to break the layout.

Tip: Use Split view whenever you're unsure where the cursor is inserted.

2 Press the Left Arrow key.

The cursor is moved to the left of the opening `<p>` tag.

3 Choose Insert > Image Objects > Image Placeholder.

The Image Placeholder dialog box appears.

4 In the Image Placeholder dialog box, type **Sidebar** in the Name field.

Type **180** in the Width field.

Type **150** in the Height field.

Click OK.

An image placeholder appears in `<div.sidebar1>` below the vertical menu.

5　Select all the text below the image placeholder. Type **Insert caption here**.

The caption placeholder replaces the text.

6　Press Ctrl-S/Cmd-S to save.

Inserting placeholder text

Let's simplify the layout by replacing the existing headings and text in the main content area.

1　Double-click to select the heading *Instructions*. Type **Insert main heading here** to replace the text.

2　Select the remaining text in `<div.content>`. Type **Insert content here** to replace the text.

3　Press Ctrl-S/Cmd-S to save.

Modifying the footer

You need to reformat the footer and insert the copyright information.

1　Double-click the `.footer` rule in the CSS Styles panel.

2　In the Type category, enter **90%** in the Type-size field and **#FFC** in the Color field.

3　In the Background category, click the browse icon and insert **images/background.jpg** in the Background-image field.

4　Click OK/Choose.

5　Choose repeat-x from Background-repeat field menu.

6　Type **#090** into the Background-color field. Click OK.

7　Select the placeholder text in the footer. Type **Copyright 2010 Meridien GreenStart, All rights reserved**.

8　Press Ctrl-S/Cmd-S to save.

The basic page layout is complete.

Checking browser compatibility

The CSS layouts included with Dreamweaver have been thoroughly tested to work flawlessly in all major browsers. However, during the lesson you made major modifications to the original layout. These changes could have ramifications in the compatibility of the code in certain browsers. Before you use this page as your project template, you should check its compatibility.

1   If necessary, open **layout.html** in Dreamweaver.

2   Choose File > Check Page > Browser Compatibility.

    When the Report box opens, there should be no issues listed.

3   To close the report, double-click the Browser Compatibility tab in the Report panel or right-click the tab and choose Close Tab Group from the context menu.

Congratulations. You created a workable basic page layout for your project template and learned how to insert additional components, image placeholders, text, and headings; adjust CSS formatting; and check for browser compatibility.

Review questions

1 What three questions should you ask about any web design project?

2 What is the purpose of using thumbnails and wireframes?

3 What is the advantage of inserting the banner as a background image?

4 How can you insert the cursor before or after an element without using Code view?

5 How does the Code Navigator assist in designing your website layout?

Review answers

1 What is the purpose of the website? Who is the customer? How did they get here? These questions, and their answers, are essential in helping you develop the design, content, and strategy of your site.

2 Thumbnails and wireframes are quick techniques for roughing out the design and structure of your site without having to waste lots of time coding sample pages.

3 By inserting the banner or other large graphics as a background image, you leave the container free for other content.

4 Select an element using its tag selector and press the Left or Right Arrow key to move the cursor before or after the selected element.

5 The Code Navigator serves the role of a CSS detective. It allows you to investigate what CSS rules are formatting a selected element and how they are applied.

6 WORKING WITH CASCADING STYLE SHEETS

Lesson Overview

In this lesson, you'll work with cascading style sheets (CSS) in Dreamweaver and do the following:

- Manage CSS rules using the CSS Styles panel

- Create new CSS rules

- Create and apply custom CSS classes

- Create descendant selectors

- Create styles for page layout elements

- Move CSS rules to an external style sheet

- Create a style sheet for print applications

 This lesson will take about 2 hours to complete. Before beginning, make sure you have copied the files for Lesson 6 to your hard drive as described in the "Getting Started" section at the beginning of the book. If you are starting from scratch in this lesson, use the method described in the "Jumpstart" section of "Getting Started."

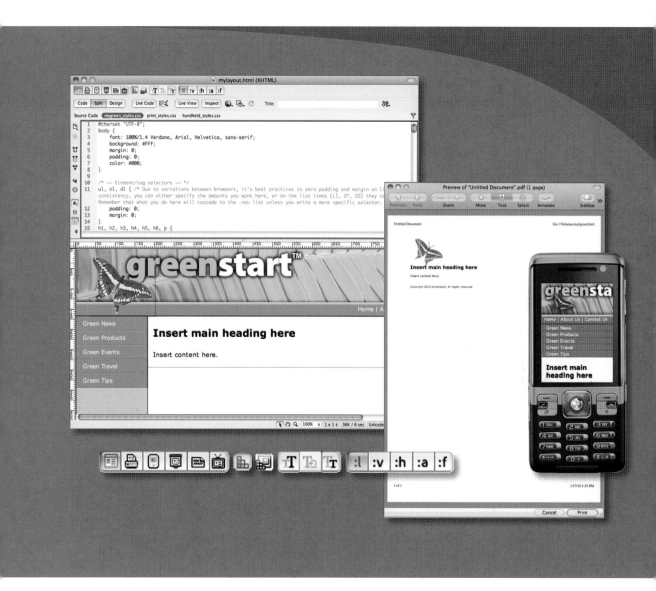

Today, pages designed in compliance with web standards separate the content from the formatting. Stored in a cascading style sheet (CSS), the formatting can be quickly changed and substituted for specific applications and devices.

Previewing a completed file

To see the finished page you will create in this lesson, you can preview it in a browser.

1   In the Files panel, expand the lesson06 folder.

2   Select the **layout_finished.html**.

3   Preview the page in your primary browser.

    Note the layout, various colors, and other formats applied to the text and page elements—all created by CSS styles.

4   In Dreamweaver, select File > Close to close **layout_finished.html**, if necessary.

Working with the CSS Styles panel

In Lesson 5, "Creating a Page Layout," you used one of the CSS layouts provided by Dreamweaver to start building your project site template page. These layouts come equipped with an underlying structure and a whole set of predefined CSS rules that establish the basic design and formatting of the page components and content. In the upcoming exercises in this lesson, you'll modify these rules and add new ones to complete the site design. But before you proceed, it's a vital aspect of your role as designer to understand the existing structure and formatting before you can effectively complete your tasks. It's important to take a few minutes at this time to examine the rules and understand what role they perform in the current document.

1   Open **mylayout.html** from the site root folder, if necessary. Or, if you are starting from scratch in this exercise, see the "Jumpstart" instructions in the "Getting Started" section at the beginning of the book.

2   Display the CSS Styles panel, if it isn't visible.

    The CSS Styles panel displays the `<style>` tag indicating that the style sheet is embedded in the `<head>` section of the document.

> ▶ **Tip:** If you don't see line numbers along the side of your Code view window, choose View > Code View Options > Line Numbers to turn on this feature.

3 Select Code view and locate the `<head>` section (starting around line 3). Locate the element `<style type="text/css">` and examine the subsequent code entries.

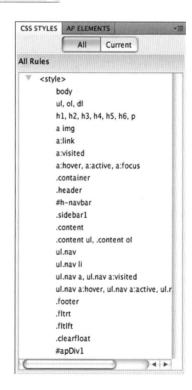

```
[Code] [Split] [Design]   [Live Code] [☰] [Live View] [Inspect] ⊙. ⊙ C    Title: Untitled Document              ⋔⋔.
3   <head>
4   <meta http-equiv="Content-Type" content="text/html; charset=UTF-8" />
5   <title>Untitled Document</title>
6   <style type="text/css">
7   <!--
8   body {
9       font: 100%/1.4 Verdana, Arial, Helvetica, sans-serif;
10      background: #FFF;
11      margin: 0;
12      padding: 0;
13      color: #000;
14  }
15
16  /* ~~ Element/tag selectors ~~ */
17  ul, ol, dl { /* Due to variations between browsers, it's best practices to zero
        padding and margin on lists. For consistency, you can either specify the amounts you
        want here, or on the list items (LI, DT, DD) they contain. Remember that what you
        do here will cascade to the .nav list unless you write a more specific selector. */
18      padding: 0;
19      margin: 0;
20  }
21  h1, h2, h3, h4, h5, h6, p {
22      margin-top: 0;   /* removing the top margin gets around an issue where margins
        can escape from their containing div. The remaining bottom margin will hold it away
        from any elements that follow. */
23      padding-right: 15px;
```

`<head>`   21K / 3 sec   Unicode 5.1 UTF-8

All the CSS rules displayed in the list are contained within the `<style>` element.

4 Note the names and order of the selectors within the CSS code.

5 Select Design view. In the CSS Styles panel, expand and examine the list of rules.

The list shows the same selector names in the same order you saw in Code view. There is a one-to-one relationship between the CSS code and the CSS Styles panel. When you create new rules or edit existing ones, Dreamweaver makes all the changes in the code for you, saving you time and reducing the possibility of code-entry errors. The CSS Styles panel is just one of the many productivity enhancements that you'll use and master in this book.

You should have 22 rules at this time—20 that came with the CSS layout, and 2 you made yourself in the previous lesson. The order of your rules may vary from this figure. The CSS Styles panel makes it easy to reorder the list.

In the last lesson, you created `<div#apDiv1>` and inserted it into the layout. The `#apDiv1` rule formats the `<div>` holding the butterfly logo and appears in the code between `<div.container>`

and `<div.header>`. But as you can see in the pictured CSS Styles panel, it appears at the bottom of all the rules. Moving this rule within the style sheet will not affect how it formats the element, but it will make it easier to find if you need to edit later.

● **Note:** The names and order of styles in your panel may vary from those pictured.

6 Select the `#apDiv1` rule and drag it directly underneath the `.container` rule.

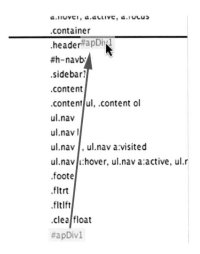

Dreamweaver has moved the rule within the list, but that's not all. It has also rewritten the code in the embedded style sheet, moving the rule to its new position. Arranging related rules together can save time later when you need to format specific elements or components. But be watchful for unintended consequences. Moving rules in the list can upset the established cascade or inheritance relationships you have already created. Review Lesson 3, "CSS Basics," if you need a refresher on these theories.

Before you move any other rules, you should first understand what function each one performs.

7 Select the body rule in the CSS Styles panel. Observe the properties and values that appear in the Property section of the panel.

Most of these settings came with the layout, although you changed the background color in the last lesson. Note how the margins and padding are set to zero.

8 Select the next `ul`, `ol`, `dl` rule and observe the values that appear.

As in the body rule, this rule sets all margin and padding values to zero. Do you know why? An experienced web designer could select each rule in turn and probably figure out the reasons for each of the formats and settings. But you don't need to resort to hiring a consultant, when Dreamweaver provides much of the information you need already.

9 Right-click the ul, ol, dl rule and choose Go to Code from the context menu.

Dreamweaver displays the document in Split view and focuses on the section of code that contains the ul, ol, dl rule. Observe the text between the opening /* and closing */ markers. This markup is called a *comment* and contains text that usually provides behind-the-scenes information that will not be displayed within the browser or affect any elements. Comments are a good way to leave handy reminders within the body of the web page or notes to yourself, or others, explaining why you wrote the code in a particular way. You'll notice that some of the comments are used to introduce a set of rules, and others are embedded in the rule itself.

10 Scroll down through the style sheet and study the comments, paying close attention to the embedded ones.

The more you understand what these predefined rules are doing, the better results you can achieve for your final site. Here's what you'll find: the rules body, .header, .container, .sidebar1, .content, and .footer define the basic structural elements of the page. The rules a:img, a:link, a:visited, a:hover, a:active, and a:focus set up the appearance and performance of the default hyperlink behavior; ul.nav, ul.nav li, ul.nav a, ul.nav a:visited, ul.nav a:hover, ul.nav a:active, and ul.nav a:focus define the look and behavior of the vertical menu. The remaining rules are intended to reset default formatting or add some desired styling as outlined in the embedded comments.

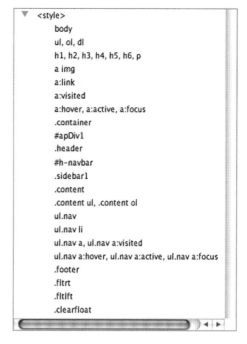

For the most part, there's nothing unacceptable, or fatal, in the current order of the rules, but keeping related rules together will pay productivity dividends later when the style sheet gets more complicated.

11 Using the CSS Styles panel, reorder the rules in the list, as shown in the figure on the right.

● **Note:** When moving rules using the CSS Styles panel, the position of comments that are not embedded may not be preserved.

Now that you are more aware of the rules and rule order, taking special care with rule order from this point forward when you create new styles is a good practice.

12 Save the file.

Creating new CSS rules

In most of the previous exercises, you merely edited the rules that were predefined in the CSS layout. In the next exercise, you will learn how to create your own custom rules for HTML elements, classes, and ids.

Creating descendant selectors

The predefined style sheet declares a rule for multiple elements that will affect all h1, h2, h3, h4, h5, h6, and p tags no matter where they appear on the page. But, if you want to target a style at a specific tag within a specific `<div>`, it requires a *descendant* selector. Dreamweaver makes it easy to create such rules.

1   Insert the cursor in the main heading in the main content area. Note the names and order of the tag selectors at the bottom of the document window.

The heading is an `<h1>` element in `<div.content>` in `<div.container>` in the body element. As described in the last exercise, when creating new rules take care about where they appear in the style sheet. Rules at the top of the sheet pass formatting to rules appearing later. Inserting a rule in the wrong place could cause the browsers to ignore it altogether.

2   Select the `.content` rule in the CSS Styles panel.

By selecting the `.content` rule first, Dreamweaver will insert the new rule immediately following it in the style sheet.

● **Note:** When the cursor is inserted into the page content, Dreamweaver will always create the compound selector for you, even if the Compound option is not displayed when the dialog box first appears.

3   In the CSS Styles panel, click the New CSS Rule (⊞) icon. If the Compound selector type is not displayed, choose it from the Selector Type menu.

The New CSS Rule dialog box opens. Typically, when the cursor is inserted into page content, the dialog box defaults to the Compound selector type and displays a descendant selector based on the location of the cursor, in this case `.container .content h1`.

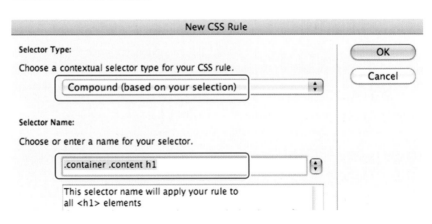

Selector Type:

Choose a contextual selector type for your CSS rule.

Compound (based on your selection)   OK   Cancel

Selector Name:

Choose or enter a name for your selector.

.container .content h1

This selector name will apply your rule to all `<h1>` elements

If you remember the CSS syntax you learned in Lesson 3, you know that this new rule will affect <h1> elements, but only when they appear within an element formatted with a class of .content, when both appear within an element formatted with a class of .container. All other <h1> elements will remain unaffected.

Since there will only be one <div.content> element in this page design, there's no need for such specificity in the rule. Whenever possible, rules should be simplified to reduce the total amount of code that needs to be downloaded. Although in this case it's only the word .container that isn't needed, unnecessary code adds up across the entire site (and Internet) overall.

4 In the New CSS Rule dialog box, click the Less Specific button. Click OK.

The word .container is removed from the Selector Name field.

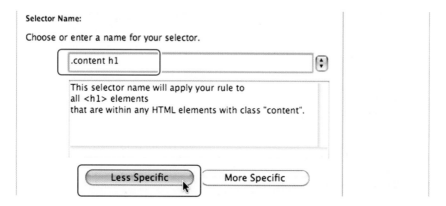

5 In the Type category of the "CSS Rule Definition For .content h1" dialog box, enter **160%** in the Font-size field.

6 In the Box category, deselect Same For All and enter **10px** in the top margin field only. Enter **5px** in the Bottom margin field. Click OK.

The main heading appears smaller in size and 10 pixels lower on the page. Note that the new rule was inserted directly after the .content rule in the CSS Styles panel.

7 Save the file.

Creating custom classes

CSS class attributes allow you to apply custom formatting to a specific element, or portion of a specific element. Let's create a class that will allow you to apply the GreenStart logo color as you did in Lesson 4, "Getting a Quick Start."

1 In the CSS Styles panel, click the New CSS Rule icon.

2 Choose Class from the Selector Type menu. Type **green** in the Selector Name field. Click OK.

Tip: When the desired styling doesn't appear as expected, use the Code Navigator to suss out the conflict.

3 In the "CSS Rule Definition For .*green*" dialog box, type **#090** in the Color field of the Type category. Click OK.

The .green rule is added to the style sheet. In most instances, a class attribute will override any default or applied styling, so it should not matter where in the style sheet it appears. However, differing, even contradictory, effects can occur when classes are combined with elements and/or ids to form compound selectors.

Dreamweaver makes it easy to apply classes. Let's apply a class to an entire element.

4 Insert the cursor anywhere in the <h1> element in <div.content>. Make sure the cursor is flashing in the element and no text is selected.

Note: You may need to refresh the page display to see the updated tag selector.

5 In the Property inspector, choose **green** from the Class menu.

All the text in the <h1> element is now formatted in green. At the bottom of the document window, <h1.green> now displays in the tag selectors.

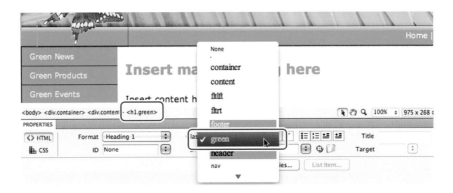

6 Switch to Code view. Examine the opening tag of <h1.green>.

```
<h1 class="green">Insert main heading here</h1>
```

The rule is applied as an attribute to the tag as <h1 class="green">. When the cursor is inserted in an existing element, Dreamweaver assumes you want to apply the class to the entire element.

Now let's remove a class from an element.

Tip: You can also apply the class by clicking the tag selector before selecting the class from the Property inspector.

7 Insert the cursor anywhere in the formatted element.

The tag selector displays <h1.green> and *green* appears in the Class menu of the Property inspector.

8 Choose None from the Class menu of the Property inspector.

The class attribute is removed from the code. The tag selector is now <h1> and *None* appears in the Class menu.

Next let's apply a class to a range of text.

9 Select the words *main heading* in the <h1> element. Choose green from the Class menu in the Property inspector.

The class is applied to the selected text using <span class="green">.

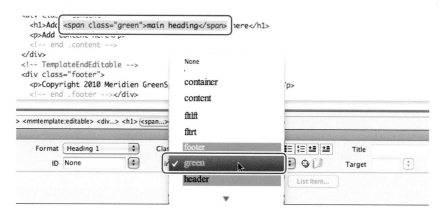

Now remove the class.

10 Switch to Design view. Insert the cursor anywhere in the formatted text. Choose None from the Class menu.

The text returns to the default formatting. When the cursor is inserted in a class-formatted element, Dreamweaver assumes you want to remove the formatting from the entire range of text.

11 Save the file.

> **Tip:** Classes can be applied and removed in either Design or Code view.

Creating custom ids

The CSS id attribute is given more specific weight in CSS styling because it is used to identify unique content on a web page and should trump all other styling. The AP div containing the butterfly logo is a good example of a unique element. The <div#apDiv1> is positioned in a specific location on the page, and you can be pretty certain you'll have only one such <div> per page. Let's modify the existing rule for this element to reflect its use in the layout.

1 Select the #apDiv1 rule in the CSS Styles panel. Right-click the selector name and choose Edit Selector from the context menu.

The selector name becomes editable in the panel list.

2 Change the name to **#logo**. Press Enter/Return to complete the editing process.

The rule name changes, but it no longer formats `<div#apDiv1>`. The layout reflects the default behavior of the unformatted element; without `height` and `width` and other key attributes, it expands to the full width of `<div.container>` and pushes `<div.header>` down below the height of the butterfly image.

To restore the layout, you have to assign the `#logo` rule to `<div#apDiv1>`.

3 Insert the cursor in `<div#apDiv1>` or click the butterfly to select it. Click the `<div#apDiv1>` tag selector at the bottom of the document window.

The Property inspector displays the properties of `<div#apDiv1>`. Note the id displayed in the Property inspector.

4 Choose logo from the ID field pop-up menu.

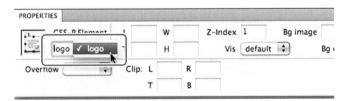

Reformatted, `<div#logo>` resumes its former size and positioning.

Classes can be used as many times as you want, but an id is supposed to be used only once per page. Although you could conceivably type one id multiple times manually yourself, Dreamweaver won't offer any help in your attempt at rule breaking. You can demonstrate this functionality with a simple test.

5 Examine the CSS Styles panel and note the available class and id selectors.

There are 10 classes and 2 ids.

6 Insert the cursor in `<div#logo>`. Click the `<div#logo>` tag selector.

The Property inspector reflects the formats of `<div#logo>`.

● **Note:** On a Mac, you may not be able to access the ID pop-up menu if no unassigned ids are available.

7 Open the ID field pop-up menu and examine the available ids.

The only id available is `logo`. As each id stored in the style sheet is used in your layout, Dreamweaver interactively removes it from the menu.

A <div> apart

An AP div is treated differently from normal <div> elements. You see this difference as soon as you insert an AP div into a document; Dreamweaver creates a rule for it automatically and assigns it attributes for width, height, position, and z-index. This doesn't happen with a normal div. In fact, the special treatment persists even after the rule is created. If you change the id of the AP div in the Property inspector, Dreamweaver will update the name of the rule in the CSS Styles panel at the same time.

However, the reverse is not true. If you change the rule name (as you did in this lesson), Dreamweaver does not change the id on the element itself. The program leaves this chore up to you.

8   Choose green from the Class field menu.

The tag selector displays <div.green#logo>.

9   Insert the cursor in the horizontal menu <div#h-navbar>.
    Click the <div#h-navbar> tag selector.

10 Open the ID menu and examine the available ids.

The only id available is h-navbar.

11 Open the Class field menu. Examine the available class attributes.

Note that the class green is still available. The Dreamweaver interface allows you to apply the same class to both <div> elements but prevents you from applying either id more than once.

12 Choose None from the Class field menu.

13 In the Property inspector, apply None to <div#logo> using the Class menu.

14 Save the file.

Creating an interactive menu

By combining descendant selectors, classes, and ids together, you can produce amazing behaviors from seemingly static elements.

1   If necessary, switch to Design view and click the Live View button.

The document window will preview the layout as it would appear in a browser. Videos, Flash animation, and JavaScript behaviors will all perform as they would on the Internet.

2 Position the cursor over the vertical navigation menu in the sidebar. Observe the behavior and appearance of the menu items.

As the mouse moves over each button, the cursor icon changes to the hand pointer, indicating that the menu items are formatted as hyperlinks. The buttons also change color momentarily as the mouse passes over each, producing a dramatic graphical experience, too. These effects are all enabled by HTML hyperlink behaviors, formatted by CSS.

Hyperlink pseudoclasses

In all, there are four *states,* or distinct behaviors, available to the <a> element that can be modified by CSS using what are called *pseudoclasses:*

- The a:link pseudoclass creates the default display and behavior of the hyperlink. The a:link pseudoclass is interchangeable with the "a" selector in CSS rules.

- The a:visited pseudoclass applies formatting after the link has been visited.

- The a:hover pseudoclass applies formatting while the cursor passes over the link.

- The a:active pseudoclass formats the link when the mouse is clicked on it.

When used, the pseudoclasses must be declared in this order to be effective. Remember, whether declared in the style sheet or not, each state has a set of default formats and behaviors.

3 Position the mouse cursor over the items in the horizontal navigation menu in <div#h-navbar>. Observe the behavior and appearance of the menu items, if any.

The pointer and background color do not change. The items are not formatted as hyperlinks yet.

4 Click the Live View button to return to the normal document display.

5 Select the word *Home* in <div#h-navbar>. Do not select the spaces on either side of the word or the vertical bars, or *pipes,* that separate the words.

Correct

Incorrect

● **Note:** In most cases, you can't create new CSS rules or format elements in the document while Live view is active.

6 Type # in the Link field of the Property inspector. Press Enter/Return.

Adding a hash mark # in the Link field creates a hyperlink placeholder and will allow you to create and test the necessary formatting for the horizontal navigation menu without having to create a complete link. Note how the text now displays the formatting of a typical text hyperlink.

7 Add hyperlink placeholders to the items *About Us* and *Contact Us.*

Be sure to select both words in each item before applying the placeholder. If you don't, each word will be treated as separate links instead of as one.

The first step in making the horizontal menu look more like the vertical one is to remove the default hyperlink underscore.

8 Insert the cursor in any of the hyperlinks in `<div#h-navbar>`. Select the `#h-navbar` rule in the CSS Styles panel. Click the New CSS Rule icon.

9 Choose Compound from the Selector Type menu, if necessary.

The Selector Name field displays `.container #h-navbar a.`

10 In the New CSS Rule dialog box, click the Less Specific button.

The `.container` class is removed from the Selector Name field.

11 Insert the cursor in the Selector Name field. Press Ctrl-A/Cmd-A to select the entire selector name. Press Ctrl-C/Cmd-C to copy the selector.

12 Press the Right Arrow key to move the cursor to the end of the selector text. Type a comma (,) and press the spacebar to insert a space. Press Ctrl-V/Cmd-V to paste the selector from the clipboard. Type `:visited` at the end of the pasted selector.

The selector should now appear as #h-navbar a, #h-navbar a:visited in the Selector Name field.

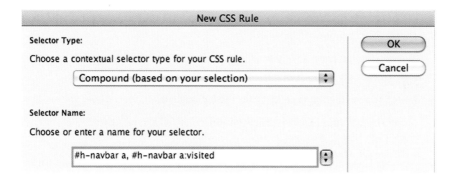

13 Click OK.

The new #h-navbar a, #h-navbar a:visited rule appears in the CSS Styles panel below the #h-navbar rule.

▶ **Tip:** If you click Apply two times in a row, the CSS Rule definition dialog box will close. If you accidentally close the dialog box before you complete the formatting, simply double-click the rule in the CSS Styles panel to reopen it.

14 In the Type category Text Decoration option, select none. Click Apply.

The underscore is removed from the hyperlinks. Let's make the text easier to read against the green background.

15 Type **#FFC** in the Color field. Click OK.

The color #FFC is easier to see on the green background color. Let's test the hyperlink properties of the items in the horizontal menu.

16 Click the Live View button. Position the cursor over the hyperlink placeholders in the horizontal menu.

The mouse icon changes to the hand pointer, indicating that the text is formatted as a hyperlink, but it has none of the flair of the vertical menu, with its changing background color. That interactive behavior is controlled by the pseudoclass a:hover. Let's use this selector to create a similar behavior.

17 Click the Live View button to return to the normal document display. Save all files.

Modifying hyperlink behavior

In this exercise, you will modify the default hyperlink behavior and add interactivity.

◖ **Note:** The a:hover state inherits much of its formatting from a or a:link. In most cases, you only need to declare values for formatting that will change when this state is activated.

1 Insert the cursor in any one of the hyperlinks in the horizontal menu. You don't need to select any characters in the link. Select the #h-navbar a, #h-navbar a:visited rule in the CSS Styles panel. Click the New CSS Rule icon.

The New CSS Rule dialog box appears with the Compound selector type displayed and the text .container #h-navbar a entered in the Selector Name field.

2 Select the Compound selector type, if necessary. Edit the Selector Name to say #h-navbar a:hover. Click OK.

The new #h-navbar a:hover rule appears in the CSS Styles panel. The "CSS Rule Definition For *#h-navbar a:hover*" dialog box appears.

3 In the Type category, type **#FFC** in the Color field.

In the Background category Background-color field, type **#0C0**. Click OK.

◖ **Note:** Adding space to the margins won't work, because margins add space outside the background color.

4 Activate Live view and test the hyperlink behavior in the horizontal menu.

The background behind the hyperlink text changes to light green as the mouse passes over it. This is a good start, but you may notice that the color change doesn't extend to the edges of the <div> or even to the pipes dividing one link from another. You can create a more interesting effect by adding a little padding to the element.

5   Deactivate Live view. Double-click the #h-navbar a:hover rule to edit it.

6   In the Box category, enter **5px** in the Padding field, with the Same For All option selected. Click OK.

7   Activate Live view and test the hyperlink behavior in the horizontal menu.

The background color of each link now extends five pixels all around the hyperlink. But there's an unintended consequence: The added padding causes the text on either side of the link to shift whenever the a:hover state is activated. The solution to this problem is actually quite simple.

8   In the CSS Styles panel Properties section, select and delete the Padding property for the rule: #h-navbar a:hover.

9   Double-click the #h-navbar a, #h-navbar a:visited rule to edit it. In the Box category, enter **5px** in the Padding field, with the Same For All option selected. Click OK.

10   Activate Live view and test the hyperlink behavior in the horizontal menu.

When the mouse moves over the links, the background color extends five pixels around the link without shifting. By adding padding to the default state of the hyperlink, the hover state inherits the extra padding and allows the background color to work as desired.

11   Save the file.

Congratulations. You've created your own version of the interactive navigation menu in <div#h-navbar>. But you may have noticed that the predefined background color selection for the a:hover state in the vertical menu doesn't match the site color scheme. To be consistent, the colors used in the site should adhere to the overall theme.

Modifying existing hyperlink behavior

As you gain more experience in web design and working with CSS, identifying design inconsistencies and knowing how to correct them becomes easier. Since you know that the *hover* state is responsible for creating the interactive link behavior, it should be a simple matter to change the background color in the vertical menu. The first step is to assess what rules pertain specifically to the vertical menu itself.

1   Insert the cursor into one of the vertical menu items. Observe the names and the order of elements in the tag selector display.

The vertical menu is using a `.nav` class applied to the `<ul>` (unordered list) element.

2   Locate any rules in the CSS Styles panel that format the `.nav` class. Is there an `a:hover` pseudoclass associated with it?

The CSS Styles panel displays the `ul.nav a:hover`, `ul.nav a:active`, `ul.nav a:focus` rule that formats the hyperlink behavior you're looking for.

3   Double-click the `ul.nav a:hover`, `ul.nav a:active`, `ul.nav a:focus` rule to edit it. Change the background color to **#0C0**. Click OK.

4   Using Live view, test the behavior of the vertical menu.

The background color of the vertical menu matches the horizontal menu and the site color scheme.

5   Save the file.

Adding visual appeal to menus

Another popular CSS trick that can give menus a bit more visual interest is to vary the border colors. By applying different colors to each border, you can give the buttons a 3-D appearance. As in the previous exercise, you first need to locate the rules formatting the elements.

1   Insert the cursor in one of the menu items and examine the tag selector display.

The menu buttons are built using `<ul.nav>`, `<li>`, and `<a>` elements. Since you know that the `<ul>` element creates the entire list, and not the individual items, you can eliminate it as a suspect.

2   Select the `ul.nav li` rule in the CSS Styles panel. Observe the attributes displayed in the Properties section of the panel.

The `ul.nav li` rule formats the basic structure of the menu button.

3   Double-click the `ul.nav li` rule.

4   Select the Border category in "CSS Rule Definition For *ul.nav li*."
Enter **solid, 1px, #0C0** in the Top border fields.
Enter **solid, 1px, #060** in the Right border fields.
Enter **solid, 1px, #060** in the Bottom border fields.
Enter **solid, 1px, #0C0** in the Left border fields.
Click OK.

By adding lighter colors to the top and left and darker colors to the right and bottom, you have created a subtle but effective three-dimensional effect.

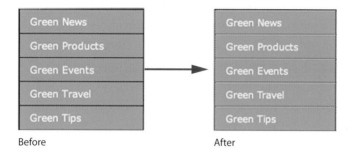

Before   After

5 Save the file.

Creating faux columns

Although multicolumn designs are very popular on the web, HTML and CSS have no built-in commands to produce true column structures in a web page. Instead, columnar designs—like the one used in the Dreamweaver CSS layouts—are simulated by using `<div>` elements and various formatting techniques, usually involving margins and the float attribute.

Unfortunately, these methods have their limitations and downsides. For example, one of the problems with the current layout in this lesson is getting both columns to display at the same height. Either one column or the other will almost always be shorter. Since the sidebar has a background color, there will be a visible gap at the bottom as content is added to the main page. There are methods, using JavaScript and other tricks, to force columns to display at equal height, but these are not fully supported by all browsers and could cause your page to break unexpectedly. Many designers sidestep the issue altogether by simply refusing to use background colors.

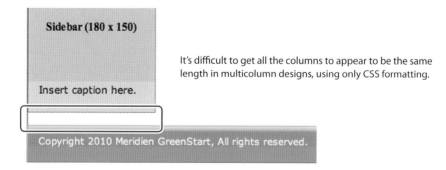

It's difficult to get all the columns to appear to be the same length in multicolumn designs, using only CSS formatting.

Instead, you will create the effect of a full-height sidebar column by using a background graphic and the repeat function. This technique works well with fixed-width website designs, like this one.

1   Insert the cursor in `<div.sidebar1>` below the vertical menu. Examine the tag selector display.

    The `<div.sidebar1>` is contained within `<div.container>` and then, together, in the body element.

2   Select the `.sidebar1` rule in the CSS Styles panel. Examine its properties.

    The `.sidebar1` rule applies a background color to the sidebar. Since the background color assigned to the `<div>` appears already to be failing to extend to the bottom of the document, the `.sidebar1` rule is not the solution to this problem. It's a good idea to remove the background color if it's not producing the desired results.

● **Note:** The Trash Can icon in the CSS Styles panel is context sensitive. It can be used to delete a rule property or the entire rule, depending on how it is invoked.

3   Select the background color reference in the Properties section of the CSS Styles panel. Click the Delete CSS Property (🗑) icon at the bottom of the panel.

    Now, you'll modify the `.container` rule to produce a background effect for the sidebar.

4   Double-click the `.container` rule. In the Background category, click the Browse button. Select **divider.gif** from the default images folder. Click OK/Choose.

5   Choose repeat-y in the Background-repeat field menu. Click OK.

    A graphic 180 pixels wide appears at the left edge of `<div.container>` and extends from the top to the bottom. Since the other `<div>` elements are contained entirely within `<div.container>`, the background appears behind them and is visible only where appropriate.

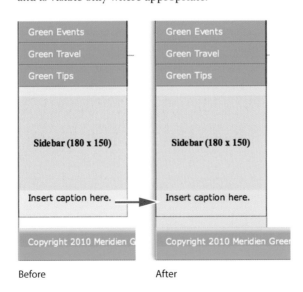

Before   After

Let's make one last tweak to the sidebar by removing the extra space that appears between the menu and image placeholder. The first step is to identify the rules that may be creating this styling.

6 Insert the cursor in the last button of the vertical menu. Right-click the button and choose Code Navigator from the context menu.

The Code Navigator appears, displaying a list of 11 CSS rules affecting this item. Chances are a margin setting is producing the spacing effect.

7 Scan the rules for a bottom-margin setting.

The ul.nav rule features a bottom-margin of 15 pixels.

8 Select the ul.nav rule in the CSS Styles panel. Select the bottom-margin setting in the Properties section. Click the Delete CSS Property (🗑) icon.

The gap between the menu and the image placeholder closes up.

9 Save the file.

Moving rules to an external style sheet

When prototyping a web page design, it's more practical to keep the CSS embedded. It makes the process of testing and uploading quick and simple. But, an internal style sheet is limited to one page. An external style sheet can be linked to any number of pages and, for most web applications, is the normal and preferred workflow. Before this page is put into production as a template, it's a good idea to move the CSS styles from the <head> section of the document to an external CSS style sheet. Dreamweaver provides the means to handle that task quickly and easily.

1 In the CSS Styles panel, select the first defined style, body. Hold the Shift key and select the last style.

2 In the CSS Styles panel, choose Move CSS Rules from the Options menu in the upper-right corner of the panel.

● **Note:** The last style in your style sheet may differ from the figure. Remember to select the last one.

You could also right-click the selected area to access the Move CSS Rules option from the context menu.

3 When the Move To External Style Sheet dialog box appears, choose A New Style Sheet in the Move Rules To options. Click OK.

The Save Style Sheet File As dialog box appears.

4 Navigate to the site root folder, if necessary. Type **mygreen_styles** in the File Name field. Click Save.

Dreamweaver adds the .css extension to the filename, moves the selected styles from the `<head>` area to the newly defined style sheet, and simultaneously inserts a link to the style sheet. Note at the top of the document window that Dreamweaver now displays the name of the external style sheet in the Related Files interface.

The last chore is to remove the no-longer-needed `<style>` tag.

5 In the CSS Styles panel, click the `<style>` entry and press Delete, or click the Trash Can icon.

If the reference does not disappear, you can right-click it and choose Delete from the context menu.

6 Choose File > Save All. Or, press Ctrl-Alt-Shift-S/Cmd-Ctrl-S to access the keyboard shortcut for the Save All command you created in Lesson 1, "Customizing Your Workspace."

▶ **Tip:** Once you move the CSS to an external file, remember to use the Save All command moving forward. Pressing Ctrl-S/Cmd-S saves only the top document in the Dreamweaver interface. Other files that are opened and referenced that have been changed are not automatically saved.

Creating style sheets for other media types

Current best practices call for the separation of presentation (CSS) from content (the HTML tags, text, and other page elements). The reason is simple: by separating the formatting, which may only be relevant for one type of medium, one HTML document can be formatted instantly for multiple purposes. More than one style sheet can be linked to a page. By creating and attaching style sheets optimized for other media, the specific browsing application can select the appropriate style sheet and formatting for its own needs. For example, the style sheet created and applied in the previous exercises was designed for a typical computer screen display.

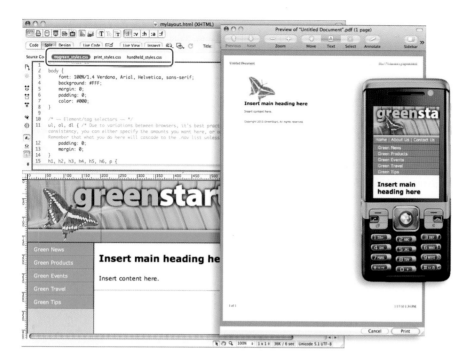

In this exercise, you'll convert a CSS screen-media file to one optimized for print. This is a popular technique for many websites today. Designers frequently include a "Print" link on pages heavy with text so that users can send the information to the printer more effectively. Print style sheets often adjust colors to work better in print, hide unneeded page elements, or adjust sizes and layouts to be more suitable for printing.

When the print queue is activated, the printing application checks for a print-media style sheet. If one is present, the relevant CSS rules are taken into account. If not, the printer defers to the rules in the screen or all-media style sheets or the CSS defaults for print.

Displaying the Style Rendering toolbar

Dreamweaver's default display medium is screen media. However, Dreamweaver has the capacity to switch how the media is rendered in Design view using the Style Rendering toolbar. With Design view's rendering of the rules in a print style sheet, you can see the effect your style rules will have on a printed page.

1   If necessary, open the **mylayout.html** file by double-clicking its filename in the Files panel.

2 Choose View > Toolbars > Style Rendering.

The Style Rendering toolbar appears above the document window. Leave it visible for the next exercise.

- **Ⓐ** Render screen media type
- **Ⓑ** Render print media type
- **Ⓒ** Render handheld media type
- **Ⓓ** Render projection media type
- **Ⓔ** Render TTY media type
- **Ⓕ** Toggle displaying of CSS styles
- **Ⓖ** Render TV media type
- **Ⓗ** Design-time style sheets
- **Ⓘ** Increase text size
- **Ⓙ** Reset text size
- **Ⓚ** Decrease text size
- **Ⓛ** Show styles for :link pseudoclass
- **Ⓜ** Show styles for :visited pseudoclass
- **Ⓝ** Show styles for :hover pseudoclass
- **Ⓞ** Show styles for :active pseudoclass
- **Ⓟ** Show styles for :focus pseudoclass

Converting an existing style sheet for print

Although you can develop a print style sheet from scratch, it's usually much faster to convert an existing screen-media style sheet. The first step is to save the existing external style sheet under a new name.

1 In the Files panel, double-click **mygreen_styles.css** to open it.

2 Choose File > Save As.

3 When the Save As dialog box opens, type **print_styles.css** in the File Name/ Save As field. Make sure the site root folder is targeted. Click Save.

4 If necessary, open **mylayout.html** from the site root folder. In the CSS Styles panel, click the Attach Style Sheet (⊜) icon.

The Attach External Style Sheet dialog box opens

5 Click Browse.

The Select Style Sheet File dialog box appears.

6 Select **print_styles.css** from the site root folder. Click OK/Choose.

7 In the Attach External Style Sheet dialog box, select the Link option for the Add As value. From the Media field menu, choose print. Click OK.

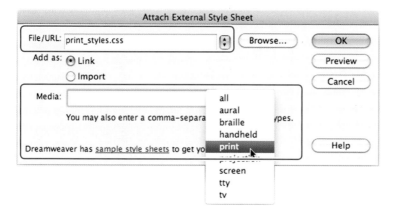

8 In the CSS Styles panel, click the All button, if necessary.

A new entry—**print_styles.css**—has been added. At the moment, both style sheets are identical. You will modify the print style sheet in the next exercise.

9 Close **print_styles.css** and **mygreen_styles.css**.

10 Save **mylayout.html**.

Hiding unwanted page areas

Using the Style Rendering toolbar, you can see your document rendered according to the print-media style rules.

1 In the Style Rendering toolbar, click the Render Print Media Type (🖶) icon.

One of the main differences between screen and print media is that interactive items on a web page are often meaningless in print. This would include all navigation elements in the horizontal and vertical menus. Using the print-media style sheet, you can hide unwanted portions of a page. For example, the horizontal menu isn't needed for printing.

Note: Remember to click the Render Screen Media Type icon when you're ready to work on screen-media formatting again.

2 In the CSS Styles panel, double-click #h-navbar in the **print_styles.css** rules.

3 In the Block category, choose none from the Display field menu. Click OK.

The entire <div#h-navbar> disappears from the document window. The <div> has not been deleted; Dreamweaver has simply stopped rendering it temporarily as long as the Print Media Type icon is selected. Let's turn off <div.sidebar1>, too.

4 In the **print_styles.css** rules, double-click .sidebar1.

5 In the Block category, choose none from the Display field menu. Click OK.

The sidebar vanishes, and the main content expands to the full width of the <div.container>. The background image is visible under the content and may make it harder to read the text.

6 In the **print_styles.css** rules, double-click .container.

7 In the Background category, delete the **divider.gif** image reference in the Background-image field. Delete repeat-y from the Background-repeat field. Click Apply.

The background image continues to display in <div.container>. Deleting the image reference is not enough. Although the print application defers to the print-media style sheet, formatting is still inherited from all referenced CSS style sheets. Even though you deleted the background image reference in the print style sheet, it's still applied in the screen styles. It won't disappear until you reset the rule by choosing none. This goes for other such rules, too.

8 Choose none from the Background-image field menu. Click Apply.

The background image vanishes. Let's check the page in Live view.

9 Click OK to complete the change. Click the Live View button.

Dreamweaver ignores the print-media styles and renders the image as if for the screen. Live view is intended for browser preview and can't render print-based styling. To properly test the page, you have to use the print preview function in an actual browser.

10 Save all files. Choose File > Preview In Browser and select your preferred browser.

11 In the browser, choose File > Print Preview.

Note: Some browsers have a different technique to access the print preview mode. You may need to choose File > Print first and access the preview function from within the print dialog box.

As you can see, the print application converted the text to black and automatically dropped all the background images and colors, but it still prints the butterfly logo and the borders. Let's eliminate the border.

12 In the **print_styles.css** rules, double-click `.container`. In the Border category, select the Same For All option in the Style section. Choose none from the Top Style field. Click OK.

13 Save all files.

14 Choose File > Preview in Browser and select your preferred browser.

15 In the browser, activate print preview.

The border has been removed successfully. You should know enough now to keep the butterfly logo from printing, too. Take a few minutes here and see if you can do it.

Removing unneeded styles

Even with the changes in the previous exercises, many rules in the two style sheets are exactly the same. To reduce file size, it's a good idea to remove rules from the print-media sheet that haven't changed or ones that don't pertain anymore. You can delete unneeded styles using the CSS Styles panel. But be careful—even though a rule hasn't changed doesn't mean it's not needed for print rendering.

1   Select all rules that format the u1.nav menu in **print_styles.css**. Click the Delete CSS Rule icon or right-click the selected rules and choose Delete from the context menu.

Since the vertical menu isn't displayed, there's no need for those rules. In fact, you can remove all rules that format hyperlink behavior, too.

2   Select all hyperlink rules in **print_styles.css** and delete them.

The hyperlinks in the horizontal and vertical menus are not printing at all, and the other rules are still identical to the ones in the screen styles and will be inherited, if supported by the print application. After deleting any rules, always test the page in the browser and in the print application.

3   Save all files.

4   Click the Render Screen Media Type (⊞) icon. Observe the screen display in Design view.

Dreamweaver renders the document for the web.

5   Click the Render For Print Media Type (🖨) icon.

Dreamweaver renders the screen using the print style sheet. You have adapted a screen-media style sheet to make a web page render more useful in print.

You have completed the basic design of the page that will be used as the project template and adapted it to print media. In the next lesson, you will learn how to convert this layout into a dynamic web template.

Review questions

1 How do you attach an existing external style sheet to a web page?

2 How can you target a specific type of formatting to content in a web page?

3 What method can you use to hide specific content on a web page?

4 How do you apply an existing CSS class to a page element?

5 What is the purpose of creating style sheets for different media?

Review answers

1 In the CSS Styles panel, choose Attach Style Sheet. In the Attach External Style Sheet dialog box, select the desired CSS file and select the media type.

2 You can create a custom class or id using descendant selectors to target formatting to specific elements or element configurations on a page.

3 In the style sheet, set the "display" property of the element, class, or id to none to hide any content you don't want to display.

4 One method is to select the element and then choose the desired style from the Class menu in the Property inspector.

5 Creating and attaching style sheets for different types of media enables the page to adapt to applications other than web browsers, like print applications.

7 WORKING WITH TEMPLATES

Lesson Overview

In this lesson, you'll learn how to work faster, make updating easier, and be more productive. You'll use Dreamweaver templates, Library items, and server-side includes to do the following:

- Create a Dreamweaver template

- Insert editable regions

- Produce child pages

- Update templates and child pages

- Create, insert, and update Library items

- Create, insert, and update server-side includes

 This lesson will take about 1 hour and 15 minutes to complete. Before beginning, make sure you have copied the files for Lesson 7 to your hard drive as described in the "Getting Started" section at the beginning of the book. If you are starting from scratch in this lesson, use the method described in the "Jumpstart" section of "Getting Started."

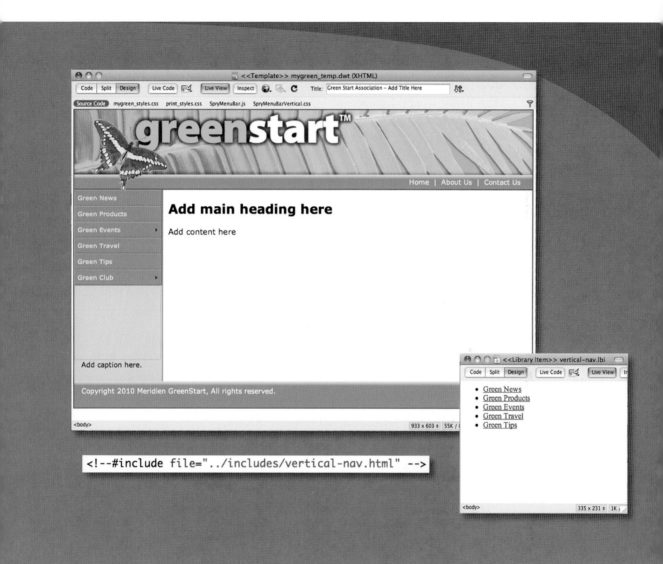

Dreamweaver's productivity tools and site
management capabilities are among its
most useful features for a busy designer.

Previewing completed files

To better understand what you will learn in this lesson, let's preview in a browser a completed page you will work on in this lesson. The completed page doesn't look much different from the previous layout you completed in Lesson 6, "Working with Cascading Style Sheets," but it contains some significant differences that you will learn about in the following exercises.

1   Open Adobe Dreamweaver CS5.

2   If necessary, press Ctrl-Shift-F/Cmd-Shift-F to open the Files panel, and select DW-CIB from the site list.

3   In the Files panel, expand the lesson07 folder. Double-click **template_finished.html** to open it. Observe the design and structure of this page.

This page was created from a template; Dreamweaver displays the name of the parent file in the upper-right corner of the document window. The layout is identical to the page completed in Lesson 6, with some notable exceptions. There are two areas on the page that display blue tabs and borders. These areas, called *editable regions*, represent the bulk of the differences between your current layout and the finished template-based one.

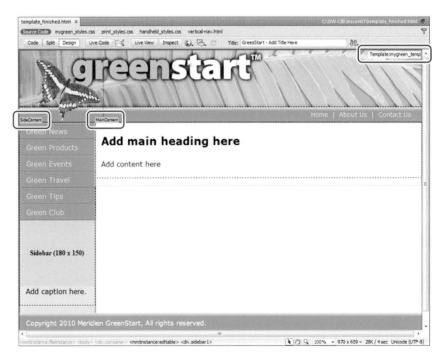

4 Move the cursor over `<div.header>`. Note the mouse icon Dreamweaver displays.

The (⊘) icon signifies that the area is locked and uneditable.

5 Select the placeholder *Add main heading here* in `<div.content>`. Type **Get a fresh start with GreenStart** to replace the text. Save the file.

The `<div.content>` element is contained in one of the blue areas labeled *MainContent*, which allows you to select and edit content therein.

6 Preview the page in your primary browser.

The browser display won't give you any clues to how this page differs from the one you created earlier—that's the beauty of a template-based page. For all intents and purposes, a template-based page is just a normal HTML file. The extra code elements that enable its special features are basically comments added and read only by Dreamweaver and other web-aware applications and should never affect its performance or display in the browser.

7 Close your browser and return to Dreamweaver. Close **template_finished.html**.

Creating a template from an existing layout

A template is a type of master page from which child pages are produced. Templates are useful for setting up and maintaining the overall look and feel of a website, while providing a means for quickly and easily producing site content. A template is different from the pages you have already completed; it contains areas that are editable and others that are not. Templates enable a workgroup environment where page content can be created and edited by several people on the team, while the web designer is able to control the page design and specific elements that must remain unchanged.

Although you can create a template from a blank page, it is far more practical, and common, to convert an existing page into a template. In this exercise, you'll create a template from your existing layout.

1 Launch Dreamweaver.

2 If necessary, open the **mylayout.html** file (which was complete at the end of Lesson 6) by double-clicking its filename in the root folder of the DW-CIB website in the Files panel. Or, if you are starting from scratch in this exercise, see the "Jumpstart" instructions in the "Getting Started" section at the beginning of the book.

The first step for converting an existing page to a template is to save the page as a template.

● **Note:** If you don't feel confident working with your own layout, use the method described in the "Jumpstart" section of "Getting Started" at the beginning of the book, and open the mylayout.html file provided in the lesson07 folder.

3 Choose File > Save as Template.

Because of their special nature, templates are stored in their own folder, Templates, that Dreamweaver automatically creates at the site root level.

▶ **Tip:** Adding the letters *temp* to the name, like adding styles to the name of the CSS file earlier, helps to visually distinguish files from one another in the site folder displays.

4 When the Save As Template dialog box appears, choose DW-CIB in the Site pop-up menu. Leave the Description field empty. (If you have more than one template in a site, a description may be useful.) Type **mygreen_temp** in the Save As field. Click Save.

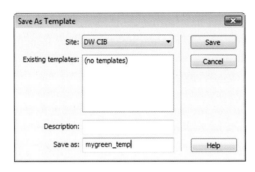

● **Note:** A dialog box may appear asking about saving the file without defining editable regions; just click Yes to save anyway. You'll create editable regions in the next exercise.

An untitled dialog box appears asking whether you want to update links.

5 Click Yes to update the links.

Since the template is saved in a subfolder, updating the links in the code is necessary so that they will continue to work properly when you create child pages later.

Although the page still looks exactly the same, you can identify a template in two ways. First, the title bar displays the term <<*Template*>>. Second, the file extension is .dwt, which stands for Dreamweaver template.

Dreamweaver templates are *dynamic* because they maintain a connection to all pages within the site that were derived from it. Whenever you add or change content within the dynamic regions of the page and save it, Dreamweaver passes those changes to all the child pages automatically, keeping them up to date. But a template can't be completely dynamic. Some sections of the page must be editable so that you can insert unique content. Dreamweaver allows you to designate certain areas of the page as *editable.*

Inserting editable regions

When you first create a template, Dreamweaver treats all the existing content as part of the master design. Child pages created from the template would be exact duplicates, except that the content would be locked and uneditable. This is great for repetitive features of a page, such as the navigation components, logos, copyright and contact information, and so on, but it's also bad because it stops you from adding unique content to each child page. You get around this barrier by defining editable regions in your template. Dreamweaver creates one editable region automatically for the `<title>` element in the `<head>` section of the page; you have to create the rest.

First, give some thought to which areas of the page should be part of the template and which should be open for editing. At the moment, two sections of your current layout need to be editable, `<div.content>` and `<div.sidebar>`. Although editable regions don't have to be limited to `<div>` elements, they are easier to manage.

1 Insert the cursor in `<div.content>`. Click the `<div.content>` tag selector.

2 Choose Insert > Template Objects > Editable Region.

3 In the New Editable Region dialog box, type **MainContent** in the Name field. Click OK.

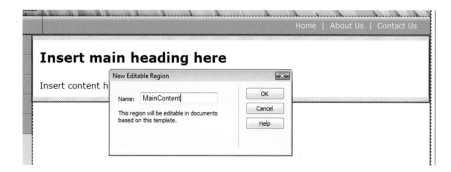

Each editable region must have a unique name, but there are no other special conventions. However, keeping them short and descriptive is a good practice. The name appears in a blue tab above the area and identifies it as an editable region.

4 Insert the cursor in `<div.sidebar1>`. Click the `<div.sidebar1>` tag selector.

5 Choose Insert > Template Objects > Editable Region.

6 In the New Editable Region dialog box, type **SideContent** in the Name field. Click OK.

Adding a title to each page is a good practice. Each title should reflect the specific content or purpose of the page, but many designers also include the name of the company or organization in the title to make it more pertinent. Adding the name in the template will save time typing it in each child page later.

7 In the Title field of the document toolbar, select the placeholder text *Untitled Document*. Type **GreenStart Association – Add Title Here** to replace the text.

● **Note:** The Update Template pages dialog box may appear when you save the file. Since there are no template pages yet, click Don't Update.

8 Press Enter/Return to complete the title. Choose File > Save.

9 Choose File > Close.

You now have two editable regions, plus an editable title that can be changed as needed when you create new child pages using this template. The template is linked to your style sheet files, so any changes in those files will be reflected in all child pages made from this template, too.

Producing child pages

● **Warning:** If you open a template in a text editor, all the code is editable, including the code for the non-editable regions of the page.

Child pages are the *raison d'être* for Dreamweaver templates. Once a child page has been created from a template, only the content within the editable regions can be updated. The rest of the page remains locked. This behavior is only supported within Dreamweaver and other web-aware HTML editors. If you open the page in a text editor, the code is fully editable.

The decision to use Dreamweaver templates for a site should be made at the beginning of the design process, so that all the pages in the site can be made as child pages of the template. That's the purpose of the layout we've built up to this point in the last two lessons: To create the basic structure of your site template.

1 Choose File > New. Or, press Ctrl-N/Cmd-N.

The New Document dialog box appears.

2 In the New Document dialog box, select the Page From Template option. Select DW-CIB in the Site list, if necessary. Select **mygreen_temp** in the Template For Site *"DW-CIB"* list.

3 Select the Update Page When Template Changes option, if necessary. Click Create.

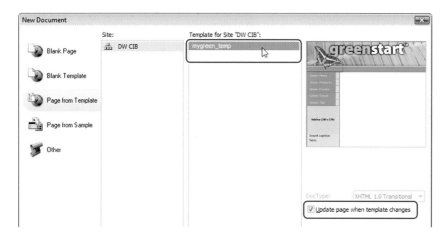

Dreamweaver creates a new page based on the template. Note the name of the template file displayed in the upper-right corner of the document window. Before modifying the page, you should save it.

4 Choose File > Save. In the Save As dialog box, navigate to the root folder for your project site. Type **about_us.html** in the File Name field. Click Save.

5 Move the cursor over the different page areas.

Certain areas, such as the header, menu bar, and footer, are locked and cannot be modified. The content in the editable regions can be changed.

6 In the Title field, select the placeholder text *Add Title Here*. Type **About Us** and press Enter/Return.

7 Select the placeholder text *Insert main heading here* in the MainContent editable region. Type **GreenStart – green awareness in action!** to replace the text.

8 In the Files panel, double-click **content-aboutus.rtf** in the lesson07 folder to open the file.

The file will open in a compatible program, such as WordPad or TextEdit.

9 Press Ctrl-A/Cmd-A to select all the text. Press Ctrl-C/Cmd-C to copy the text.

10 Switch back to Dreamweaver. Select the placeholder text *Insert content here* in the MainContent region. Press Ctrl-V/Cmd-V to paste the text.

The pasted text will replace the placeholder copy.

11 In the SideContent region, double-click the image placeholder. In the Select Image Source dialog box, select **shopping.jpg** from the default images folder. Click OK.

12 Select the placeholder text *Insert caption here* and replace the text with **When shopping for groceries, buy fruits and vegetables at farmers markets to support local agriculture.**

13 Save the file.

14 Click the Live View button to preview the page.

As you can see, there is no indication that this template child page is any different from any other standard web page. There's no limit to the content you can insert into the editable regions: text, images, tables, Flash video, and so on.

15 Click the Live View button to return to standard document display. Choose File > Close.

Updating a template

Templates can automatically update any child pages made from that template. But only areas outside the editable regions will be updated. In the current template, the horizontal navigation menu is part of the template, while the vertical menu was included in the SideContent editable region. Let's make some changes in the template to learn how a template is updated:

1 Choose Window > Assets.

    The Assets panel appears. Typically, it is grouped with the Files panel. The Assets panel gives you immediate access to a variety of components and content available to your website.

2 In the Assets panel, click the Template category (⬚) icon. Click the refresh (↻) icon if no templates appear in the list.

    The panel changes to display list and preview windows for site templates. The name of your template appears in the list.

3 Right-click **mygreen_temp** and choose Edit from the context menu.

    The template opens.

4 Select the text *Home* in the horizontal menu. Type **GreenStart Home** to replace the text.

5 Select the text *News* in the vertical menu. Type **Headlines** to replace the text.

6 Select and replace the text *Insert* with the word **Add** wherever it appears in the MainContent or SideContent editable regions.

7 Save the file.

The Update Template Files dialog box appears. The file name **about_us.html** appears in the update list.

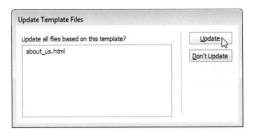

▶ Tip: If the log window does not open automatically, select the Show Log option to open it.

8 Click the Update button.

The Update Pages dialog box appears. The log window at the bottom of the dialog box displays a report detailing which pages were successfully updated and which ones were not.

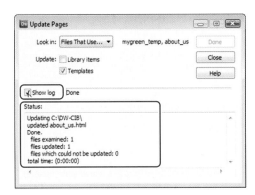

9 Close the Update Pages dialog box.

10 Choose File > Open Recent > **about_us.html**. The file **about_us.html** opens. Observe the page and note any changes.

The changes made to the horizontal menu are reflected in this file, but the changes to the sidebar and main content areas were ignored and the content you added to both areas remain unaltered. That way, you can safely make changes and add content to the editable regions without worrying that the template will delete all your hard work. While at the same time, the boilerplate elements of the header, footer and horizontal menu all remain consistently formatted and up to date based on the status of the template.

11 Click the document tab for **mygreen_temp.dwt** at the top of the document window to switch to the template file.

12 Delete the word *GreenStart* from the Home link in the horizontal menu.

13 Save the template and update linked files.

14 Click the tab for **about_us.html** to switch back. Observe the page and note any changes.

The horizontal menu has been updated. Dreamweaver even updates linked documents that are open at the time. The only concern is that the changes have not been saved; the document tab shows an asterisk, which means the file has been changed and is unsaved. If Dreamweaver or your computer were to crash at this moment, the changes would be lost and you would have to update the page manually, or wait until the next time you make changes to the template to take advantage of the automatic update feature.

15 Select File > Save All.

Tip: Always use the Save All command whenever you have multiple files open that have been updated by a template.

There's only one issue with the template as it stands now, and it's going to be an even bigger problem as you add more pages to the site. The vertical menu lies in the editable region SideContent and, as you have seen, it will not update automatically when the template is changed.

There are many possible ways to fix the problem; here are two:

- Remove the editable region markup from `<div.sidebar1>` to make it part of the template boilerplate and insert a stand-alone editable region inside the `<div>` below the vertical menu.

- Insert a dynamic content element—such as a Dreamweaver Library item or server-side include—in place of the vertical menu that could be updated independently of the region.

Let's explore option number two in the next exercise.

Using Library items

Library items are reusable bits of HTML—paragraphs, links, copyright notices, tables, images, navigation bars, and so on—that you use frequently within a website. You can use an existing page element or create original Library items from scratch and add copies of them where needed. They act similarly to a template—when you make changes to a Library item, Dreamweaver automatically updates every page that uses that item.

Creating a Library item

In this exercise, you'll create a Library item from the vertical menu and add it to the template.

1 Click the document tab for **mygreen_temp.dwt** at the top of the document window to switch to the template file, or open the file, if necessary.

2 Insert the cursor in the vertical menu. Click the `<ul.nav>` tag selector.

3 Choose Window > Assets to display the Assets panel, if necessary.

4 Click the Library category (📖) icon.

No items appear in the Library.

Note: Don't be too surprised if your Asset panel shows one or more Library items. Although you have not created any yourself, .lbi files are located in various lesson subfolders. If you click the Refresh Site List icon in the Assets panel, Dreamweaver will search all the folders in the current site and create a list of these items.

5 Click the New Library Item (➕) icon at the bottom of the panel.

A dialog box appears explaining that the Library item may not look the same when placed in other documents because style sheet information is not included.

6 Click OK. Type **vertical-nav** in the Library item name field.

When you click OK, Dreamweaver does three things simultaneously. First, it creates a Library item from the selected menu code and inserts an *Untitled* reference to it in the Library list, allowing you to name it. Second, it replaces the existing menu with the Library item code. And, third, it creates a folder at the site root level called Library where this and other items are stored. In Lesson 17, "Publishing to the Web," you will learn more about what files need to be uploaded, or published, to the Internet.

Note: This folder doesn't need to be uploaded to the server.

7 Save the template and update linked files. Observe the Update Pages report.

Dreamweaver indicates that it didn't update the **about_us.html** file, so you'll have to insert the Library item manually.

8 Click the tab for **about_us.html** to bring this page to the front. Insert the cursor into the vertical menu in the SideContent region. Observe the tag selectors.

The tag selectors display <ul.nav>. The tag selector confirms the report that the page was not updated and that the vertical menu is still being created by the original code.

9 Click the <ul.nav> tag selector to select the vertical menu.

10 In the Assets panel, select the vertical-nav item in the Library category. Click the Insert button.

The `<ul.nav>` is replaced by `<mm.libitem>`. The template and **about_us.html** are both using the Library item.

11 Position the cursor over the vertical menu. Observe the mouse icon.

The (🚫) icon signifies that the area is uneditable.

12 Click the `<mm.libitem>` tag selector. Switch to Code view. Insert your cursor in the selected code.

```
<mmtinstance:editable> <div.sidebar1> <mm:libitem>
```

The code for the Library items is highlighted in a different color and enclosed in some special markup, but it's otherwise unchanged. The opening tag is:

```
<!-- #BeginLibraryItem "/Library/vertical-nav.lbi" -->
```

The closing tag is:

```
<!-- #EndLibraryItem -->
```

But be careful. While the Library item is locked in Design view, Dreamweaver doesn't prevent you from editing the code in Code view.

13 Select the text *Headlines* in the code. Press Delete.

```
<div class="sidebar1"><!-- #BeginLibraryItem "/Library/vertical-nav.lbi" -->
<ul class="nav">
  <li><a href="#">Green </a></li>
  <li><a href="#">Green Products</a></li>
  <li><a href="#">Green Events</a></li>
  <li><a href="#">Green Travel</a></li>
  <li><a href="#">Green Tips</a></li>
</ul>
<!-- #EndLibraryItem --><img src="images/shopping.jpg" alt="" name="Sidebar"
```

14 Save the file and preview the page in a browser.

The browser displays the page with the edited menu. You may be wondering why no warning dialogs appeared and why you weren't prevented from making the change. But the news isn't entirely bad. Dreamweaver is keeping track of the Library item and your edits, intentional or otherwise. As you will see shortly, the change you made will be short-lived.

15 Choose File > Close All.

Finally, a dialog appears warning you that you have made changes to code that was locked. It further explains that the original code will be restored the next time you update the template or Library item.

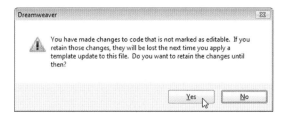

16 Click Yes to preserve your manual edits. Save all changes.

17 Right-click vertical-nav in the Library list and choose Update Site from the context menu.

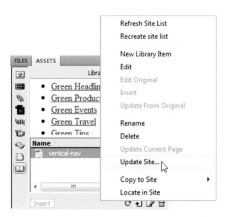

The Update Pages dialog box appears.

18 Click Start.

Dreamweaver updates any pages in the site that use the Library item and reports the results of the process. At least one page should be updated.

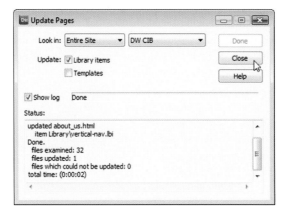

19 Click Close to exit the dialog box

20 Click **about_us.html** in the Welcome Screen to reopen the file.

21 Click the Live View button to preview the page.

The menu has been restored to the original code. Library items allow you to insert repeating content throughout the site and update it without having to open the files individually.

Updating Library items

Templates, Library items, and the server-side includes exist for one reason: to make it easy to update web page content. Let's update the menu Library item.

1 In the Library category list in the Assets panel, double-click the vertical-nav item.

2 Switch to Code view. Select the text *Headlines* and type **News** to replace it.

```
<li><a href="#">Green News</a></li>
<li><a href="#">Green Products</a></li>
<li><a href="#">Green Events</a></li>
<li><a href="#">Green Travel</a></li>
<li><a href="#">Green Tips</a></li>
```

3 Choose File > Save.

The Update Library Items dialog box appears.

4 Click Update.

The Update Pages dialog box appears and reports which pages were successfully updated and which ones were not.

5 Click Close to close the Update Pages dialog box.

6 Click the Live View button. Observe the vertical menu.

The vertical menu has been updated successfully. Let's check the template.

7 Click the Live View button to restore standard view.

8 In the Assets panel, click the Templates category (⊞) icon. Double-click **mygreen_temp** in the Template window to open the file. Observe the vertical menu in Live view.

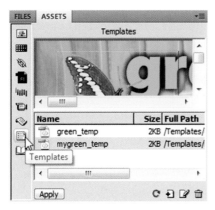

The menu in the template was updated, too.

You've completed updates to the current site files using Library items. As you can see, using Library items and templates can save you a lot of time when you want to update pages. And, Dreamweaver still has one more trick up its productivity sleeve: server-side includes.

Using server-side includes

Server-side includes (SSI) are like Library items in some ways. They are reusable bits of HTML—paragraphs, links, copyright notices, navigation bars, tables, images, and so on—that you use frequently. The main differences between Library items and SSIs are in the way they are handled in the page code and then managed within the site.

For example, a complete copy of the Library item must be inserted in the page's code *before* it's uploaded to the web. (That's why the Library items themselves don't have to be stored on the server.) Then, each affected page must be updated and then uploaded before the change takes effect on the Internet.

Unlike the Library items, SSIs must be stored on the web, preferably in your site folder. In fact, the code the SSI contains doesn't appear anywhere in the page itself, only a reference to its file name and path location. The SSI appears only when the page is accessed by a visitor and rendered by the browser. This function has advantages and disadvantages.

On the plus side, server-side includes are the most efficient and timesaving way to add reusable HTML snippets to a large number of pages. They are faster and easier to work with than either templates or Library items. The reason is simple: It only takes a single file containing a menu or piece of important content—once edited and uploaded—to update the entire site.

On the downside, dozens or even hundreds of pages on your site could depend on one file to operate correctly. Any error in the code or path name, even a minor one, could cause your entire site to fail. For small sites, Library items can be a perfectly workable solution. For large sites, it would be hard to live without SSIs.

In this exercise, you will create an SSI and add it to a page in your site.

Creating server-side includes

An SSI is an HTML file stripped clean of any superfluous code.

1 Choose File > New. Select Blank Page from the Category section. In the Page Type list, choose HTML. In the Layout list, select <none>. Click Create.

2 Click the document tab for **about_us.html** to bring this page to the front, or open it from the site root folder.

3 Insert the cursor in the vertical menu. Click the <mm.libitem> tag selector. Switch to Code view.

Note how the entire Library item is selected.

4 Select all the code for <ul.nav>, but do not include the Library item markup. Press Ctrl-C/Cmd-C to copy the code.

```
22      <div class="sidebar1"><!-- #BeginLibraryItem "/Library/vertical-nav.lbi" -->
23      <ul class="nav">
24          <li><a href="#">Green News</a></li>
25          <li><a href="#">Green Products</a></li>
26          <li><a href="#">Green Events</a></li>
27          <li><a href="#">Green Travel</a></li>
28          <li><a href="#">Green Tips</a></li>
29      </ul><!-- #EndLibraryItem --><img src="" alt="" name="Sidebar" width="180"
        height="150" class="hide4hh" id="Sidebar" />
```

● **Note:** As long as they are part of a library item, you won't be able to use the <ul.nav> tag selector to grab the correct code elements. Dreamweaver ignores the internal markup of a Library item within the layout.

5 Click the Untitled document tab for the new file. Switch to Code view, if necessary.

Note how the Untitled document is a completely formed web page. However, the <head> and <body> sections are not needed in the SSI and could actually cause problems if inserted into another page.

6 Press Ctrl-A/Cmd-A to select all the code in the new file. Press Ctrl-V/Cmd-V to replace the code with <ul.nav>.

Only the code for <ul.nav> appears in the document window.

7 Choose File > Save. Navigate to the site root folder. In the Save As dialog box, click the Create New Folder button. Name the folder **includes**. Select the newly created includes folder, if necessary. Type **vertical-nav.html** in the File Name field. Click Save.

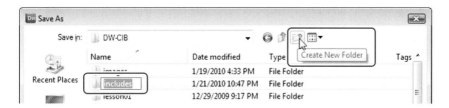

8 Close **vertical-nav.html**.

You have completed the SSI for the vertical menu. In the next exercise, you will learn how to insert it into a web page.

Inserting server-side includes

On a live website, you would upload the includes folder to the server along with any HTML snippets it contained. A command inserted in the code of any page on your site would make a *call* to the server to add the HTML snippet in the indicated location. The include command will look something like this:

```
<!--#include file="includes/vertical-nav.html" -->
```

You can see that it consists of an include command and the path location to the SSI file. Depending on the type of server you are using, the exact include command may vary. It will also affect the file extension you use for both the SSI and web page file itself. The include behavior is considered a dynamic function and typically requires a file extension that supports these capabilities. If you save the file with the default .htm or .html extension, you may find that the browser won't load the SSI. In the following example, you'll use the extension .shtml, which supports SSI functionality. Later, you'll build pages using the .asp, .cfm, and .php extensions for data publishing. These extensions support SSI capabilities by default.

Before you insert the SSI in the template or any other page, make sure that Dreamweaver's Preferences are set to show the included file in Design view.

1   Press Ctrl-U/Cmd-U to edit Dreamweaver Preferences. Or, choose Edit > Preferences (Windows)/Dreamweaver > Preferences (Mac) to display the Preferences dialog box.

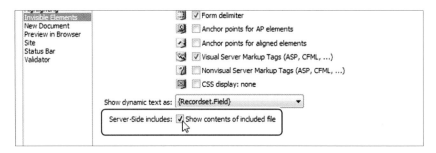

2   From the Category list, select Invisible Elements. Select the Show Contents Of Included File option, if necessary. Click OK.

The SSI can be seen in Design view and in Live view, in Dreamweaver. However, it may not render in a browser while it is still located on your hard drive. To test it properly, you may have to upload it to a server configured to work with SSIs first.

Next, let's insert the SSI.

3   Click the tab for **about_us.html** to bring this page to the front, or open it from the site root folder.

4   Insert your cursor in the vertical menu. Click the <mm.libitem> to select the Library item. Press Delete to remove the entire item.

The vertical menu disappears.

5   Without moving the cursor, select Insert > Server-Side Include.

6   Select **vertical-nav.html** from the includes folder. Click OK.

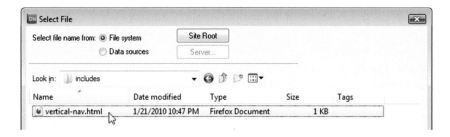

The vertical menu reappears, but there's one significant difference. The code for the menu is not actually resident in this file.

7 Switch to Code view. Observe the code where the menu should appear.

The code for `<ul.nav>` has been replaced by the `include` command and the path to **vertical-nav.html**. Although the code is not present, the menu will look and function normally.

```
<!-- TemplateBeginEditable name="SideContent" -->
<div class="sidebar1">
    <!--#include file="../includes/vertical-nav.html" -->
    <img src="" alt="" name="Sidebar" width="180" height="150" class="hide4hh"
id="Sidebar" />
    <p class="hide4hh">Add caption here.</p>
    <!-- end .sidebar1 -->
</div>
<!-- TemplateEndEditable --><!-- TemplateBeginEditable name="MainContent" -->
```

8 Click the Live View button to preview the page. Test the functionality of the vertical menu.

The menu appears and behaves as expected.

9 Select File > Save As. Name the file **about_us.shtml**.

As long as you didn't miss the additional "s" in the extension, you just created an another version of **about_us.html**, and left the original file unchanged. Without the new extension, the SSI may not appear at all when it's uploaded to a web server. As it is, you'll also discover that the SSI probably can't even be tested in your primary browser.

SSIs need specific server functionality to manage and load them into a browser. To test them on your local hard drive requires that you install and run a *testing server*. Since you won't learn about testing servers until Lesson 14, "Working with Online Data," you'll have to be content testing SSIs in Live view for now.

So, far, you've created a server-side include and inserted it on a page in the site. In the next exercise, you'll learn how easy it is to update a file that uses an SSI.

Updating server-side includes

Although working with templates and Library items offers vast improvements in productivity, it can also be a tedious chore. Changes made must be saved and updated to all the appropriate pages, and then each newly updated page must be uploaded to the server. When the change involves hundreds of pages, the problem is compounded. On the other hand, when using SSIs, the only file that must be changed, saved, and uploaded is the include file itself. Quick and tidy.

Let's change the include file and see how Dreamweaver handles the change.

1   Choose File > Open Recent > **vertical-nav.html**.

2   Insert the cursor at the end of the last bullet, *Green Tips*. Press Enter/Return to insert a new list item. Type **Green Club** on the new line.

3   Select the text *Green Club* and type # in the Link field of the Property inspector to create a hyperlink placeholder.

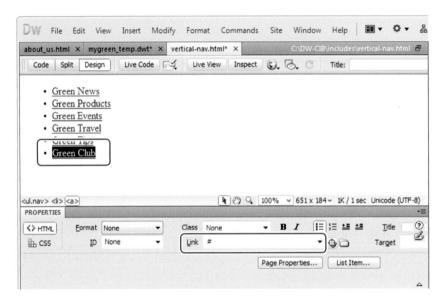

You have added a new menu item, complete with hyperlink placeholder.

4   Click the tab for **about_us.html** to bring this page to the front, or open it from the Files panel. Observe the vertical menu.

The menu has not changed here, yet.

5   Click the tab for **vertical-nav.html** to bring this page to the front. Save the file.

▶ **Tip:** In most cases, Dreamweaver will update the SSI instantly. If it doesn't, simply press F5 to refresh the display, or check to make sure you actually saved (and uploaded) the SSI, as needed.

6   Examine the vertical menu in **about_us.html**.

The menu has changed. You should also notice one more thing: The file tab at the top of the document window doesn't show an asterisk indicating that the file has changed and needs to be saved. Why? It's because the SSI is not really part of the file. So, when the code was changed in **vertical-nav.html** it had no impact on the file.

7 Close all files.

You've created a server-side include, added it to a page, and updated it. Many other web-page elements—such as logos, menus, privacy notices, and banners—can be made into easily maintained server-side includes.

Sorry, no SSIs for now

A *server-side include* is a logical and important element for any web designer. So, you may be wondering why we're not adding the SSI to the current project template that you just completed. The reason is simple: you won't be able to see the SSI in a browser without a testing server as long as it's stored only on your local hard drive. So, for convenience sake, we'll stick to Library-based components in the current workflow. However, once you have a full-fledged testing server installed and operating, feel free to permanently replace any appropriate Library items with equivalent SSIs.

Dreamweaver's productivity tools—templates, Library items, and server-side includes—help you build pages and automatically update sites quickly and easily. In the upcoming lessons, you will use the newly completed template to create files for the project site. Although choosing to use templates and the other productivity tools is a decision you should make when first creating a new site, it's never too late to use them to speed up your workflow and make site maintenance easier.

Review questions

1 How do you create a template from an existing page?

2 Why is a template dynamic?

3 What must you add to a template to make it useful in a workflow?

4 How do you create a child page from a template?

5 What are the differences and similarities of Library items and server-side includes?

6 How do you create a Library item?

7 How do you create a server-side include file?

Review answers

1 Choose File > Save as Template and enter the name of the template in the dialog box.

2 A template is dynamic because it maintains a connection to all pages derived from it within a site. When the template is updated, it can pass the changes to the dynamic areas of the child pages.

3 You must add editable regions to the template; otherwise unique content can't be added to the child pages.

4 Choose File > New, and in the New Document dialog box select Pages From Templates. Locate the desired template and click Create. Or, right-click the template name in the Assets > Template category and choose New From Template.

5 Both are used to store and present reusable code elements and page components. But while the code for Library items is inserted fully in the targeted page, the code for server-side includes is only inserted in the page by the server, dynamically.

6 Select the content on the page that you want to add to the Library. Click the Insert button at the bottom of the Library category of the Assets panel, and then name the Library item.

7 Open a new, blank HTML document. Enter the desired content. In Code view, remove any page elements from the code except the content you want included. Save the file.

8 WORKING WITH TEXT, LISTS, AND TABLES

Lesson Overview

In this lesson, you'll create several web pages from your new template and work with headings, paragraphs, and other text elements to do the following:

- Enter heading and paragraph text
- Insert text from another source
- Create bulleted lists
- Create indented text
- Insert and modify tables
- Check spelling in your website
- Search and replace text

 This lesson will take about 2 hours and 10 minutes to complete. Before beginning, make sure you have copied the files for Lesson 8 to your hard drive as described in the "Getting Started" section at the beginning of the book. If you are starting from scratch in this lesson, use the method described in the "Jumpstart" section of "Getting Started."

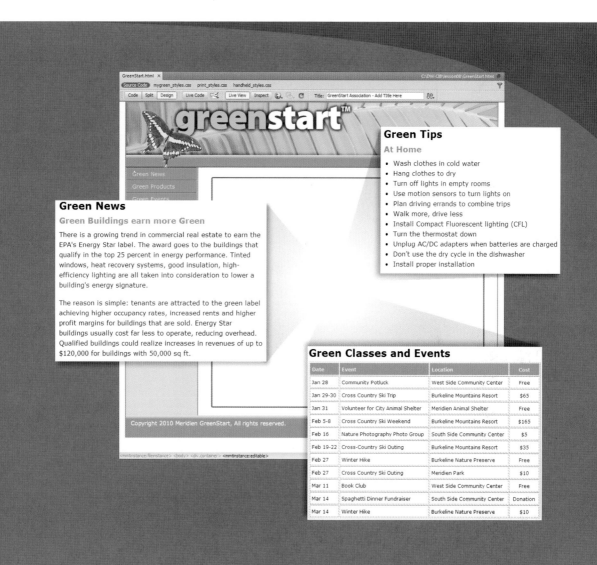

Green News

Green Buildings earn more Green

There is a growing trend in commercial real estate to earn the EPA's Energy Star label. The award goes to the buildings that qualify in the top 25 percent in energy performance. Tinted windows, heat recovery systems, good insulation, high-efficiency lighting are all taken into consideration to lower a building's energy signature.

The reason is simple: tenants are attracted to the green label achieving higher occupancy rates, increased rents and higher profit margins for buildings that are sold. Energy Star buildings usually cost far less to operate, reducing overhead. Qualified buildings could realize increases in revenues of up to $120,000 for buildings with 50,000 sq ft.

Green Tips

At Home

- Wash clothes in cold water
- Hang clothes to dry
- Turn off lights in empty rooms
- Use motion sensors to turn lights on
- Plan driving errands to combine trips
- Walk more, drive less
- Install Compact Fluorescent lighting (CFL)
- Turn the thermostat down
- Unplug AC/DC adapters when batteries are charged
- Don't use the dry cycle in the dishwasher
- Install proper installation

Green Classes and Events

Date	Event	Location	Cost
Jan 28	Community Potluck	West Side Community Center	Free
Jan 29-30	Cross Country Ski Trip	Burkeline Mountains Resort	$65
Jan 31	Volunteer for City Animal Shelter	Meridien Animal Shelter	Free
Feb 5-8	Cross Country Ski Weekend	Burkeline Mountains Resort	$165
Feb 16	Nature Photography Photo Group	South Side Community Center	$5
Feb 19-22	Cross-Country Ski Outing	Burkeline Mountains Resort	$35
Feb 27	Winter Hike	Burkeline Nature Preserve	Free
Feb 27	Cross Country Ski Outing	Meridien Park	$10
Mar 11	Book Club	West Side Community Center	Free
Mar 14	Spaghetti Dinner Fundraiser	South Side Community Center	Donation
Mar 14	Winter Hike	Burkeline Nature Preserve	$10

Dreamweaver provides numerous tools for creating, editing and formatting web content, whether it's created within the program or imported from other applications.

Previewing a completed file

To get a sense of the file you will work on in the first part of this lesson, let's preview the completed pages in the browser.

1   Launch Adobe Dreamweaver CS5, if necessary. Close any files currently open if Dreamweaver is running.

2   If necessary, press Ctrl-Shift-F/Cmd-Shift-F to open the Files panel, and select DW-CIB from the site list.

3   In the Files panel, expand the lesson08 folder.

Dreamweaver allows you to open one or more files at the same time.

4   Select **contactus_finished.html**. Press Ctrl/Cmd and select **events_finished.html**, **news_finished.html**, and **tips_finished.html**.

By pressing Ctrl/Cmd before you click, you can select multiple non-consecutive files.

5   Right-click any of the selected files. Choose Open from the context menu.

All four files open. Tabs at the top of the document window identify each file.

6   Click the **news_finished.html** tab to bring it to the top.

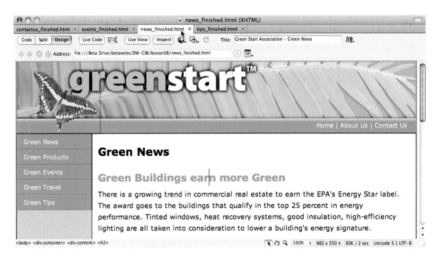

Note the headings and text elements used.

7 Click the **tips_finished.html** tab to bring it to the top.

Note the bulleted list elements used.

8 Click the **contactus_finished.html** tab to bring it to the top.

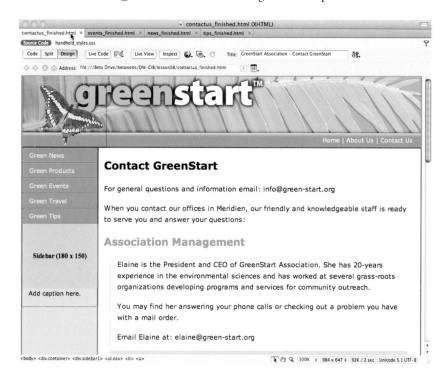

Note that text elements are indented and formatted.

9 Click the **events_finished.html** tab to bring it to the top.

Note the two table elements used. In each of the pages, there are a variety of elements used, including headings, paragraphs, lists, bullets, indented text, and tables. In the following exercises, you will create these pages and learn how to format each of these elements.

10 Choose File > Close All.

Importing text

In this exercise, you'll create a new page from the site template and then insert heading and paragraph text from a text document.

1 Choose Window > Assets to display the Assets panel. In the Template category, right-click **mygreen_temp** and choose New From Template from the context menu.

A new page is created based on the site template.

2 Save the file as **news.html** in the site root folder.

3 In the Files panel, double-click **green_news.rtf** in the lesson08 > resources folder.

The file opens in a compatible program. The text is unformatted and features extra lines between each paragraph, as described in Lesson 4, "Getting a Quick Start."

4 In the text editor or word processing program, press Ctrl-A/Cmd-A to select all the text. Press Ctrl-C/Cmd-C to copy the text.

5 Switch back to Dreamweaver. Select the placeholder heading *Add main heading here* in `<div.content>` and type **Green News** to replace it.

6 Select the placeholder paragraph text *Add content here*. Press Ctrl-V/Cmd-V to paste the text from the clipboard.

The clipboard text replaces the placeholder. The text contains news items separated by headings.

7 Save the file.

Creating headings

In HTML, the tags—`<h1>`, `<h2>`, `<h3>`, `<h4>`, `<h5>`, and `<h6>`—create headings. Any browsing device, whether it is a computer, a Braille reader, or a cell phone, interprets text formatted with any of these tags as a heading. Headings organize HTML pages into meaningful sections with helpful titles, just as they do in books. Following the semantic meaning of HTML tags, the news content begins with a heading "Green News" formatted as an `<h1>`. To be semantically correct, only one such heading should be used per page. All other headings should descend in order from this one. Since each news story has equal importance, they all can begin with a second-level heading, or `<h2>`. At the moment, all the pasted text is formatted as `<p>` elements. Let's format the news headings as `<h2>` elements.

1 Select the text *Green Buildings earn more Green* and choose Heading 2 from the Format menu in the Property inspector.

Tip: If the Format menu is not visible, you need to select the HTML mode of the Property inspector.

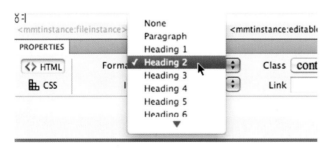

The text will be formatted as an `<h2>` element.

2 Repeat step 1 with the text *Shopping green saves energy, Recycling isn't always Green,* and *Fireplace: Fun or Folly?*

All the selected text should now be formatted as <h2> elements. Let's create a custom rule for this element to set it off from the other headings.

3 Insert the cursor in any of the newly formatted <h2> elements.
Choose Window > CSS Styles to open the CSS Styles panel, if necessary.

4 Select the .content h1 rule in **mygreen_styles.css** in the CSS Styles panel before you click the New CSS Rule icon.

▶ **Tip:** A good designer carefully manages the naming and order of CSS rules. By selecting a rule in the panel before clicking the New CSS Rule icon, Dreamweaver inserts the new rule immediately after the selection. If the new rule doesn't appear in the proper location, just drag it to the desired position.

5 Choose Compound from the Selector Type menu. Click the Less Specific button once. Click OK.

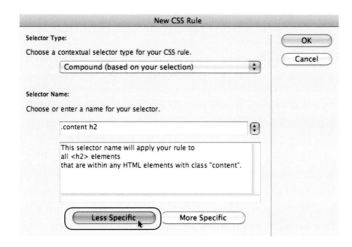

The "New CSS Rule Definition For .*content h2*" dialog box appears.

6 In the Type category, enter **140%** for the Font-size field and **#090** in the Color field.

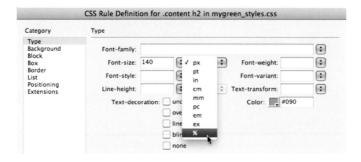

7 In the Box category, enter **5px** only in the Bottom margin field. Click OK.

● **Note:** By default, each heading tag—<h1>, <h2>, <h3> and so on—is formatted smaller than the preceding tag. This formatting reinforces the semantic importance of each tag. Although size is an obvious method of indicating hierarchy it's not a requirement; feel free to experiment with other styling techniques, such as color, indenting, borders and background shading to create your own hierarchical structure.

8 In the document Title field, select the placeholder text *Add Title Here.*
Type **Green News** to replace the text.
Press Enter/Return to complete the title.

9 Save the file.

Creating lists

Text should be formatted to add meaning, organization, and clarity to the content. In the same way, list and blockquote elements carry with them additional semantic meaning.

Lists are the workhorses of the web because they are easier to read than blocks of dense text and also help users find answers quickly. In this exercise, you will make an unordered list.

1 Choose Window > Assets to bring the Assets panel to the front. In the Template category, right-click **mygreen_temp** and choose New From Template from the context menu.

A new page is created based on the template.

2 Save the file as **tips.html** in the site root folder.

3 In the document Title field, select the placeholder text *Add Title Here.*
Type **Green Tips to Save Money and Energy** to replace the text.
Press Enter/Return to complete the title.

4 In the Files panel, double-click **green_tips.rtf** in the lesson08 > resources folder.

5 In the text editor or word processing program, press Ctrl-A/Cmd-A to select all the text. Press Ctrl-C/Cmd-C to copy the text.

6 Switch back to Dreamweaver. Select the placeholder heading *Add main heading here* in `<div.content>` and type **Green Tips** to replace it.

7 Select the placeholder paragraph text *Add content here.* Press Ctrl-V/Cmd-V to paste the text from the clipboard.

The text consists of three individual lists of tips to save energy and money at home, at work, and in the community. First, let's format the headings that identify the tip categories.

8 Select the text *At Home* and format it as a Heading 2.

9 Repeat step 8 with the text *At Work* and *In the Community*.

The remaining text is currently formatted entirely as <p> elements. Dreamweaver makes it easy to convert this text into an HTML list. Lists come in two flavors: ordered and unordered.

10 Select all the <p> formatted text between the headings *At Home* and *At Work*. In the Property inspector, click the Ordered List (⊟) icon.

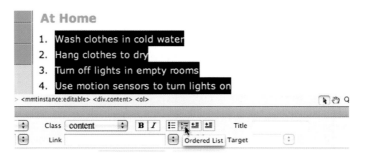

An ordered list adds numbers automatically to the entire selection. Semantically, it prioritizes each item, giving them an intrinsic value relative to one another. As you may see, this list doesn't seem to be in any particular order. Each item is more or less equal to the next one. An unordered list is another method of formatting a list when the items are in no particular order. Before you change the formatting, let's take a look at the markup.

11 Switch to Split view. Observe the list markup in the Code section of the document window.

▶ **Tip:** The easiest way to select the entire list is to use the <ol> tag selector.

The markup consists of two elements: <ol> and <li>. Note how each line is formatted as an <li> *list item*. The <ol> parent element begins and ends the list and designates it as an ordered list. Changing the formatting from numbers to bullets is simple and can be done in Code or Design view.

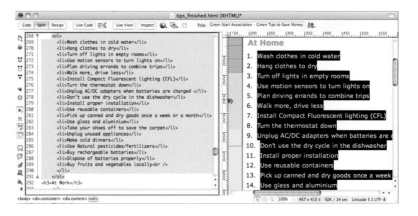

Before changing the format, ensure that the formatted list is still entirely selected.

12 In the Property inspector, click the Unordered List (▤) icon.

All the items are now formatted as bullets. Observe the list markup. The only thing that has changed is the parent element. It now says <ul> for *unordered list*.

13 Select all the <p> formatted text between the headings *At Work* and *In the Community*. In the Property inspector, click the Unordered List (▤) icon.

14 Repeat step 13 with all the text following the heading *Around the Community*.

All three lists are now formatted with bullets.

15 Select File > Save.

▶ **Tip:** You could also change the formatting by editing the markup manually in the Code view window. But, don't forget to change both the opening and closing parent elements.

Creating text indents

Today, many designers use the <blockquote> element as an easy way to indent headings and paragraph text. Semantically, the <blockquote> element is intended to identify long sections of text quoted from other sources. Visually, text formatted thusly will appear indented and set off from the regular paragraph text and headings. But, if you want to comply with web standards, you should leave this element for it intended purpose, and instead use custom CSS classes when you want to indent text, as you will in this exercise.

1 Create a new page from the template **mygreen_temp**. Save the file as **contact_us.html** in the site root folder.

2 In the document Title field, select the placeholder text *Add Title Here*.
Type **Contact GreenStart** to replace the text.
Press Enter/Return to complete the title.

3 Switch to the Files panel and double-click **contact_us.rtf** in the lesson08 folder.

4 In the text editor or word processing program, press Ctrl-A/Cmd-A to select all the text. Press Ctrl-C/Cmd-C to copy the text.

5 Switch back to Dreamweaver. Select the placeholder heading *Add main heading here* in <div.content> and type **Contact GreenStart Association** to replace it.

6 Select the placeholder paragraph text *Add content here*. Press Ctrl-V/Cmd-V to paste the text from the clipboard.

The text consists of five department sections, including headings, descriptions, and email addresses for the managing staff of GreenStart.

7 Select the text *Association Management* and format it as a Heading 2.

8 Repeat step 7 for the text *Education and Events*, *Transportation Analysis*, *Research and Development*, and *Information Systems*.

To indent a single paragraph, you can create and apply a custom class. In this case, you'll insert the paragraphs into a `<div>` element to help better organize the information graphically.

9 Select the three subsequent descriptive paragraphs ending with Elaine's email address after the heading *Association Management*. Don't include the heading in this selection.

10 If necessary, select Window > Insert to open the Insert panel. Choose the Layout category in the Insert panel. Click the Insert Div Tag button.

The Insert Div Tag dialog box appears. The Insert menu displays Wrap Around Selection.

11 Insert the cursor in the Class field. Type **profile** and click OK.

The selected text is inserted into a new `<div>` element. The tag selector displays `<div.profile>`. Before inserting the other sections into a similar `<div>` element, let's create the CSS formatting.

12 Insert the cursor anywhere in `<div.profile>`. Select `.content h2` in the CSS Styles panel. Click the New CSS Rule icon.

13 In the New CSS Rule dialog box, click Less Specific once to remove `.container` from the Selector Name field. The selector name field should display `.content .profile`. Click OK.

14 Select the Box category.

Enter **25px** in the Right and Left Margins only. In the Bottom margin only, enter **15px**.

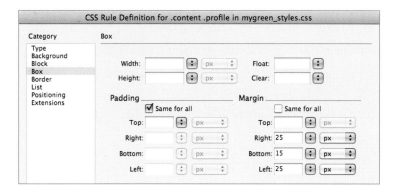

15 In the Border category, enter the following specifications for the Bottom border only: **solid**, **10px**, **#CADAAF**.

16 Enter the following specifications for the Left border only: **solid**, **2px**, **#CADAAF**. Click OK.

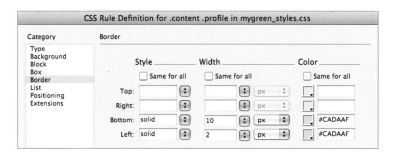

The border helps to visually group the indented text under its heading.

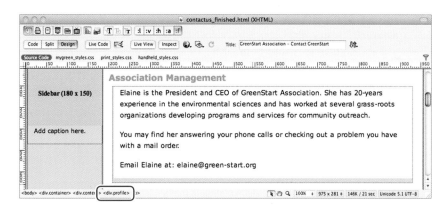

17 Select the descriptive paragraphs after the heading: *Education and Events, Transportation Analysis.* Click the Insert Div Tag button.

The Insert Div Tag dialog box appears. The Insert field displays: *Wrap Around Selection.*

18 Choose **profile** from the Class field menu. Click OK.

The paragraphs are inserted in a new `<div.profile>`.

19 Repeat steps 17 and 18 for the text after each department heading: *Research and Development*, and *Information Systems.*

Each section is indented and displays the custom border.

20 Save all files.

Creating and styling tables

Before the advent of CSS, HTML offered few tools to execute effective page designs. Instead, web designers resorted to using images and tables used to create page layouts. Today, tables are eschewed for page design and layout purposes for a few reasons. Tables are hard to create, format, and modify. They can't adapt easily to different screen sizes or types. And, certain browsing devices and screen readers don't see the comprehensive page layouts, they only see tables for what they actually are—rows and columns of data.

When CSS debuted and was promoted as the preferred method for page design, some designers came to believe that tables were bad altogether. That was a bit of an overreaction. Although tables are not good for page layout, they are very good, and necessary, for displaying many types of data, such as product lists, personnel directories, and time schedules to a name a few.

1 Create a new page from the template **mygreen_temp**. Save the file as **events.html** in the site root folder.

2 In the document Title field, select the placeholder text *Add Title Here.*
Type **Green Events and Classes** to replace the text.
Press Enter/Return to complete the title.

Dreamweaver enables you to create tables from scratch, to copy and paste them from other applications, or to create them instantly from data supplied by database or spreadsheet programs.

Creating tables from scratch

Dreamweaver makes it easy to create tables from scratch.

1 Select the placeholder heading *Add main heading here* in `<div.content>` and type **Green Events and Classes** to replace it.

2 Select the placeholder paragraph text *Add content here*. Press Delete.

3 Choose Insert > Table.

The Table dialog box appears. The size and specifications of tables, like most HTML elements, can be controlled by HTML attributes or CSS. Although best practices lean heavily toward using CSS for its power and flexibility, nothing beats the down-and-dirty convenience of HTML. When you enter values in this dialog box, Dreamweaver applies them via HTML attributes.

4 Enter **2** in the Rows field and **4** in the Columns field. Enter **90** in the Table Width field. Choose **percent** from the Table Width menu. Enter **0** in the Border thickness field. Click OK.

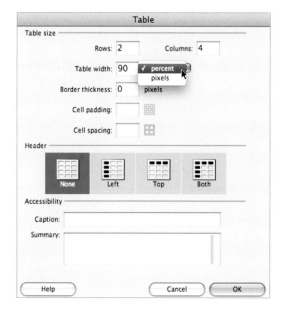

A four-column, two-row table appears below the heading. The table is ready to accept input.

5 Insert the cursor in the first cell of the table. Type **Date** and press Tab to move into the next cell in the first row.

6 In the second cell, type **Event** and press Tab. Type **Location** and press Tab. Type **Cost** and press Tab to move the cursor to the first cell of the second row.

7 In the second row, type **May 1** (in cell 1), **May Day Parade** (in cell 2), **City Hall** (in cell 3), and **Free** (in cell 4).

Inserting additional rows in the table is easy.

8 Press Tab to insert a new blank row in the table.

If this is too slow, Dreamweaver allows you to insert multiple new rows at once.

9 Select the `<table>` tag selector at the bottom of the document window.

The Property inspector displays the properties of the current table, including the total number of rows and columns.

10 Select the number 3 in the Rows field. Type **10** and press Enter/Return to complete the change.

Dreamweaver adds seven new rows to the table.

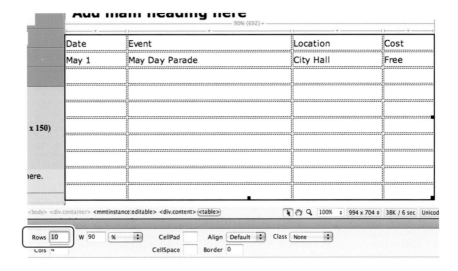

Copying and pasting tables

Dreamweaver also allows you to move tables from other HTML files or even other programs, using copy and paste.

1 Open the Files panel and double-click **calendar.html** in the lesson08 folder to open it.

<blockquote>● **Note:** Dreamweaver allows you to copy and paste tables from other programs, although you'll find that this function doesn't work with every program.</blockquote>

This HTML file will open in its own tab in Dreamweaver. Note the table structure; it has four columns and numerous rows.

2 Insert the cursor in the table. Click the `<table>` tag selector. Press Ctrl-C/Cmd-C to copy the text.

Sep 14	Book Club	East Side Community Center	Free
Oct 16	Day hike at the Dunes	Shoreline Park	$10
Oct 18	Volunteer for Homeless Shelter	North Side Community Center	Free
Oct 30	Halloween Haunted Hike	West Side Park	$10
Nov 14	Nature Photography Photo Group	South Side Community Center	$5
Dec 18	Holiday Party	West Side Community Center	Free

`<bod` `> <table>` `< r> <td>`

PROP

| | Table | | Rows 30 | W | | pixels ◆ | CellPad | | Align Default ◆ |

3 Click the **events.html** tab to bring the file to the front.

4 Insert the cursor in the table. Select the `<table>` tag selector. Press Ctrl-V/Cmd-V to paste the table.

The new table element completely replaces the existing table.

Green Classes and Events

Date	Event	Location	Cost
Jan 28	Community Potluck	West Side Community Center	Free
Jan 29-30	Cross Country Ski Trip	Burkeline Mountains Resort	$65
Jan 31	Volunteer for City Animal Shelter	Meridian Animal Shelter	Free
Feb 5-8	Cross Country Ski Weekend	Burkeline Mountains Resort	$165

`<body> <div.container> <mmtinstance:editable> <div.content> <h1>`   100% ◆ 994 x 705 ◆ 45K / 7 sec Unicode 5.1

5 Save the file.

Styling tables with CSS

Right now, your table aligns to the left, touching the edge of <div.content>, and may or may not stretch all the way across the element. Tables can be formatted by HTML attributes or by CSS rules. Using CSS enables you to control table formatting across the entire site using only a handful of rules.

1 Select the <table> tag selector. Select the .content .profile rule in the CSS Styles panel, and then click the New CSS Rule icon.

The New CSS Rule dialog box appears.

2 Choose Compound from the Selector Type menu, if necessary. Click Less Specific once to remove .container from the Selector Name field. Click OK.

Before you apply formatting to the table, you should know what other settings are already affecting the element and what ramifications new settings could have to your overall design and structure. For example, the .content rule sets the width of the element to 770 pixels. Other elements such as <h1> and <p> feature left padding of 15 pixels. If you apply widths, margins, and/or padding that total up to a number larger than 770 pixels, you could inadvertently break the careful structure of your page design.

3 In the Type category, enter **80%** in the Type-size field.

⦿ **Note:** Adding the width to the margin totals 760 pixels, 10 pixels less than the current width of <div.content>. Keep this in mind going forward in case other settings conflict with the table specifications.

4 In the Box category, enter **740px** in the Width field. Enter **15px** only in the Left Margin field.

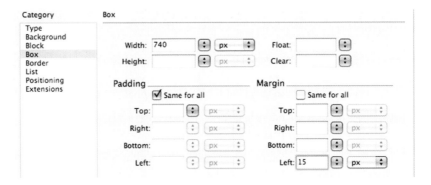

5 In the Border category, enter the following specifications only in the Bottom border fields: **solid**, **3px**, and **#060**. Click OK.

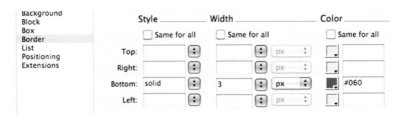

The table resizes, moves away from the left edge of `<div.content>`, and display a dark green border at the bottom. You have applied the desired styling to specific table properties, but you can't stop there. The default formatting of the tags that make up table markup is a hodgepodge of different settings that are honored haphazardly in various browsers. You'll find that the same table can be displayed differently in every browser.

One setting that may cause trouble is the HTML-based `cellspacing` attribute that functions with a margin-like quality between individual cells. If you leave this attribute blank, some browsers will insert a small space between cells and actually split any cell borders in two. In CSS, this attribute is handled by the `border-collapse` property. If you don't want the table borders to be split inadvertently, you need to include this setting in the styling. Unfortunately, this is one of the few specifications you can't access within the CSS Rule Definition dialog box.

6   Choose Window > CSS Styles to reveal the CSS Styles panel, if necessary. Select the `.content table` rule and observe the Properties section of the panel.

The Properties section displays the current settings for the `.content table` rule.

7   Click the Add Property link at the bottom of the list of properties. Type **border-collapse** and press Tab to move the cursor to the Value column field. Type **collapse** and press Enter/Return to complete the property.

Note: You won't find the `border-collapse` property in the pop-up menu, so you have to type it yourself. Once you type the property name, the value menu will then populate properly with the available options.

In Design view you may not see any difference in how the tables are displayed, but don't let that dissuade you from the need for this attribute.

8   Save all files.

The `.content table` rule you just created will format the overall structure of every table inserted into `<div.content>` on any page using this style sheet throughout the site. But the formatting isn't complete, yet. The widths of the individual columns are not controlled by the `<table>` element. To control the column widths you need to look elsewhere.

Styling table cells

Just as for tables, specifications for columns can be applied by HTML attributes or CSS, with similar advantages and disadvantages. Formatting for columns is applied through two elements that create the individual cells: <th> for *table header* and <td> for *table data*. The table header is a handy element that you can use to differentiate titles and header content from regular data.

It's a good idea to create a generic rule to reset the default formats of the <th> and <td> elements. Later, you will create custom rules to apply to specific columns and cells.

1 Insert the cursor into any cell of the table. Select the `.content table` rule before you click the New CSS Rule icon.

2 Choose Compound from the Selector Type menu, if necessary. Click Less Specific once to remove `.container` from the Selector Name field. Edit the Selector Name to say `.content td, .content th` and click OK.

The simplified selector will work fine.

3 In the Block category, choose **left** from the Text-align field menu.

4 In the Box category, enter **5px** in all Padding fields.

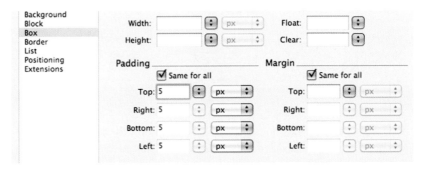

5 In the Border category, enter the following specifications only in the Top Border fields: **solid**, **1px**, and **#090**. Click OK.

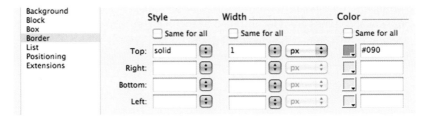

A thin green border appears above each row of the table, making the data easier to read. To see the border properly, you may need to preview the page in Live view first. Headers are usually formatted in bold to help them stand out from the normal cells. You can make them stand out even more by giving them a touch of color.

6 Select `.content td, .content th` in the CSS Styles panel. Click the New CSS Rule icon. Choose Compound from the Selector Type menu, if necessary. Type `.content th` in the Selector Name field. Click OK.

7 In the Type category, enter **#FFC** in the Color field.

8 In the Background category, enter **#090** in the Background-color field. Click OK.

The rule is created, but it still needs to be applied. Dreamweaver makes it easy to convert the existing `<td>` elements into `<th>` elements.

9 Insert the cursor into the first cell of the first row of the table. In the Property inspector, select the Header option. Note the tag selector.

● **Note:** Remember that the order of the rules affects the style cascade and how and what formats are inherited.

The cell is filled with green. When you click the check box, Dreamweaver automatically rewrites the markup converting the existing `<td>` to `<th>` and thereby applies the CSS formatting. This functionality will save you lots of time over editing the code manually. You can also convert multiple cells at one time.

10 Insert the cursor into the second cell of the first row. Drag to select the remaining cells in the first row. Or, you can select an entire row at once by positioning the cursor at the left edge of the table row and clicking when you see the black selection arrow appear.

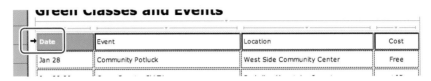

Green Classes and Events			
→ Date	Event	Location	Cost
Jan 28	Community Potluck	West Side Community Center	Free

11 In the Property inspector, select the Header option to convert the table cells to header cells.

The whole first row is filled with green as the table cells are converted to header cells.

12 Save all files.

Controlling column width

Unless otherwise specified, empty table columns will divide the available space between them equally. But once you start adding content to the cells, all bets are off—the table seems to get a mind of it own and divvies up the space in a different way. It usually gives columns that contain more data more space.

This behavior may or may not be your intention or achieve an acceptable balance, so to control the width of table columns you could use HTML attributes or custom CSS classes. When you create custom styles to format column widths, one idea is to base the rule names either on the width value itself or on the content, or subject, of the column.

● **Note:** Rule names can't start with numerals or punctuation characters, except for a period, which indicates a class or hash (#), which indicates an id.

1 Select the `.content th` rule in the CSS Styles panel and then click the New CSS Rule icon. Choose Compound from the Selector Type menu. Delete any text in the Selector Name field, type **`.content .w100`**, and click OK.

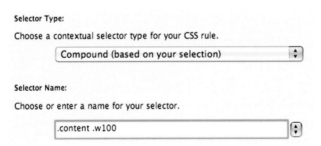

Selector Type:

Choose a contextual selector type for your CSS rule.

Compound (based on your selection) ▲▼

Selector Name:

Choose or enter a name for your selector.

.content .w100 ▲▼

In the new value for the Selector Name, the *w* stands for *width* and *100* indicates the value.

2 In the Box category, enter **100px** in the Width field. Click OK.

Controlling the width of a column is quite simple. Since the entire column must be the same width, you have to apply a width specification only to one cell. If cells in a column have conflicting specifications, typically the largest width wins. Let's apply a class to control the width of the Date column.

3 Insert the cursor into the first cell of the first row of the table. Select the `<th>` tag selector. In the Property inspector, choose **w100** from the Class menu.

▶ **Tip:** Be sure to click the tag selector, otherwise Dreamweaver may apply the class to the cell content instead of the `<th>` element.

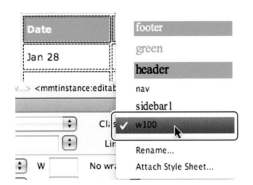

The first column resizes to a width of 100 pixels. The remaining columns automatically divvy up the available space. Column styling can also specify text alignment as well as width. Let's create a rule for the content in the Cost column.

Note: If you apply a narrow width, remember that the cell can't be any smaller than the largest word or graphic element contained within it.

4 Select the `.content .w100` rule in the CSS Styles panel and click New CSS Rule. Choose Compound from the Selector Type menu. Delete any text in the Selector Name field and type `.content .cost`. Click OK.

Obviously, this rule is intended for the Cost column. But don't add the width value to the name as you did before; that way you can change the value in the future without worrying about changing the name (and the markup), as well.

5 In the Block category, choose **center** from the Text-align field menu.

6 In the Box category, enter **75px** in the Width field. Click OK.

Unlike with the previous example, to apply text alignment to the contents of the entire column, you must apply the class to every cell.

7 Click in the first cell of the Cost column and drag down to the last cell of the column to select all the cells. Or, position the cursor over the top of the column and click using the black arrow to select the entire column at once. Choose `.cost` from the Class menu in the Property inspector.

The Cost column resizes to a width of 75 pixels, and the text aligns to the center. Now if you want to change only the Cost column, you have the ability to do so.

8 Save all files.

Inserting tables from other sources

Tables can also be created from data exported from databases, spreadsheets, and delimited files. In this exercise, you will create a table from data exported from MS Excel to a comma-separated values (CSV) file.

1   Insert the cursor anywhere in the table. Select the `<table>` tag selector. Press the right Arrow key to move the cursor after the closing `</table>` tag in the code.

2   Choose Insert > Table Objects > Import Tabular Data.

The Import Tabular Data dialog box appears.

3   Click the Browse button and select **classes.csv** from the lesson08 > resources folder.
Click Open.

Comma should be automatically selected in the Delimiter menu.

4   In the Table Width option, select Fit to Data. Delete any values appearing in the other fields not mentioned already, some of these fields will apply HTML attributes instead of CSS styling. Click OK.

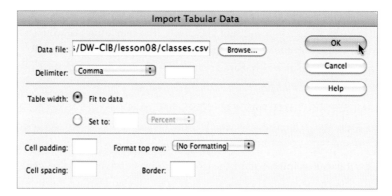

A new table—containing a class schedule—appears below the first. The new table consists of five columns with multiple rows. The first row contains header information but is still formatted as normal table cells.

5   Select the first row of the class schedule. In the Property inspector, select the Header option.

The first row appears in green with reversed text. You'll notice that the text is wrapping awkwardly in the last three columns. You will use the class `.cost` for the Cost column in the new table, but the other two will need custom classes of their own.

6   Select the Cost column as you did in the previous exercise. In the Property inspector, choose `.cost` from the Class menu.

7 In the CSS Styles panel, right-click the `.content .cost` rule and choose Duplicate from the context menu.

8 Change the Selector Name to **`.content .day`** and click OK.

9 Apply `.content .day` to the Day column in the Classes table, as in step 6.

10 Duplicate `.content .day` and name the new `.content .length` rule and click OK. Apply it to the Length column in the Classes table.

By creating custom classes for each column, you have the means to modify each column individually. One more rule is needed to format the Class column. This column requires only a generic rule to apply a more appealing width.

11 Right-click the `.content .w100` rule and duplicate it. Name the new rule **`.content .w150`** and click OK. Edit the new rule and change the Width to **150px** in the Box category. Apply the new rule only to the Class header cell.

> ▶ **Tip:** When applying a width value, only one cell needs to be formatted.

12 Save all files.

Adjusting vertical alignment

If you study the content of the Class table, you will notice that many of the cells contain paragraphs that wrap to multiple lines. When cells in a row have differing amounts of text in them, the shorter content is aligned vertically to the middle of the cell. Many designers find this behavior unattractive and prefer to have the text all align to the tops of the cells. As with most of the other attributes, vertical alignment can be applied by HTML attributes or CSS. To control the vertical alignment with CSS, you can add the specification to an existing rule.

Exploring Deep Ecology	An eight-session course examining our core values and how they affect the way we view and treat the earth.	4 weeks	F	$40
Future Food	Explores food systems and their impacts on culture, society and ecological systems.	4 weeks	Tu-Th	$80
The Impact of Globalization	This class explores the affect of global trade on local environments and economies throughout the world.	6 weeks	Tu	$60

1 Double-click the `.content th, .content td` rule to edit it.

The `<th>` and `<td>` elements style the text stored in the table cells.

▶ **Tip:** Some designers like to leave the text in `<th>` cells aligned to the middle or even the bottom. If this was the case, you'd need to create separate rules for each element.

2 In the Block category, choose top from the Vertical-align field menu. Click OK.

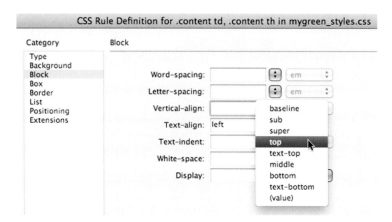

All the text in both tables now aligns to the top of the cells.

3 Save all files.

Adding and formatting `<caption>` elements

The two tables you inserted on the page contain different information but run into each other on the screen in a confusing manner. To help users differentiate between the two sets of data, let's add a title to each and a bit of extra spacing. To create this title, you could use an HTML heading to introduce each table, or an element devised especially for this purpose. The `<caption>` element was especially designed to identify the content of HTML tables. To use it, you'll insert it as a child of the `<table>` element.

1 Insert the cursor in the first table. Select the `<table>` tag selector. Switch to Code view.

By selecting the table in Design view, Dreamweaver automatically highlights the code in Code view, making it easier to find.

2 Locate the opening `<table>` tag. Insert the cursor directly after this tag. Type **`<caption>`** or select it from the code-hinting menu when it appears.

3 Type **2010 Event Calendar**, and then type `</` to close the element.

4 Switch to Design view.

The caption is complete and inserted as a child element of the table.

5 Repeat steps 1 and 2 for the second table. Type **2010 Class Schedule**, and then type </ to close the element.

6 Switch to Design view.

The captions are relatively small, and they're lost against the color and formatting of the table. Let's beef them up a bit with a custom CSS rule.

7 Insert the cursor in either caption. Click the New CSS Rule icon.

8 Choose Compound from the Selector Type menu, if necessary. Click Less Specific once to remove .container from the Selector Name field. Click OK.

9 In the Type category, enter **140%** in the Font-size field. Enter **1.2em** in the Line-height field. Choose **bold** from the Font-weight field menu. Enter **#090** in the Color field.

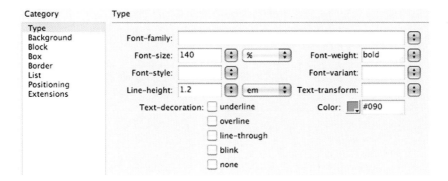

10 In the Box category, enter **20px** only in the Top margin field. Click OK.

11 Save all files.

12 Examine your work using Live view or a browser.

Formatting the tables and the captions with CSS has made them much easier to read and understand. Feel free to experiment with the size and placement of the caption and specification settings that affect the tables. In Lesson 14, "Working with Online Data," you will learn how to use tables to create dynamic web pages.

Spell checking web pages

It's important to ensure that the content you post to the web is error free. Dreamweaver includes a robust spell checker capable of identifying commonly misspelled words and creating a custom dictionary for nonstandard terms.

1 Click the **contact_us.html** tab to bring the document to the front, or open it from the site root folder.

2 Insert the cursor in the main heading *Contact GreenStart Association* in `<div.content>`. Choose Commands > Check Spelling.

Spell-checking starts wherever the cursor has been inserted. If the cursor is located lower on the page, you will have to restart the spell check at least once to examine the entire page.

3 The Check Spelling dialog box highlights the word *GreenStart*, which is the name of the association. You could click Add To Personal to insert the word into your custom dictionary, but for now click Ignore All, which will skip over other occurrences of the name during this check

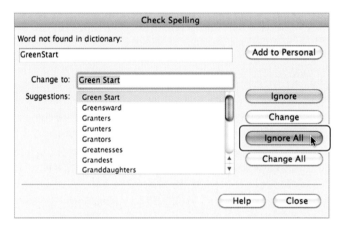

4 Next, Dreamweaver highlights the word *email*, which is listed in the dictionary spelled as *e-mail*. If your company uses the hyphenated spelling, go ahead and click Change, otherwise click the Ignore All again.

5 Dreamweaver highlights the domain for the email address *info@green-start.org*. Click Ignore All. Click Ignore All again when it stops on the name of the town (*Meridien*).

6 Dreamweaver highlights the word *Asociation*, which is missing an *s*. To correct the spelling, locate the correctly spelled word (Association) in the Suggestions list and double-click it.

7 The next word the spell check stops on is *grassroots*, which is in the dictionary as two words. The word is a compound noun made from two separate words. If you look it up, many dictionaries will show it with a hyphen between the two words. To make this type of change, add the hyphen in the Change To field so that the correction reads **grass-roots** and click Change.

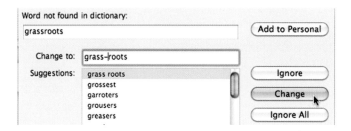

8 Continue the spell check to the end. Correct any misspelled words and ignore proper names, as necessary. If a dialog prompts you to start the check from the beginning, click Yes.

9 Save the file.

Finding and replacing text

The ability to find and replace text is one of Dreamweaver's most powerful features. Unlike other programs, Dreamweaver can find almost anything, anywhere in your site, including text, code, and any type of white space that can be created in the program. You can limit the search to just the rendered text in Design view, the underlying tags, or the entire markup. Advanced users can enlist powerful pattern-matching algorithms called *regular expressions* to perform the most sophisticated find-and-replace operations. And, then Dreamweaver takes it one step further, by allowing you to replace the targeted text or code, with similar amounts of text, code, and white space.

In this exercise, you'll learn some important techniques for using the find and replace feature.

1 Click the **events.html** tab to bring it to the front, or open the file from the site root folder.

There are several ways to identify the text or code you want to find. One way is simply to type it in the field manually. In the events table, the name *Meridien* was spelled incorrectly as *Meridian*. Since *Meridian* is an actual word, the spell checker won't flag it as an error and give you the opportunity to correct it. So, you'll use find and replace to make the change instead.

2 Switch to Design view, if necessary. Insert the cursor in the heading *Green Events and Classes.* Choose Edit > Find And Replace.

The Find And Replace dialog box appears. The Find field is empty.

3 Type **Meridian** in the Find field. Type **Meridien** in the Replace field. Choose Current Document from the Find In menu and choose Text from the Search menu.

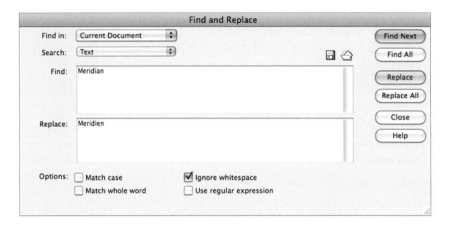

4 Click Find Next.

Dreamweaver finds the first occurrence of *Meridian.*

5 Click Replace.

Dreamweaver replaces the first instance of *Meridian* and immediately searches for the next instance. You can continue to replace the words one at a time, or choose to replace all occurrences.

Superpowerfindelicious!

Note the options in the Find In and Search menus. The power and flexibility of Dreamweaver shines brightest here. The Find And Replace command can search in selected text, the current document, all open documents, in a specific folder, in selected files of the site, or the entire current local site. But as if those options aren't enough, Dreamweaver also allows you to target the search to the source code, text, advanced text, or even to a specific tag.

6 Click Replace All.

If you replace the words one at a time, Dreamweaver inserts a one-line notice at the bottom of the dialog box that tells you how many items were found and how many were replaced. When you click Replace All, Dreamweaver closes the Find and Replace dialog box and opens the Search report panel and lists all the changes made.

7 Right-click on the Search report tab and select Close Tab Group from the Context menu.

Another method for targeting text and code is to select it *before* activating the command. This method can be used in either Design or Code view.

8 In Design view, locate and select the first occurrence of the text *Burkeline Mountains Resort* in the Location column of the Events table. Choose Edit > Find And Replace.

The Find And Replace dialog box appears. The selected text is automatically entered into the Find field by Dreamweaver. This technique is even more powerful when used in Code view.

9 Close the Find And Replace dialog box. Switch to Code view.

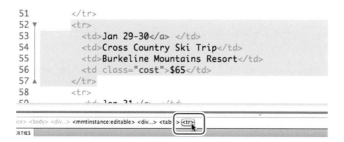

10 With the cursor still inserted in the text *Burkeline Mountains Resort*, click the `<tr>` tag selector at the bottom of the document window.

11 Choose Edit > Find And Replace. Observe the Find field.

The Find And Replace dialog box appears. The selected code is automatically entered into the Find field by Dreamweaver, including the line breaks and white space. The reason this is so amazing is because there's no way to enter this type of markup in the dialog manually.

12 Select the code in the Find field. Press Delete to remove it. Type **\<tr>** and press Enter/Return to insert the line break. Observe what happens.

Pressing Enter/Return did not insert a line break; instead it activated the Find command and finds the first occurrence of the \<tr> element. In fact, you can't manually insert any type of line break within the dialog.

You probably don't think this is much of a problem, since you've already seen how Dreamweaver inserts text/code when it's selected first. Unfortunately, the method used in step 8 doesn't work with large amounts of text or code.

13 Close the Find And Replace dialog box. Click the \<table> tag selector.

The entire markup for the table is selected.

14 Choose Edit > Find And Replace. Observe the Find field.

This time Dreamweaver did not transfer the selected code into the Find field. To get larger amounts of text or code into the Find field, and to enter large amounts of replacement text and code, you need to use copy and paste.

15 Close the Find And Replace dialog box. Select the table, if necessary. Press Ctrl-C/Cmd-C to copy the markup.

16 Press Ctrl-F/Cmd-F to activate the Find And Replace command. Insert the cursor in the Find field, press Ctrl-V/Cmd-V to paste the markup.

The entire \<table> selection is pasted into the Find field.

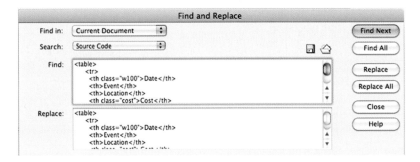

17 Insert the cursor into the Replace field and press Ctrl-V/Cmd-V.

The entire selection is pasted into the Replace field. Obviously, the two fields contain identical markup, but it illustrates how easy it would be to change or replace large amounts of code.

18 Close the Find And Replace dialog box. Save all files.

In this lesson you created four new pages and learned how to import text from other sources. You formatted text as headings and lists, and then styled it using CSS. You inserted and formatted tables and added captions to each. And, you reviewed and corrected text using Dreamweaver's spell check and find and replace tools.

Review questions

1 How do you format text to be an HTML heading?

2 Explain how to turn paragraph text into a ordered list and then an unordered list.

3 Describe two methods for inserting HTML tables into a web page.

4 What element controls the width of a table column?

5 Describe three ways to insert content in the Find field.

Review answers

1 Use the Format field menu in the Property inspector to apply HTML heading formatting.

2 Highlight the text with the cursor and click the Ordered List button in the Property inspector. Then click the Unordered List button to change the formatting to bullets.

3 You can copy and paste a table from another HTML file or a compatible program. And, you can insert a table by importing the data from a delimited file.

4 The width of a table column is controlled by the <td> element that creates the individual table cell.

5 You can type text into the field, select it before you open the dialog box and allow Dreamweaver to insert the selected text, and you can copy and paste the text or code into the field.

9 WORKING WITH IMAGES

Lesson Overview

In this lesson, you'll include images in your web pages in the following ways:

- Inserting an image
- Using Bridge to import Photoshop or Fireworks files
- Using Photoshop Smart Objects
- Copying and pasting an image from Photoshop

This lesson will take about 60 minutes to complete. Before beginning, make sure you have copied the files for Lesson 9 to your hard drive as described in the "Getting Started" section at the beginning of the book. If you are starting from scratch in this lesson, use the method described in the "Jumpstart" section of "Getting Started."

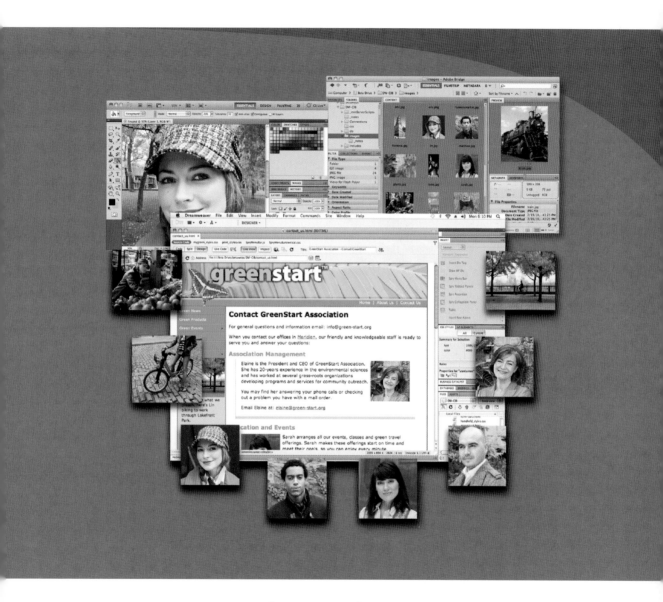

Dreamweaver provides many ways to insert and adjust graphics, both within the program and in tandem with other Creative Suite tools such as Adobe Bridge, Adobe Fireworks, and Adobe Photoshop.

Reviewing web image basics

The web is not as much a place as it is an experience. And, essential to that experience are images and graphics—both still and animated—that populate most websites. In the computer world, graphics fall into two main categories: *vector* and *raster*.

Vector graphics

Vector graphics are created by math. They act like discrete objects, allowing you to reposition and resize them as many times as you want without affecting or diminishing their output quality. The best application of vector art is wherever geometric shapes and text are used to create artistic effects. For example, most company logos are built from vector shapes.

Vector graphics excel in line art, drawings, and logo art. Raster technology works better for storing photographic images.

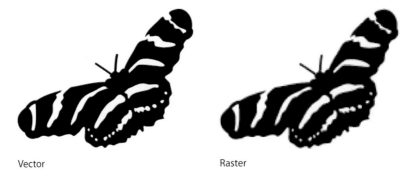

Vector   Raster

Vector graphics are typically stored in AI, EPS, PICT, or WMF file formats. Unfortunately, most web browsers don't support these formats. The format that is supported is SVG, which stands for *Scalable Vector Graphic*. The simplest way for you to get started with SVG would be to create a graphic in your favorite vector-drawing program—like Adobe Illustrator or CorelDRAW—and then export it to this format. If you are good at programming, you may want to try creating SVG yourself, using Extensible Markup Language (XML). Check out www.w3schools.com/svg to find out more about creating SVG yourself.

Raster graphics

Although SVG has definite advantages, web designers primarily use raster-based images in their web designs. Raster images are built from *pixels*, which stands for *picture elements*. Pixels have three basic characteristics:

- They are perfectly square in shape.
- They are all the same size.
- They display only one color at a time.

Raster-based images are usually composed of thousands, even millions, of different pixels arranged in rows and columns, in patterns that create the illusion of an actual photo or drawing. It's an illusion, because there is no real photo on the screen, just a bunch of pixels that fool your eyes into seeing an image. And, as the quality of the image increases, the more realistic the illusion becomes. Raster-image quality is based on three factors: resolution, size, and color.

Raster images are built of thousands or even millions of pixels that produce the illusion of a photograph.

Resolution

Resolution is the most well known of the factors affecting raster image quality. It is the expression of image quality measured in the number of pixels that fit in one inch (ppi). The more pixels you can fit in one inch, the more detail you can depict in the image. But better quality comes at a price. An unfortunate byproduct of higher resolution is larger file size. That's because each pixel must be stored as bytes of information within the image file—information that has real overhead in computer terms. More pixels mean more information, which means larger files.

Resolution has a dramatic effect on image output. The web image on the left looks fine in the browser but doesn't have enough quality for printing.

72 ppi

300 ppi

Luckily, web images only have to be optimized to look best on computer screens, which are mostly based on a resolution of 72 ppi. This is low compared to other applications—like printing—where 300 dpi is considered the lowest acceptable quality. The lower resolution of the computer screen is an important factor keeping most web image files down to a reasonable size for downloading from the Internet. Because web pages are intended for viewing and not printing, the pictures don't have to have any resolution higher than 72 ppi.

Size

Size refers to the vertical and horizontal dimensions of the image. As image size increases, more pixels are required to create it, and therefore the file becomes larger. Since graphics take more time to download than HTML code, many designers in recent years have replaced graphical components with CSS formatting to speed up the web experience for their visitors. But keeping image size small is one of the best ways to ensure snappy downloads. You won't find too many websites that depend on full-page graphics, for example.

Although these two images share the identical resolution and color depth, you can see how image dimensions can affect file size.

300 KB

1.1 MB

Color

Color refers to the color space or *palette* that describes each image. Computer screens can display only a fraction of the colors that the human eye can see. And, different computers and applications display varying levels of color, expressed by the term *bit depth*. Monochrome, or 1-bit, color is the smallest space, displaying only black and white, with no shades of gray. Monochrome is used mostly for line-art illustrations, blueprints, and to reproduce handwriting.

The 4-bit color space describes up to 16 total colors. Additional colors can be simulated by a process called *dithering*, where the available colors are interspersed and juxtaposed to create an illusion of more color. This color space was created for the first color computer systems and game consoles. Because of its limitations, this palette is seldom used today.

The 8-bit palette offers up to 256 total colors or 256 shades of gray. This is the basic color system of all computers, mobile phones, game systems, and handheld devices. This color space also includes what is called the web-safe color palette. *Web-safe* refers to a subset of 8-bit colors that are supported on both Macintosh and Windows computers. Most computers, game consoles, and handheld devices now support higher color palettes, but 8-bit is the fallback for all web-compatible devices.

Today, smart phones and handheld games usually support the 16-bit color space. This palette is called *high color* and sports a grand total of 65,000 colors. Although this sounds like a lot, 16-bit color is not considered good enough for most graphic design purposes or professional printing.

The highest color space is 24-bit color, which is called *true color*. This system generates up to 16.7 million colors. It is the gold standard for graphic design and professional printing. Several years ago a new color space was added to the mix: 32-bit color. It doesn't offer any additional colors, but it provides an extra eight bits for an attribute called *alpha transparency*.

Here you can see a dramatic comparison of three color-spaces and what the total number of available colors means to image quality.

24-bit color   8-bit color   4-bit color

Alpha transparency enables you to designate parts of graphics as fully or partially transparent, which allows you to create graphics that seem to have rounded corners or curves and eliminate the white bounding box typical of raster graphics.

As with dimensions, color-depth can dramatically affect image file size. With all other aspects being equal, an 8-bit image is over 7 times larger than a monochrome image. And, the 24-bit version is over 3 times larger than the 8-bit image. The key to effective use of images on a website is finding the balance of resolution, size, and color to achieve the desired optimal quality.

Raster image file formats

Raster images can be stored in a multitude of file formats, but web designers have to be concerned with only three: GIF, JPEG, and PNG. These three formats are optimized for the Internet and compatible with most browsers. However, they are not equal in capability.

GIF

GIF (graphic interchange format) was one of the first raster image file formats designed specifically for the web. It has changed only a little in the last 20 years. GIF supports a maximum of 256 colors (8-bit palette) and 72 ppi, so it's used mainly for web interfaces, buttons, graphical borders, and such. But it does have several interesting features that keep it pertinent for today's web designers: index transparency and animation.

JPEG

JPEG, also written JPG, is named for the Joint Photographic Experts Group that created the image standard back in 1992 as a direct reaction to the limitations of the GIF file format. JPEG is a powerful format that supports unlimited resolution, image dimensions, and color depth. Because of this, most digital cameras use JPEG as their default file type for image storage. It's also the reason most designers use JPEG on their websites for images that must be displayed in high quality.

But for pixel-based images, high quality—as described earlier—usually means large file size. Large files take longer to download to your browser. So, why is the format so popular on the web? JPEG's claim to fame comes from its patented user-selectable image compression algorithm that can reduce file size as much as 95 percent. JPEG images are compressed each time they are saved and then decompressed before they are opened and displayed.

Unfortunately, there's a downside to all this compression. Too much compression damages image quality. This type of compression is called *lossy*, because it loses quality each time. In fact, it can damage an image so much that the image can be rendered useless. Each time designers save a JPEG image, they face a trade-off between image quality and file size.

PNG

PNG (Portable Network Graphic) was developed in 1995 because of a looming patent dispute involving the GIF format. At the time it looked as if designers and developers would have to pay a royalty for using the .gif file extension. Although that issue blew over, PNG has found many adherents and a home on the Internet because of its capabilities.

PNG combines many of the features of GIF and JPEG and then adds a few of its own. For example, it offers support for unlimited resolution, 32-bit color, and full alpha and index transparency. It also provides lossless compression, which means you can save an image in PNG format and not worry about losing any quality each time you open and save the file. That's the good news.

The bad news is that although the format has been around for over 10 years, its features—such as alpha transparency—are not fully supported in older browsers.

Previewing the completed file

To get a sense of the files you will work on in this lesson, let's preview the completed pages in the browser.

1 Launch Adobe Dreamweaver CS5.

2 If necessary, press Ctrl-Shift-F/Cmd-Shift-F to open the Files panel and select DW-CIB from the site list.

3 In the Files panel, expand the lesson09 folder.

4 Open the **contactus_finished.html** and **news_finished.html** files from the lesson09 folder and preview the pages in your primary browser.

The page includes several images, as well as a Photoshop Smart Object image.

5 Close your browser and return to Dreamweaver.

Inserting an image

Images are key components of any web page, both for developing visual interest and for telling stories. Dreamweaver provides numerous ways to populate your pages with images, using built-in commands and even using copy and paste. One method is to insert the image using Dreamweaver tools.

1 In the Files panel, open the **contact_us.html** file from the site root folder, which you completed in Lesson 8, "Working with Text, Lists, and Tables."

An image placeholder appears in `<div.sidebar1>` to indicate where an image should be inserted.

2 Double-click the image placeholder labeled "Sidebar (180 x 150)."

The Select Image Source dialog box appears.

Note: If you are starting from scratch in this chapter, use the Jumpstart instructions in the "Getting Started" section at the beginning of the book.

3 Select **biking.jpg** from the site images folder. Click OK/Choose.

4 In the Image Tag Accessibility Attributes dialog box, in the Alternate Text field, type **Bike to work to save gas** and click OK. If this dialog box does not appear, you can add this text using the Alt field in the Property inspector. Remember, Alt text appears whenever images can't be displayed.

5 To give your image a caption, select the placeholder text *Insert caption here* and type **We practice what we preach, here's Lin biking to work through Lakefront Park**.

You've successfully inserted an image using one technique, but you have another technique available. Alternatively, you can add an image to the page using the Assets panel.

6 Insert the cursor at the beginning of the first paragraph under the heading *Association Management* in `<div.content>`. The cursor should be inserted before the name *Elaine*.

7 Choose Window > Assets to display the Assets panel, if necessary. Click the Images category (📷) icon to display a list of all images stored within the site.

8 Locate and select **elaine.jpg** in the list.

A preview of **elaine.jpg** appears in the Assets panel. The panel lists the image name, dimensions in pixels, and file type, as well as its directory path.

9 Note the dimensions of the image: 150 pixels by 150 pixels.

10 At the bottom of the panel, click the Insert button.

Note: The Images window shows all images stored in the site, even ones outside the site's default image folder; so you may see listings for images stored in the lesson subfolders, too.

▶ **Tip:** Dreamweaver also allows you to drag the image icon from the Assets panel to the page.

Note: If more than one file appears with the same name in the Assets panel, make sure you select the image stored in the default images folder.

The image appears at the current cursor location.

11 In the Image Tag Accessibility Attributes dialog box, type **Elaine, Meridien GreenStart President and CEO** in the Alternate Text field and click OK.

12 Choose File > Save.

You inserted Elaine's picture in the text, but it doesn't look very nice at its current position. In the next exercise, you will adjust the image position using a CSS class.

Adjusting image positions with CSS classes

The <img> element is an inline element, by default. That's why you can insert images into paragraphs and other elements. When the image is taller than the font size, the image will increase the vertical space for the line in which it appears. As with most solutions, there is a way to adjust its position using HTML attributes or CSS.

1 In the layout, select **elaine.jpg**. From the Align menu in the Property inspector, choose Right.

The image shifts to the right side of the paragraph and drops down into the text, with the text wrapping around it to the left.

2 Select the <img> tag selector. Switch to Code view. Observe the attributes within the beginning <img> tag.

The opening tag includes an align="right" attribute. This technique works fine, but it creates a lot more trouble for you if you wish to adjust this formatting later. A better solution uses CSS.

3 Select the image again, if necessary. From the Align menu in the Property inspector, choose Default.

The image returns to its insertion point.

4 From the Class menu in the Property inspector, select fltrt.

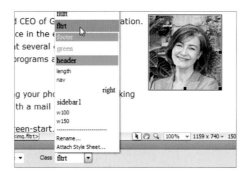

The image moves back to the right, as before. The classes fltrt (short for float right) and fltlft (short for float left) are included in each of the Dreamweaver predefined CSS layouts. They apply a CSS property that produces the same effect as the HTML Align attribute, but one that will be easier to modify across the entire site, if necessary.

Working with the Insert panel

The Insert panel duplicates key menu commands and has a number of buttons that make inserting images both quick and easy.

1 Insert the cursor at the beginning of the first paragraph under the heading *Education and Events.*

2 Choose Window > Insert to display the Insert panel, if necessary.

3 In the Insert panel, choose the Common category.

   Click to open the Images button.

   The button offers seven options: Image, Image Placeholder, Rollover Image, Fireworks HTML, Rectangular Hotspot, Oval Hotspot, or Polygon Hotspot. A *hotspot* is basically a hyperlink enabled by a user-defined area drawn on an image.

Note: If you don't see the Insert panel docked on the right side of the screen, it may open as a toolbar at the top of the document window, as it does in the Classic workspace for example.

4 From the pop-up menu, choose Image.

   The Select Image Source dialog box appears.

5 Select **sarah.jpg** from the default images directory and note the dimensions of the image: 150 pixels by 150 pixels. Click OK/Choose.

6 In the Image Tag Accessibility Attributes dialog box, type **Sarah, GreenStart Events Coordinator** in the Alternate Text field and click OK.

7 Apply the fltlft class to this image.

   The image drops down into the paragraph on the left side with the text wrapping to the right.

8 Save the file.

Another way to insert images in your web page is by using Adobe Bridge.

Using Adobe Bridge

Adobe Bridge CS5 is an essential tool for web designers that can quickly browse directories of images and other supported assets, as well as manage and tag files with keywords and labels. Bridge is fully integrated with Dreamweaver: You can launch it from within Dreamweaver and drag images directly from Bridge into your layouts.

1   Insert the cursor at the beginning of the first paragraph under the heading *Transportation Analysis.*

2   Choose File > Browse in Bridge.

Adobe Bridge launches. The interface in Bridge can be set up to your liking and saved as a custom workspace.

3   Click the Folders tab to bring the Folders panel to the top. If necessary, choose Window > Folders Panel, if the panel isn't visible. Navigate to the folder designated as your default site images folder on your hard drive. Observe the names and types of files displayed in the folder.

Bridge displays a thumbnail image of each file in the folder. Bridge can display thumbnails for all types of graphic files, including AI, BMP, EPS, GIF, JPG, PDF, PNG, SVG, and TIF, among others.

4   Click **eric.png**. Observe the Preview and Metadata panels. Note the dimensions, resolution, and color space of the image.

The Preview panel displays a high-quality preview of the selected image.

Bridge also has capabilities for helping you locate and isolate specific types of files.

5   Choose Window > Filter Panel to display the panel, if it's not visible.

The Filter panel displays a default set of data criteria—such as file type, ratings, keywords, date created, and so forth—that are then populated automatically by the contents of a particular folder. You can filter the contents to these criteria by clicking one or more of these items.

6   In the Filter panel, expand the File Type criteria. Select the JPEG File criterion.

A check mark appears beside the JPEG File criterion. The PNG file you selected earlier is no longer visible. The Content panel displays only JPEG files.

7   In the File Type criterion, select GIF Image.

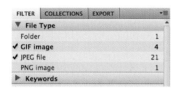

A check mark appears beside the GIF Image criterion. The Content panel now displays only GIF and JPEG files. Bridge enables you to insert files instantly into other Creative Suite applications.

8   Select **eric.jpg** in the Content panel. Note the dimensions in the Metadata panel: 150 pixels by 150 pixels. Choose File > Place > In Dreamweaver.

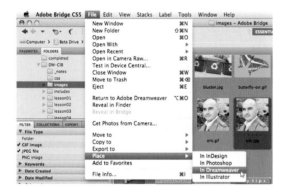

Your computer switches back to Dreamweaver automatically.

9   In the Image Tag Accessibility Attributes dialog box, type **Eric, Transportation Research Coordinator** in the Alternate Text field and click OK.

The **eric.jpg** image appears in the Dreamweaver layout at the last position of the cursor.

10 Apply the fltrt class to this image. Save the file.

Dreamweaver is not limited only to the file types GIF, JPEG, and PNG; it can work with other file types, too. In the next exercise you will learn how to insert a Photoshop document (PSD) into a web page.

Inserting incompatible file types

Although most browsers will display only the web-compatible image formats described earlier, Dreamweaver allows you to choose from many different formats to insert into the layout. The program will then automatically convert the file to a compatible format on the fly.

1   Insert the cursor at the beginning of the first paragraph under the heading *Research and Development.*

2   Choose Insert > Image. Navigate to lesson09 > resources on your hard drive. Select **lin.psd** and note the image dimensions. Click OK/Choose.

The Image Preview dialog box appears. The Image Preview dialog box acts as an intermediary that will convert the file to the necessary format.

3   Note the image type displayed in the Format menu. Open the Format menu.

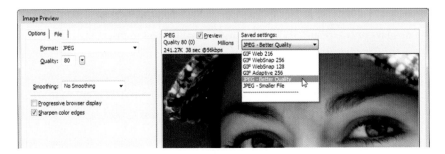

The Format drop-down menu offers five options: GIF, JPEG, PNG 8, PNG 24, and PNG 32.

4   Choose JPEG. Note the Quality setting.

The default setting for JPEG is usually at 80 percent. This quality setting produces a high-quality image with a moderate amount of compression. You can raise the compression level to reduce the file size, but as described earlier, this can adversely affect image quality.

5   Before you experiment with the Quality setting, note the text displayed above the image preview.

This information reports valuable statistics about the current state of the image and tells you how big the file is and how long it will take to download using a specified connection speed.

6 Change the Quality value to **50**. Press Tab to effect the change.

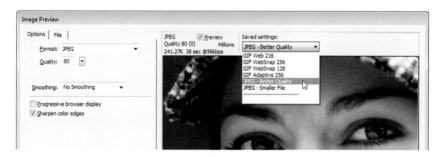

The change in quality may not be observable in the image preview, but it had a noticeable effect on the file size and download speed. Compression affects images differently based on many factors, including color, contrast, and composition. An amount of compression that is acceptable in one image may ruin another.

7 Change the Quality value to **10**. Press Tab to effect the change.

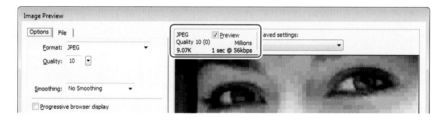

At 10, the compression has severely affected the image quality. Few images would be usable at this compression level. But you can see that the high compression has also reduced the file size and download time dramatically.

8 Change the Quality value to **80**.

The image preview returns to its earlier quality. You can adjust the setting up and down as many times as you want as long as the dialog box is open. But once you click OK, this dialog box will effect permanent changes to the image.

9 Click the File tab in the upper left to switch the mode of the dialog box. Note the values in the Scale fields.

As you plainly see, the PSD image is much larger than any of the previously used images. The image is at 100 percent of its original size, 600 pixels by 600 pixels. The width of this image would definitely break the layout of your page if it were inserted at its current size. Fortunately, the Image Preview dialog box has the ability to resample and resize this image. If you recall, the images inserted previously were 150 pixels by 150 pixels.

10 Select the value in the Width field. Type **150** to replace the value and press Tab to move to the Height field.

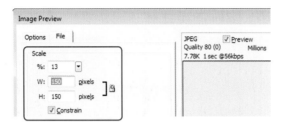

Note that the Height field changes to 150 if the Constrain option is selected. The image preview changes to reflect the new size.

● **Note:** When an image has to be converted this way, Dreamweaver usually saves the converted image into the default site images folder. This is not the case when the images inserted are web-compatible. So, before you insert an image you should be aware of its current location in the site and move it to the proper location, if necessary.

11 Click OK.

The Save Web Image dialog box appears with the name *lin* entered in the Save As field. Dreamweaver will add the .jpg extension to the file automatically, too.

12 If necessary, navigate to the default site images folder. Click Save.

The Image Tag Accessibility Attributes dialog box appears.

13 Enter **Lin, Research and Development Coordinator** in the Alternate Text field. Click OK.

The image appears in Dreamweaver at the cursor position.

14 Apply the flt1ft class to this image. Save the file.

The image appears in the layout, but there's something different about it. An icon appears in the upper-left corner of the image that identifies this image as a Photoshop Smart Object.

Working with Photoshop Smart Objects

Unlike other images, Smart Objects maintain a connection to a Photoshop (PSD) file. If the PSD file is altered in any manner and then saved, Dreamweaver will identify those changes and provide the means to update the web image used in the layout. In fact, a single PSD file can be placed in one or more pages as a Smart Object and then updated in one action.

1 If necessary, open **contact_us.html**. Scroll down to the image **lin.jpg** in the Research And Development section. Observe the icon in the upper-left corner of the image.

The icon indicates the image is a Smart Object. The circular green arrows indicate that the original image is unchanged. If you want to resize or resample the image, you can simply double-click it to reopen the Image Preview dialog. Because the image is still tied to the original image at its full size and resolution, you will be able to scale the image's size and quality up or down.

To make substantive changes to the image, you will have to open it in Photoshop. (If you don't have Photoshop installed, copy lesson09 > resources > smartobject > **lin.jpg** into the lesson09 > resources folder to replace the original image and then skip to step 6.)

2 Right-click **lin.jpg**. Choose Edit Original With > Photoshop from the context menu.

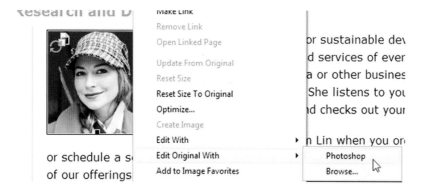

Photoshop launches—if it is installed on your computer—and loads the file.

> **Note:** Dreamweaver and Photoshop can work with the existing quality of an image only. If your initial image quality is unacceptable, you may not be able to fix it in Photoshop. You will have to re-create the image or pick another.

3 In Photoshop, choose Window > Layers to display the Layers panel, if necessary. Observe the names and states of any existing layers.

The image has two layers: Lin and New Background. New Background is turned off.

4 Click the eye (👁) icon for the New Background layer to display its contents.

The background of the image changes to show a scene from a park.

5 Save the Photoshop file.

6 Switch back to Dreamweaver.

In a moment or two, the Smart Object icon in the upper-left corner changes to indicate that the original image has been changed. You don't have to update this image at this time. You can leave the out-of-date image in the layout for as long as you want, Dreamweaver will continue to monitor its status as long as it's in the layout. But for this exercise, you want to update the image.

7 Right-click the image and choose Update From Original from the context menu.

This Smart Object and any other instances of it also change to reflect the new background.

8 Save the file.

As you can see, Smart Objects have advantages over a more typical image workflow. For images that are frequently updated, using a Smart Object can simplify updating the website in the future.

Copying and pasting images from Fireworks and Photoshop

As you build your website, you will need to edit and optimize many images before you use them in your site. Adobe Fireworks and Adobe Photoshop are both excellent programs for performing these tasks. A common workflow is to manually export the finished GIF, JPEG, or PNG to the default images folder in your website when you're done working on it. But Dreamweaver allows you to copy and paste images from either program directly into your layout. The steps are nearly identical for both; feel free to use the program you are most familiar with in this exercise.

1 Launch Adobe Fireworks or Adobe Photoshop, if necessary. Open **matthew.tif** from the lesson09 > resources folder. Observe the Layers panel.

   The image has only one layer. In Fireworks, you can select multiple layers and copy and paste them into Dreamweaver. In Photoshop, you will have to merge or flatten layers before you copy and paste them.

2 Press Ctrl-A/Cmd-A to select the entire image. Press Ctrl-C/Cmd-C to copy the image.

3 Switch to Dreamweaver. Scroll down to the Information Systems section in **contact_us.html**. Insert the cursor at the beginning of the first paragraph in this section.

4 Press Ctrl-V/Cmd-V to paste the image from the clipboard.

   The Image Preview dialog box appears.

5 Click the File button to switch the mode of the dialog box. Change the Width to **150**. Click OK.

   The height changes automatically to match. The Save Web Image dialog box opens with the name *matthew* already displayed in the Save As field.

6 In the Save Web Image dialog box, click Save.

> ● **Note:** Raster images can be scaled down in size without losing quality, but the opposite is not true. Unless a graphic has a resolution higher than 72 ppi, it may not be possible to scale it larger without noticeable degradation.

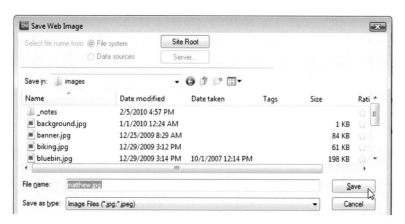

Dreamweaver will add the .jpg extension to the file automatically.

The Image Description (Alt Text) dialog box appears.

7   Enter **Matthew, Information Systems Manager** in the Image Description (Alt Text) field. Click OK.

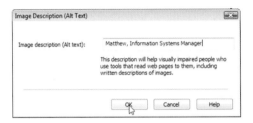

The image appears in the layout at the cursor location. Although this image came from Fireworks or Photoshop, it's not "smart" like a Photoshop Smart Object and can't be updated automatically. It does, however, keep track of the location of the original image if you want to edit it later.

8   In the layout, right-click the image **matthew.jpg** and choose Edit Original With > Browse from the context menu.

▶ **Tip:** The executable program file is usually stored in the Program Files folder in Windows and in the Applications folder on a Mac.

9   Navigate to and select the program file for Fireworks or Photoshop on your hard drive. Click Open.

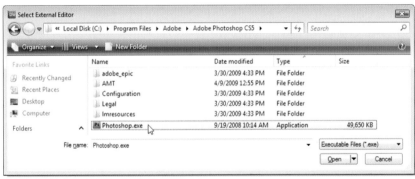

The program launches and displays the original TIF file. You can make changes to the image and copy and paste it into Dreamweaver by repeating steps 2 through 7. Although there's no way to automatically replace the image, as with Smart Objects, there's a more efficient way than using copy and paste. Photoshop users should skip to step 11.

10 **In Fireworks:** Choose File > Image Preview. Switch to File mode in the Image Preview dialog box. Choose JPEG – Better Quality from the Saved Settings menu and change the Width field to **150px**. Click Export. Skip to step 12.

The Height field changes to match the width. The Export dialog box appears.

11 In Photoshop: Choose File > Save For Web And Devices. Choose JPEG – High from the Preset menu. Change the Image Size Width field to **150px**. Click Save.

The height field changes to match the width. The Save Optimized As dialog box appears.

12 Navigate to the default site images folder and click the file **matthew.jpg**.

The name **matthew.jpg** appears in the Save As field of the Export/Save Optimized As dialog box.

13 Click Export/Save.

14 Switch back to Dreamweaver. Scroll down to view **matthew.jpg** in the Information Systems section.

No further action is needed to update the image in the layout because you saved the new image over the original file. As far as Dreamweaver is concerned, the file hasn't changed at all. This method saves you several steps and avoids any potential typing errors.

15 Apply the `fltrt` class to this image. Save the file.

Copy and paste is just one of the handy methods for inserting images. Dreamweaver also allows you to drag images into your layout.

Tip: Clicking the name inserts the existing filename and avoids any spelling or typing errors, which is vital for Unix-based web servers.

Inserting images by drag and drop

Most of the programs in the Creative Suite offer drag-and-drop capabilities, and Dreamweaver is no exception.

1 Open the **news.html** file you created in the last lesson from the site root folder.

2 Choose Window > Files to display the Files panel, if necessary. For this exercise, the panel should be docked. Click the Collapse button to dock the panel, if necessary.

3 Navigate to and expand the images folder.

4 Drag **city.jpg** from the panel to the beginning of the first paragraph under the heading *Green Buildings earn more Green*.

The Image Tag Accessibility Attributes dialog box appears.

5   In the Alternate Text field, enter **Green buildings are top earners**. Click OK.

6   Apply the class fltlft to the image. Save the file.

It takes a steady hand and a little practice to perfect your drag-and-drop technique, but it's a good way to get images into your layout quickly.

Optimizing images with the Property inspector

Optimized web images balance dimensions and quality with file size. Sometimes you may need to optimize graphics that have already been placed on the page. Dreamweaver has built-in features that can help you achieve the smallest possible file size while preserving image quality. In this exercise, you'll use tools in Dreamweaver to scale, optimize, and crop an image for the web:

1   Insert the cursor at the beginning of the first paragraph under the heading *Shopping green saves energy*. Choose Insert > Image. Select **farmersmarket.jpg** from the site images folder and click OK/Choose.

2   In the Alternate Text field, enter **Buy local to save energy**. Click OK.

3   Apply the class fltrt to the image.

The image is large and poorly composed. You can use tools in Dreamweaver to fix the image composition.

4   If necessary, choose Window > Properties to display the Property inspector.

Whenever an image is selected, image-editing options appear in the lower-right corner of the Property inspector. The buttons here allow you to edit the image in Fireworks or Photoshop, or adjust various settings in place. See the sidebar "Dreamweaver's graphic tools" for an explanation of each button.

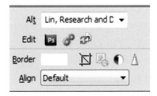

There are two ways to reduce the dimensions of an image in Dreamweaver. The first method changes the size of the image temporarily by imposing user-defined dimensions.

5   In the layout, select **farmersmarket.jpg**. In the Property inspector, change the image width to **200** and the height to **300**.

Although the dimensions entered are not correct for this image, it resizes anyway. A circular arrow appears beside the Width and Height fields, indicating that the image dimensions have been modified manually.

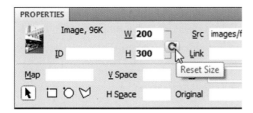

6   Click the circular arrow.

The image returns to its original size. You should avoid this method for reducing the image dimensions because it has no beneficial effect on file size or download speed.

The image can also be resized interactively.

7   Hold the Shift key (which constrains the operation to proportional scaling) and drag the lower-right corner to scale the image down to a width of **300**.

The circular arrow appears in the Property inspector.

8   In the Property inspector, click the Resample (▣) icon. Click OK.

A dialog box appears, indicating that the change will be permanent.

Dreamweaver can also crop images.

9   Click the Crop (◲) icon.

Crop handles appear on the image.

▶ **Tip:** As you scale the image, the Property inspector gives a real-time display of the image dimensions.

10 Crop the image to remove unwanted areas. Press Enter/Return to finalize the change.

11 Save the file.

In this lesson, you learned how to insert images and Smart Objects into a Dreamweaver page, work with Adobe Bridge, copy and paste from Fireworks and Photoshop, and use the Property inspector to edit images.

There are numerous ways to create and edit images for the web. The methods examined in this lesson show but a few of them and are not meant to recommend or endorse one method over another. Feel free to use whatever methods and workflow you desire, based on your own situation and expertise.

Dreamweaver's graphic tools

All of Dreamweaver's graphic tools are accessible from the Property inspector when an image is selected. Here are the six tools:

Edit—Sends the selected image to the defined external graphics editor. You can assign a graphics editing program to any given file type in the File Types/Editors category of the Preferences dialog box. The button's image changes according to the program chosen. For example, if Fireworks is the designated editor for the image type, a Fireworks icon is shown; if Photoshop is the editor, you'll see a Photoshop icon.

Edit Image Settings—Opens the current image in the Image Preview dialog box. In addition to providing access to the optimization features used in this exercise, the Image Preview dialog box can be used to crop images and modify animated GIF settings.

Update From Original—Renders a Smart Object to the newly selected size. The underlying Photoshop file is unchanged.

Crop—Removes the unwanted parts of an image. When the Crop tool is selected, a bounding box with a series of handles appears within the current image. You can adjust the bounding box size by dragging the handles. When the box outlines the desired portion of the image, double-click the graphic to remove those parts of the image that are outside the bounding box.

Resample—Rescales a resized image. The Resample tool is active only when an image has been resized.

Brightness And Contrast—Adjusts an image that may be too light or too dark. A dialog presents two sliders—for brightness and contrast—that can be adjusted independently. A live preview is available so that you can evaluate adjustments before committing to them.

Sharpen—Affects the definition of image edges by raising or lowering the contrast of pixels on a scale from 0 to 10. As with the Brightness And Contrast tool, Sharpen offers a real-time preview.

You can undo all graphics operations by choosing Edit > Undo until the containing document is closed or you quit Dreamweaver.

Review questions

1 What are the three factors that determine raster image quality?

2 What file formats are specifically designed for use on the web?

3 Describe at least two methods for inserting an image into a web page using Dreamweaver.

4 True or false: All graphics have to be optimized outside of Dreamweaver.

5 What is the advantage of using a Photoshop Smart Object over copying and pasting an image from Photoshop?

Review answers

1 Raster image quality is determined by resolution, image dimensions, and color depth.

2 The compatible image formats for the web are GIF, JPEG, and PNG.

3 One method to insert an image into a web page using Dreamweaver is to use the Insert panel. Another method is to drag the graphic file into the layout from the Files panel. Images also can be copied and pasted from Photoshop. Images can be inserted from Adobe Bridge.

4 False. Images can be optimized even after they are inserted into Dreamweaver by using the Image Preview dialog box. Optimization can include rescaling, changing format, or fine-tuning format settings.

5 A Smart Object can be used multiple times in different places on a site, and each instance of the Smart Object can be assigned individual settings. All copies remain connected to the original image. If the original is updated, all the connected images are immediately updated as well. When you copy and paste all or part of a Photoshop file, however, you get a single image that can have only one set of values applied to it.

10 WORKING WITH NAVIGATION

Lesson Overview

In this lesson, you'll apply several kinds of links to page elements by doing the following:

- Creating a text link to a page within the same site

- Creating a link to a page on another website

- Creating an e-mail link

- Creating an image-based link

- Creating a Spry navigation menu

 This lesson will take about 2 hours and 45 minutes to complete. Before beginning, make sure you have copied the files for Lesson 10 to your hard drive as described in the "Getting Started" section at the beginning of the book. If you are starting from scratch in this lesson, use the method described in the "Jumpstart" section of "Getting Started."

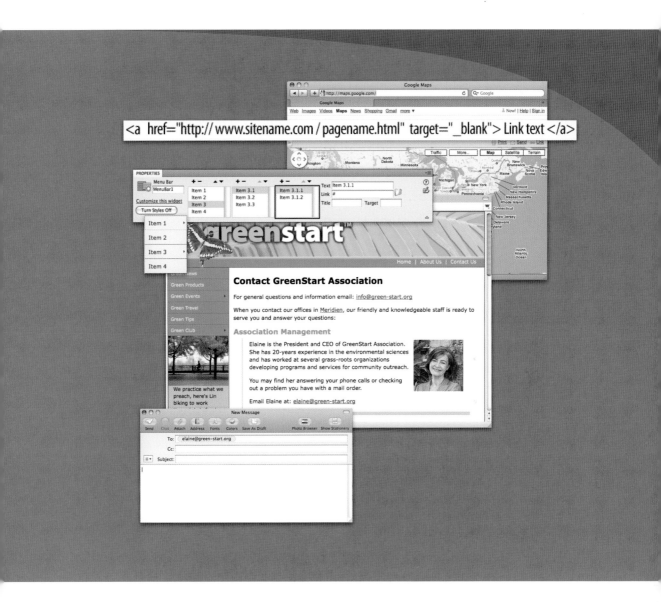

Dreamweaver can create and edit many types of links—ranging from hyperlinks to e-mail links—and does so with ease and flexibility.

Hyperlink basics

The World Wide Web, and the Internet in general, would be a far different place without the hyperlink. Without hyperlinks, HTML would simply be "ML" for *markup language*. The *hypertext* in the name refers to the functionality of the hyperlink. So what is a hyperlink?

A hyperlink, or link, is a reference to a resource available on the Internet, or within your own computer. The resource can be anything that can be stored on and displayed by a computer, such as a web page, image, movie, sound file, and so on. A hyperlink creates an interactive behavior specified by HTML, or the programming language you're using, and is enabled by a browser or other application.

An HTML hyperlink consists of the anchor <a> element and one or more attributes.

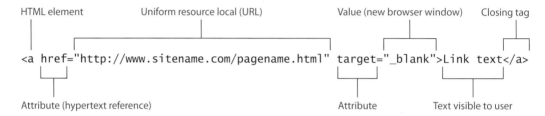

Internal and external hyperlinks

The simplest hyperlink is one that takes the user to another part of the same document, or another document stored in the same folder or hard drive. This type is called an *internal* hyperlink. An *external* hyperlink is designed to take the user to a document or resource outside your hard drive, website, or web host.

Internal and external hyperlinks work differently, but they both have one thing in common. Both are enabled in HTML by the <a> anchor element. This element designates the *address* of the destination, or target, of the hyperlink and can specify how it functions using several attributes. You will learn how to create and modify the <a> element in the exercises that follow.

Relative vs. absolute hyperlinks

The hyperlink address can be written in two different ways. When you refer to a target by where it is stored in relation to the current document, it is called a *relative* link. This is like telling someone that you live next door to the blue house. If someone was driving down your street and saw the blue house, they know where you live. But, it really doesn't tell them how to get to your house, or even to your neighborhood. A relative link frequently will consist of the resource name and perhaps the folder it is stored within, such as **logo.jpg** or **images/logo.jpg**.

Sometimes, you need to spell out precisely where a resource is located. In those instances, you need an *absolute* hyperlink. This is like telling someone you live at 123 Main Street in Meridien. This is usually the case when you refer to resources outside your website. An absolute link includes the entire URL of the target, such as http://forums.adobe.com/index.jspa, that may direct the user to a specific file or just a folder within the site.

There are advantages and disadvantages to both types of links. Relative hyperlinks are faster and easier to write but may not work if the document containing them is saved in a different folder or location in the website. Absolute links always work no matter where the containing document is saved, but they can fail if the targets are moved or renamed. A simple rule that most web designers follow is to use relative links for resources within a site and absolute links for resources outside the site.

Previewing your completed file

To see the final version of the file you will work on in this lesson, let's preview the completed page in the browser.

1 Launch Adobe Dreamweaver CS5.

2 If necessary, press Ctrl-Shift-F/Cmd-Shift-F to open the Files panel, and select DW-CIB from the site list.

3 In the Files panel, expand the lesson10 folder.

4 Right-click **aboutus_finished.html** in the Files panel, choose Preview In Browser, and select your preferred browser to preview the file.

   The file **aboutus_finished.html** appears in your default browser. This page features only internal links in both the horizontal and vertical menus.

▶ **Tip:** Firefox and Internet Explorer usually display the hyperlink destination in a thin strip in the lower-left corner of the screen, called the status bar.

▶ **Tip:** If you don't see the status bar in Firefox, choose View > Status Bar to turn it on. In Internet Explorer, choose View > Toolbars > Status Bar to turn it on.

5 Position the cursor over the *Contact Us* link in the horizontal menu. Observe the browser to see if it's displaying the link's destination anywhere on the screen.

The browser shows the link destination in the status bar.

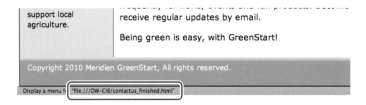

6 In the horizontal navigation menu, click the *Contact Us* link.

The browser loads the Contact Us page, replacing the About Us page. The new page includes internal, external, and e-mail links.

7 Position the cursor over the *Meridien* link in the main content area. Observe the status bar.

The status bar displays the link http://maps.google.com.

8 Click the *Meridien* link.

A new browser window appears and loads Google Maps. The link is intended to show the visitor where the Meridien GreenStart offices are located. You can even include address details or the company name in this link so that Google can load the exact map and directions, if desired.

Note how the browser opened a separate window or document tab when you clicked the link. This is a good behavior to use when directing visitors to resources outside your site. Since the link opens in a separate window, your own site is still open and ready to use. It's especially helpful if your visitors are unfamiliar with your site and may not know how to get back to it once they click away.

9 Close the Google Maps window.

The GreenStart Contact Us page is still open. Note that each employee has an e-mail link.

10 Click an e-mail link for one of the employees.

The default mail application will launch on your computer. If you have not set up this application to send and receive mail, the program will usually start a wizard to help you set up this functionality. If the e-mail program is set up, a new message window will appear with the e-mail address of the employee automatically entered in the To field.

● **Note:** Many web visitors don't use e-mail programs installed on their computers. They use web-based services like AOL, Gmail, Hotmail, and so on. For these types of visitors, e-mail links like the one you tested won't work. To learn how to receive info from visitors without relying on client-based e-mail, see Lesson 13, "Working with Forms."

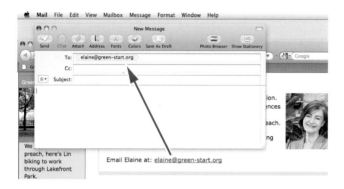

11 Close the new message window and exit the e-mail program.

12 Switch back to the browser. Position the cursor over the vertical menu. Hover over each of the buttons and examine the behavior of the menu.

The menu looks similar to the one you created in Lessons 5, "Creating a Page Layout," and Lesson 6, "Working with Cascading Style Sheets," but there's a new behavior that didn't exist before. Some of the buttons have submenus.

13 Hover on the *Green Events* link and then click the submenu link *2010 Class Schedule.*

The browser loads the Green Events page and automatically jumps down to the table containing the 2010 class schedule. As you can see, hyperlinks not only can target a specific page, they can target a specific item on the page to help visitors move quickly up and down long pages.

14 Click the *Return to Top* link that appears above the class schedule.

The browser jumps back to the top of the page.

15 Close the browser and switch to Dreamweaver.

Creating internal hyperlinks

Dreamweaver makes it easy to create hyperlinks of all types. In this exercise, you'll create text-based links to pages in the same site through a variety of methods.

1 In the Files panel, double-click the **about_us.html** file in the site root folder to open it. Or, if you are starting from scratch in this lesson, follow the "Jumpstart" instructions in the "Getting Started" section at the beginning of the book.

2 In the horizontal menu, try to select the *Home* text.

The horizontal menu was not added to an editable region in Lesson 7, "Working with Templates," so it's considered part of the template and is locked. To add a hyperlink to this menu item, you'll have to open the template.

● **Note:** If you're using the method described in the "Jumpstart" section of "Getting Started," preexisting files may display the lesson number, such as mygreen_temp_10.dwt.

3 Choose Window > Assets. In the Assets panel, click the Template (⊞) icon. Right-click **mygreen_temp** in the list and choose Edit from the context menu.

4 In the horizontal menu, select the *Home* text.

The horizontal menu is editable in the template.

5 If necessary, choose Window > Properties to open the Property inspector. Examine the contents of the Link field in the Property inspector.

To create links, the HTML tab must be selected in the Property inspector. The Link field shows a hyperlink placeholder *#*. The home page doesn't exist yet. But links can be created by manually typing the name of the file or resource.

6 Select the hash mark (#) in the Link field. Type **../index.html** and press Enter/Return to complete the link.

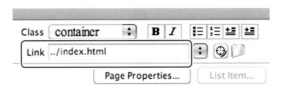

You've created your first text-based hyperlink. Since the template is saved in a subfolder, you need to add the path element "../" to the filename so that the link properly resolves once the template pages are updated. The "../" tells the browser or operating system to look in the parent directory of the current folder. Dreamweaver will rewrite the link when the template is applied to a page, depending on where the containing page is saved.

Note: The link won't have the typical hyperlink appearance because of the special formatting you applied to this menu in Lesson 6.

Dreamweaver offers interactive ways to create links, too.

7 In the horizontal menu, select the text *About Us*.

8 Click the Browse For File (icon) icon, adjacent to the Link field. When the Select File dialog box opens, select **about_us.html** from the site root folder. Make sure that the Relative To menu is set to Document. Click OK/Choose.

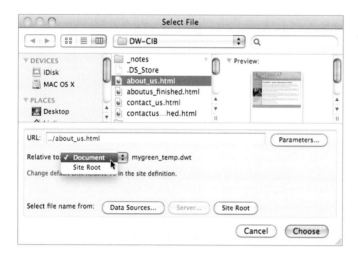

The hyperlink placeholder is replaced by the text "../about_us.html". Now, let's try a more visual approach.

9 In the horizontal menu, select the *Contact Us* text.

You can select any range of text to create a link, from one character to an entire paragraph or more; Dreamweaver will add the necessary markup to the selection.

10 Click the Files tab to bring the panel to the top, or choose Window > Files.

11 In the Property inspector, drag the Point To File (icon) icon—next to the Link field—to **contact_us.html** in the site root folder displayed in the Files panel.

Tip: If a folder in the Files panel contains a page you want to link to but the folder is not open, drag the Point To File icon over the folder and hold it in place to expand that folder so that you can point to the desired file.

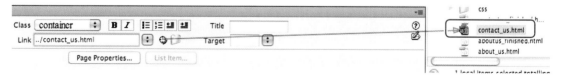

Dreamweaver enters the filename and any necessary path information into the Link field. To apply the links to all the pages formatted by this template, just save the page.

12 Choose File > Save.

The Update Template Files dialog box appears. You can choose to update pages now or wait until later. You can even update the template files manually, if desired.

▶ **Tip:** If you don't see the update report, select the Show Log option.

13 Click Update.

Dreamweaver updates all pages created from the template. The Update Pages dialog box appears and displays a report listing the pages that were updated.

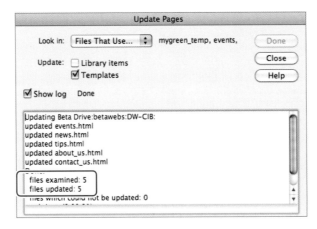

14 Close the Update Pages dialog box. Close **mygreen_temp.dwt**.

Note the asterisk in the document tab for **about_us.html**. This indicates that the page has changed but has not been saved.

15 Save **about_us.html** and preview it in the default browser. Position the cursor over the text *About Us* and *Contact Us*.

When the template was saved, it updated the locked regions of the template, adding the hyperlinks.

16 Click the *Contact Us* link.

The Contact Us page replaces the About Us page in the browser.

17 Click the *About Us* link.

The About Us page replaces the Contact Us page. The links were added even to pages that weren't open at the time.

18 Close the browser and switch to Dreamweaver.

You learned three methods for creating hyperlinks with the Property inspector: typing the link manually, using the Browse For File function, and using the Point To File tool.

Creating an image-based link

Links can also be applied to images. Image-based links work like any other hyperlink and can direct users to internal or external resources. In this exercise, you will create and format an image-based link that will direct users to the organization's About Us page.

1   Open the Assets panel and click the Template (☐) icon.
    Double-click **mygreen_temp** to open it.

2   Select the butterfly image at the top of the page. In the Property inspector, click the Browse For File icon next to the Link field.

3   Select **about_us.html** in the site root folder. Click OK/Choose.

    The text *about_us.html* appears in the Link field.

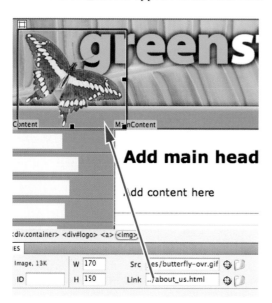

4   In the Alt field of the Property inspector, replace the existing text with **Click to learn about Meridien GreenStart** and press Enter/Return.

5   Save the template. Click Update.

    The Update Pages dialog box appears, reporting how many pages were updated.

Note: Normally an image formatted with a hyperlink would display a blue border, similar to the blue underscore text links get. But the predefined CSS that came with the layout includes an **a img** rule, which sets this default border to None.

6 Close the Update Pages dialog box. Open **contact_us.html**, if necessary, and preview it in the default browser. Position the cursor over the butterfly image. Test the image link.

Clicking the image loads **about_us.html** in the browser.

7 Switch back to Dreamweaver. Close the template file.

Creating an external link

The pages you linked to in the previous exercise were stored within the current site. You can also link to any page, or other resource, stored on the web if you know the full web address, or URL. In this exercise, you'll apply an external link to existing text.

1 Click the document tab for **contact_us.html** to bring it to the top, or open it from the site root folder.

2 In the second paragraph <p> element in the MainContent region, select the word *Meridien*.

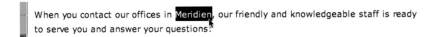

You'll link this text to the site Google Maps. If you don't know the URL of a particular site, there's a simple trick to obtain it.

Tip: For this trick, you can use any search engine.

3 Launch your favorite browser. In the URL field, type **google.com** and press Enter/Return.

4 In the search field, type **Google Maps** and press Enter/Return. Locate the link for Google Maps in the search report and click it.

Google Maps will appear in the browser window.

5 Select the entire URL that appears at the top of the document window. Press Ctrl-C/Cmd-C to copy this link.

6 Switch to Dreamweaver. In the Property inspector, insert the cursor in the Link field of the Property inspector and press Ctrl-V/Cmd-V to paste the link and press Enter/Return.

The text displays the standard formatting for a hyperlink.

7 Save the file and preview it in the default browser. Test the link.

When you click the link, the browser takes you to the opening page of Google Maps, assuming you have a connection to the Internet. But there was a problem: Clicking the link replaced the Contact Us page in the browser; it didn't open a new window as in the earlier example. To make the browser open a new window, you need to add a simple HTML attribute to the link.

8 Switch to Dreamweaver. Insert the cursor in the *Meridien* link text, if necessary.

9 Choose _blank from the Target field menu.

10 Save the file and preview the page in the default browser. Test the link.

This time a new separate window opens for Google Maps.

11 Close the browser windows and switch back to Dreamweaver.

As you can see, Dreamweaver makes it easy to create links to internal or external resources.

Setting up e-mail links

Another type of link is the e-mail link, but instead of taking you to another page it opens the visitor's e-mail program instead. It can create an automatic, pre-addressed e-mail message from your visitors for customer feedback, product orders, or other important communications. The code for an e-mail link is slightly different from the normal hyperlink and—as you probably guessed already—Dreamweaver can create the proper code for you automatically.

1 If necessary, open **contact_us.html**.

2 Select Elaine's e-mail address (**elaine@green-start.org**) and press Ctrl-C/ Cmd-C to copy the text.

3 Choose Insert > Email link.

The Email Link dialog box appears. The selected text is automatically entered into the Text field.

▶ **Tip:** If the text is selected before you access the dialog box, Dreamweaver will enter the text in the field for you automatically.

4 Insert the cursor in the Email field and press Ctrl-V/Cmd-V to paste the e-mail address. Click OK. Examine the Link field in the Property inspector.

Dreamweaver has inserted the e-mail address into the Link field and did one more thing. As you can see, it also entered the text *mailto:* in front of the address. This text changes the link to an e-mail link that will automatically launch the visitor's default e-mail program.

5 Save the file and preview it in the default browser. Test the e-mail link.

The default e-mail program launches and creates an e-mail message. If there is no default e-mail program, your computer's operating system will launch an available e-mail program or ask you to identify one.

6 Close any e-mail program or related dialog boxes or wizards that are opened. Switch to Dreamweaver.

Client-based vs. server-side functions

The e-mail link you just created relies on software installed on the visitor's computer, such as Outlook, Entourage, or Apple Mail. Such applications are referred to as *client-based*, or client-side, functionality. The e-mail link won't work, however, if a user sends his or her mail via an Internet application—such as Hotmail or Gmail—and doesn't have a desktop e-mail application set up.

Another detraction is that open e-mail links like this can be picked up easily by spambots that roam the Internet. If you want to ensure that you'll get feedback from every user who wants to send it, you should rely on functionality supplied by your server, instead. Web-based applications for capturing and passing data are referred to as *server-side* functionality. Using server-side scripts and proprietary languages—such as ASP, ColdFusion, and PHP—it's relatively easy to capture data and return it by e-mail or even insert it directly into a hosted database. You'll learn some of these techniques in Lesson 13, "Working with Forms," and Lesson 15, "Building Dynamic Pages with Data."

Targeting page elements

As you add more content on a page, it gets longer and more difficult to navigate. Typically, when you click a link to a page, the browser window displays the page starting at the very top. Whenever possible, it's a good idea to provide convenient methods for users to link to a specific point on a page.

There are two methods for targeting specific content or page structures: one uses a *named anchor* and the other an ID attribute. In this exercise, you'll learn how to do both.

1 Open **events.html**.

2 Scroll down to the table that contains the 2010 class schedule.

   When users move down this far on the page, the navigation menus are out of sight and unusable. The farther they read down the page, the farther they are from the primary navigation. Before users can navigate to another page, they have to use the browser scroll bars or the mouse scroll wheel to get back to the top of the page. Adding a link to take users back to the top can vastly improve their experience on your site. Let's call this type of link an internal *targeted* link.

   Internal targeted links have two parts: the link itself and the target element. It doesn't matter which one you create first.

3 Insert the cursor in the Class table. Select the `<table>` tag selector. Press the Left Arrow key to move the cursor before the opening `<table>` tag.

4 Type **Return to Top** and select the text.
   In the Property inspector, choose Paragraph from the Format menu.

   The text is inserted between the two tables and is formatted as a `<p>` element. Let's center the text.

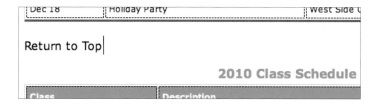

5 In the CSS panel, click the New CSS Rule icon.

6 Choose Class from the Selector Type menu.
   In the Selector Name field, type **ctr**.
   Click OK.

7 In the Block category, choose Center from the Text-align field menu. Click OK.

8 Select the tag selector for the paragraph element *Return to Top*. In the Property inspector Class menu, choose ctr.

The text *Return to Top* is aligned to the center. The tag selector now says `<p.ctr>`.

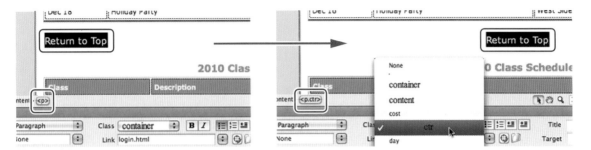

▶ **Tip:** In some browsers you need only type the hash mark (#) to enable this function. The browser will jump to the top of the page whenever an unnamed anchor is referenced. Unfortunately, other browsers will ignore them altogether. So, it's important to use a target element, as well.

9 In the Link field, type **#top** and press Enter/Return.

By using #top you have created a link to a target within the current page. This target doesn't exist yet. Dreamweaver refers to the target element as a named anchor. When users click the *Return to Top* link, the browser window will jump to the position of the anchor. For this named anchor to work properly, you need to insert it as high on the page as possible.

10 Scroll to the top of **events.html**. Position the cursor over the header element.

The mouse icon indicates that this part of the page (and its related code) is uneditable because the header and horizontal navigation menu are based on the site template. It's important to put the named anchor at the very top or part of the page may be obscured when the browser jumps to the target. The best solution, in this case, is to add the named anchor to the template.

Creating a named anchor

By adding the named anchor to the template, you will be able to use it throughout the site, wherever you want to add a link back to the top of the page.

1 Open the Assets panel. Click the Template (▣) icon. Double-click **mygreen_temp** to open it.

2 Insert the cursor in `<div.header>`. Choose Insert > Named Anchor.

3 Type **top** in the Anchor Name field. Click OK.

An anchor icon appears in the header. Don't worry, it won't be visible in the browser.

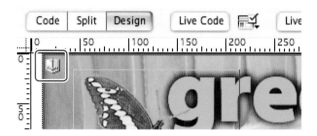

▶ **Warning:** The related anchor code should have zero impact on any text content or page layout; however, odd things have been known to occur in certain types of structures. If your page layout is affected adversely by inserting the anchor code in one place, try inserting it elsewhere.

4 Save the file and update all template pages. Close the template.

5 Switch to **events.html**, if necessary. Save the file and preview it in the default browser.

6 Scroll down to the Class table. Click the *Return to Top* link.

The browser jumps back to the top of the page.

Now that the named anchor has been inserted in every page of the site by the template, you can copy the *Return to Top* link and paste it wherever you want to add this functionality.

7 Switch to Dreamweaver. Insert the cursor in the *Return to Top* link. Select the `<p.ctr>` tag selector. Press Ctrl-C/Cmd-C.

8 Scroll down to the bottom of **events.html**. Insert the cursor in the Class table and select the `<table>` tag selector. Press the Right Arrow key to move the cursor after the closing `</table>` tag. Press Ctrl-V/Cmd-V.

The `<p.ctr>` element and link appear at the bottom of the page.

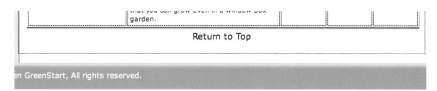

9 Save the file and preview it in the browser. Test both *Return to Top* links.

Both links can be used to jump back to the top of the document. In the next exercise, you'll learn how to use element attributes as link targets.

Using ID attributes as link targets

Named anchors can be used anywhere you want to create a link. But you don't need to add the extra code if there's a handy element nearby that you can add an ID attribute to.

1   If necessary, open **events.html**. Insert the cursor anywhere in the Events table and select the `<table>` tag selector.

The Property inspector displays the attributes of the Events table.

2   Open the ID field menu in the Property inspector.

There are no IDs available to apply to the table, but it's easy to create a new one.

● **Note:** An ID can be applied to any HTML element. They don't have to be referenced in the style sheet at all.

3   Insert the cursor in the ID field. Type **calendar** and press Enter/Return.

The tag selector now displays `<table#calendar>`. Since IDs are unique identifiers, they can be used in place of named anchors for targeting specific content on a page. Don't forget to create an ID for the Class table, too.

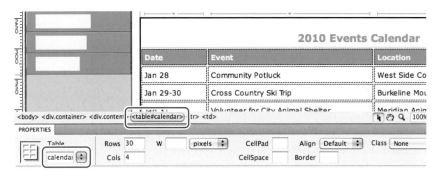

● **Note:** When creating IDs, remember that they have to be unique names.

4   Select the Class table as in step 1. Insert the cursor in the ID field. Type **classes** and press Enter/Return.

The tag selector now displays `<table#classes>`. You'll learn how to link to these IDs in the next exercise.

5   Save the file.

Inserting Spry menu bars

The existing vertical menu is currently targeting pages within the site. It's a good start, but it could be better. In the example at the beginning of this lesson, the menu in the finished page enabled you to navigate directly to specific content in the site. These links were displayed as a submenu in the vertical menu.

Although your current menu doesn't have this functionality, you could add it to the existing code yourself if you were handy with JavaScript and CSS. But why go to all that bother when Dreamweaver offers everything you need in a prebuilt widget. A widget performs a specific set of functions in a browser enabled by programming that combines HTML code, CSS, and JavaScript, otherwise known as Ajax and Adobe's Spry framework.

Learning about Ajax and Spry

The early Internet was dominated by sites and applications that simply re-created existing products and services online. Web 2.0 ushered in a new era in Internet usability and interactivity. The concept behind Web 2.0 was to break down the existing barriers between customer and service, to make the online experience seamless.

The prime technology driving Web 2.0 is known as Ajax, which stands for Asynchronous JavaScript and XML. If you've ever scrolled through a Google Map or browsed a photo collection on Flickr, you've experienced what Ajax can do.

The key term in the Ajax acronym is *asynchronous*, which means "not at the same time." Normally, viewing pages on the web is a very linear process: You load a page and the browser displays it and everything remains unchanged until you reload the page or load a new page. In other words, if you don't reload the entire page, you can't change any of the information on the page.

Ajax throws out those old rules. Using JavaScript and XML data, Ajax-driven pages can actually update data on the fly without reloading the whole page. This makes the user experience much smoother and more interactive. Data can change at any time, either when it's updated on the server or when prompted by the user.

Most implementations of Ajax require an advanced knowledge of JavaScript and a great deal of hand coding. To ease the learning curve, Adobe has developed the Spry framework, which integrates Ajax seamlessly with Dreamweaver CS5. There are four sets of Spry tools:

- **Spry Data**—Incorporates HTML or XML data into any web page and allows for the interactive display of data. You will work with a Spry Data set in Lesson 14, "Working with Online Data."

- **Spry Effects**—Extends the Dreamweaver behavior library with advanced functionality to interactively affect page elements. Spry Effects include the ability to fade, reveal, slide, highlight, and shake targeted page components.

- **Spry Form widgets**—Combines form elements, such as text fields and lists, with JavaScript validation functions and user-friendly error messages. You will work with Spry Form widgets in Lesson 13, "Working with Forms."

- **Spry Layout widgets**—Provides a series of sophisticated layout controls, including Tabbed and Accordion panels. In Lesson 11, "Adding Interactivity," you will work with Spry Accordion widgets.

Visit Adobe Labs at http://labs.adobe.com/technologies/spry if you'd like to peek under the hood and learn more about Spry and how it works.

To create the menu and behavior you experienced earlier, you will have to replace the existing vertical menu with one of Dreamweaver's Spry widgets. Spry menu bars are an easy and powerful way to insert advanced functionality in your site without having to perform all the coding by hand.

1 If necessary, open **events.html**. Click the vertical menu. Select the `<mm:libitem>` tag selector. Press Delete.

2 Choose Window > Insert to display the Insert panel, if necessary. Choose Spry from the category menu of the Insert panel. Click the Spry Menu Bar button.

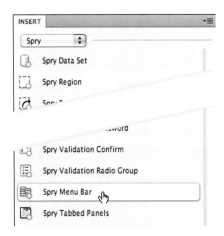

3 In the Spry Menu Bar dialog box, select Vertical and click OK.

A new vertical menu appears in the sidebar. Note the blue bar that appears directly above the menu displaying the name MenuBar1. The menu features four items and a default set of formatting. You will adjust the width and appearance of the menu in the next exercise. Dreamweaver provides special formatting capabilities geared toward Spry widgets. To access these capabilities, select the blue bar above the widget.

4 Click the blue bar above the Spry menu.

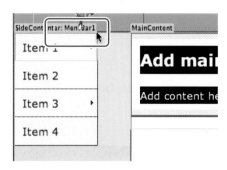

The Property inspector displays a special interface you can use to add, delete, and modify links within the menu.

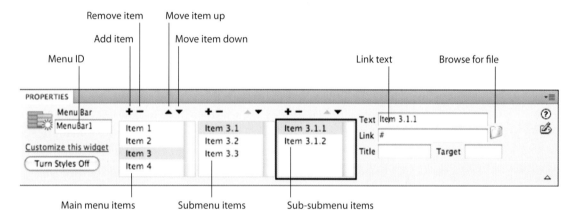

5 Before customizing the menu bar, choose File > Save. If Dreamweaver asks you about copying dependent files, click OK.

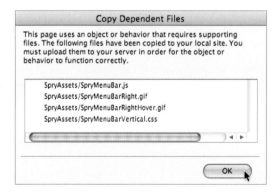

Dreamweaver inserts a folder called SpryAssets into your site root folder that will contain necessary components for any Spry widget. Custom CSS and

JavaScript files needed for the menu bar will be added to this folder, too. When files are added to the folder, Dreamweaver will automatically link the web page to them.

The Spry menu bar can be modified directly within the Property inspector.

6 In the first column of the Property inspector, click Item 1 to select it. In the Text field, select the *Item 1* text. Type **Green News** to replace it and press Enter/Return to complete the change.

The text *Green News* appears in the first menu item on the screen and in the Property inspector. The Property inspector also provides the means to add the hyperlink to the item.

7 In the Property inspector, click the Browse (⬜) icon.

8 Select **news.html** in the site root folder. Click OK/Choose.

The text *news.html* is entered in the field. In this case, Dreamweaver did not insert the text "../" into the link. That's because the file you are working in at the moment is stored in the site root folder and doesn't require this path element.

Note that the Green News button features three subitems in the Property inspector. Note the triangle icon on the button in the menu. This graphic indicates to the user that the button contains a submenu. Dreamweaver makes it easy to add or delete subitems.

9 Click Item 1.1 to select it. Click the Remove Item (➖) icon above the column to delete the subitem.

Item 1.1 is removed from the list.

10 Delete Item 1.2 and Item 1.3.

When the last subitem is removed, Dreamweaver automatically removes the submenu icon from the Green News button.

11 Select Item 2 and change the text field to read **Green Products**.

There is no Products page to link to yet, but this doesn't stop you from entering the filename in the Link field manually.

12 Select the hash mark (#) and type **products.html** in the Link field. Press Enter/Return to complete the change.

13 Select Item 3. Change the Text field to read **Green Events** and link the item to **events.html** in the site root folder.

Note that the Green Events button features three subitems and two sub-subitems. You'll use the submenu to link to the Events and Class tables.

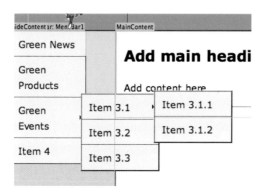

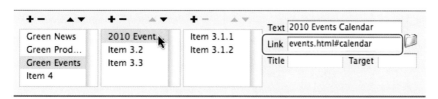

14 Select Item 3.1 and change the Text field to read **2010 Events Calendar**. In the Link field, browse and select **events.html** from the site root folder.

The link at the moment will merely open and display the page starting at the very top as normal. To target the Events table, you need to add the ID you created earlier to the link code.

15 In the Link field, insert the cursor at the end of the filename **events.html**. Type **#calendar** and press Enter/Return.

The text now reads *events.html#calendar* in the Link field. The 2010 Events Calendar item features two subitems of its own.

16 Select and delete Item 3.1.1 and Item 3.1.2 in the Property inspector.

> ▶ **Warning:** Whenever you manually type hyperlink names and path information, keep track of the exact spelling and other details you use. When the target file is created later, make sure it matches. Typos and differences in case can cause links to fail.

17 Change Item 3.2 to read **2010 Class Schedule** and enter **events.html#classes** in the Link field.

Before you test the link functionality, let's finish the rest of the menu.

18 Delete Item 3.3.

19 Change Item 4 to **Green Travel** and enter **travel.html** in the Link field.

You have re-created four of the five items from the original menu, but there's still one missing. The Property inspector makes it simple to add new menu items.

20 Click the Add Item (✚) icon above the first column to add a new item.

A new **Untitled Item** appears at the bottom of the list.

21 Replace the text *Untitled Item* with **Green Tips** and link the item to **tips.html** in the site root folder.

22 Save the file.

● **Note:** Notice that the subitem isn't wide enough to display the link text on one line. You will adjust the width of the subitem in an upcoming exercise.

23 Save all files and preview **events.html** in the browser. Check out the menu behavior and test the subitem links to 2010 Events Calendar and 2010 Class Schedule.

The menu behavior is similar to that of the menu you tested at the beginning of this lesson. When you hover on the Green Events item, a submenu pops open showing you links to the events calendar and class schedule. When the link is clicked, the browser jumps down to each table automatically.

24 Switch back to Dreamweaver.

The completed Spry menu appears in the sidebar. In the next exercise, you'll learn how to modify this menu by hand.

Modifying Spry menus directly

Although it may look like magic, Spry components are built with everyday HTML and CSS. Most widgets can be modified directly in Code or Design view, if desired.

1 Open **events.html**, if necessary. In the Property inspector, click the Turn Styles Off button.

In Design view, you see the list is displayed without CSS formatting. Note how the list is formatted differently, correlating to the main and subitem levels of the menu. Some may find it easier to work in the document window instead of in the Property inspector. The menu can now be edited as you would any other HTML list. It's a simple matter now to add a new link.

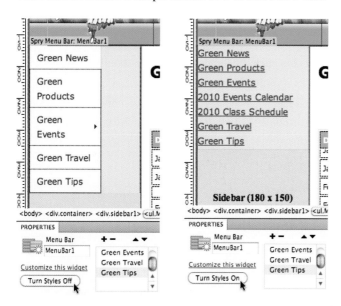

2 Insert the cursor at the end of the bulleted text *Green Tips* and press Enter/Return to insert a new line.

The new line is formatted as a list item. Let's add a link to a tentative new page in the site.

3 Type **Green Club** and select the text.

The text is part of the list, but it's not a hyperlink yet.

4 In the Link field of the Property inspector, type # and press Enter/Return to create a link placeholder.

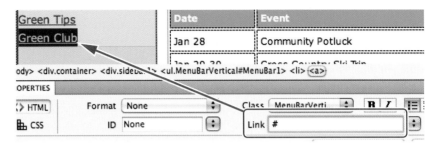

You can even add subitems using this method. Since the club is for members only, let's add a login page as a subitem.

5 Insert the cursor at the end of the text *Green Club*. Press Enter/Return to insert a new line. Type **Member Login** and select the text. In the Link field of the Property inspector, enter #.

Note how it is formatted identically to the main level items.

6 In the Property inspector, click the Blockquote button to indent the text.

The text *Member Login* doesn't indent as you might expect. In fact, it's difficult to tell that anything has happened at all. The change was subtle, but if you watched the tag selectors and examine the bullets carefully you'll see that *Member Login* is formatted in the same way as the subitems 2010 Events Calendar and 2010 Class Schedule.

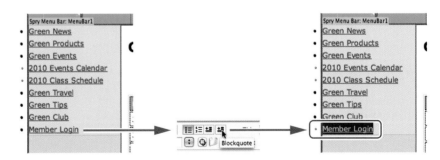

▶ **Tip:** If you don't see the Turn Styles On button, insert the cursor anywhere in the Spry-based menu and click the blue bar above it to select it again.

7 In the Property inspector, click the Turn Styles On button to return to the styled appearance.

When you turn the formatting back on, you may notice that the Green Club item doesn't show the submenu icon, as Green Events does.

8 Insert the cursor in the Green Club item. Examine the tag selector.

The tag selector shows <a> for a normal hyperlink element.

9 Insert the cursor in the Green Events item. Examine the tag selector.

The tag selector shows `<a.MenuBarItemSubmenu>`. Because you didn't use the Spry interface to add the subitem, Dreamweaver didn't apply a needed class to the Green Club parent element. This class applies CSS formatting for the submenu, including the submenu icon. You can apply the class using the Property inspector.

10 Insert the cursor in the Green Club item. Select the `<a>` tag selector. Choose MenuBarItemSubmenu from the Class menu.

The button is properly formatted now and displays the submenu icon. As you can see, the Spry interface offers several advantages over hand coding.

11 Save the file.

Whenever Dreamweaver saves a document containing Spry components, it inserts the dependent CSS and JavaScript files in the SpryAssets folder for you automatically. If you delete a component and the dependent files are no longer needed, Dreamweaver deletes any link reference to them from the document code. The Spry interface and automatic file management are two more reasons why you want to use Dreamweaver in any HTML-based workflows.

Customizing the appearance of the Spry menu bar

As you can see, the Spry menu bar offers a way to create a sophisticated, professional-looking menu quickly and easily. Styling a Spry component is no different than styling the original HTML menu it replaced. You'll need to modify both the width and styling of this menu to make it conform to the layout and the site color scheme. It's important to remember that Spry elements are normally styled by their own CSS files.

1 Open **events.html**, if necessary. Open the CSS Styles panel and scroll to the bottom of the list of style sheets.

A new style sheet—**SpryMenuBarVertical.css**—has been added by Dreamweaver.

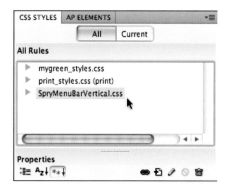

2 Expand the **SpryMenuBarVertical.css** style sheet.

This style sheet includes the formatting instructions for the Spry vertical menu. You should feel confident enough by now in your CSS skills to modify the style sheet without any help. Feel free to try, or simply follow these instructions.

3 Insert the cursor in the Green News item in the Spry menu. Press Ctrl-Alt-N/ Cmd-Opt-N to open the Code Navigator or click the Code Navigator (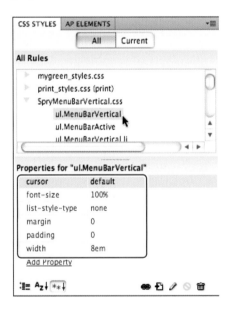) icon when it appears.

The Code Navigator window appears, listing the style sheets and rules that format this item.

4 Examine the list of CSS rules that format this item. Pay special attention to the rules in **SpryMenuBarVertical.css**.

5 Using the cursor, hover over each rule in this style sheet until you identify the properties you'll need to modify.

You're looking for rules that specifically apply to width, color, and hyperlink behavior.

6 In the CSS Styles panel, click the `ul.MenuBarVertical` rule and examine its properties.

This rule sets the width of the `<ul>` element to 8 ems. Since the current site is based on a fixed-width layout, these settings should be changed to match.

Em or ex? It's all relative

An em is a relative measurement system used in graphic design, based on the width of a capital letter *M* in the current default font for the site. An ex is a measurement based on the size of the lowercase *x*. Designers use ems and exes when they want to format a text container to preserve certain line breaks. A container width specified in ems will scale along with the text as it gets larger. A container set to a fixed width won't scale as the text gets larger; to fit, the text has to wrap to additional lines.

Fixed-width containers: text reflows

> Four score and seven years ago our fathers brought forth, up on this continent, a new nation, conceived in Liberty, and dedicated to the proposition that all men are created equal.

> Four score and seven years ago our fathers brought forth, up on this continent, a new nation, conceived in Liberty, and dedicated to the proposition that all men are created equal.

Em-width containers: no reflow

> Four score and seven years ago our fathers brought forth, up on this continent, a new nation, conceived in Liberty, and dedicated to the proposition that all men are created equal.

> Four score and seven years ago our fathers brought forth, up on this continent, a new nation, conceived in Liberty, and dedicated to the proposition that all men are created equal.

That's because the em measurement is based on the size of the font and not on an arbitrary pixel or other fixed measurement. This means if the user chooses to override your chosen font size in the browser, any web structure based on ems or exes will scale up or down proportionally to adapt to the new font size. This way, line breaks will be preserved and text-based menus won't break or reflow as the text enlarges, as they will in designs using pixels or fixed measurements.

Width set in pixels: text wraps

Width set in ems: everything scales

Note: Whenever you set the width of a container using absolute measurements, like pixels or points, you should anticipate that the container, and your layout, may break when visitors override your chosen settings to enlarge the text. Fortunately, most modern browsers now magnify the web page rather than simply enlarge the text.

7   Change the width value to **180px**.

The `ul.MenuBarVertical` rule establishes the maximum size of the menu, but because `<ul>` is not a block-level element the width of the menu is actually controlled by a different rule. Only one other rule specifies a width setting for the first-level items: `ul.MenuBarVertical li`.

8   In the CSS Styles panel, select `ul.MenuBarVertical li` and change the width to **180px** in the Properties section.

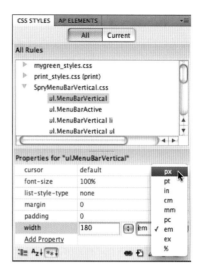

After the change, `<div.content>` may drop down below `<div.sidebar1>` in Design view, as shown in the figure.

Broken CSS layouts frequently occur during site development. Good web designers can put on their detective hats and usually track down the problem after a few minutes of investigation.

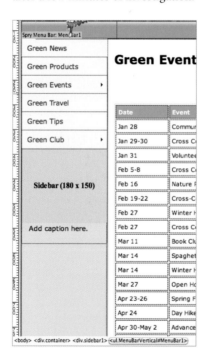

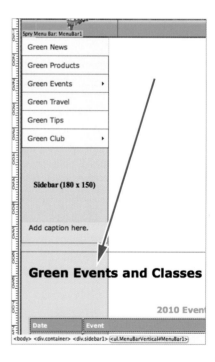

Since the border doesn't serve a purpose in the current design, let's delete it.

CSI (Crime Scene Investigator): Dreamweaver

On fixed-width sites like this one, when the structure breaks, typically it's a specification of one of the structural elements causing the conflict. As you experienced in Lesson 5, "Creating a Page Layout," if there's not enough space in the container for both `<div>` elements, one will shift down to where there's more room. Since you didn't modify any of the styles created before you inserted the menu, the culprit is almost certainly part of this Spry component.

By examining the menu CSS, you'll discover that it features a rule that adds a 1-pixel border around the entire menu. This adds 2 pixels to the total width of the menu, which was just set to 180 pixels in width. As you have already learned, widths, borders, margins, and padding all must be accounted for in your structural design. Since the site uses a containing `<div>` set to a width of 950 pixels, all the widths, borders, margins, and padding of the contained elements *combined* must equal less than that measurement. Here are several methods to fix the problem:

- Change the width of `<div.container>`.
- Change the width of `<div.sidebar1>`.
- Change the width of `<div.content>`.
- Change the width of the Spry menu bar.
- Delete the border.

9 There are two `ul.MenuBarVertical` rules in the Spry CSS. Select the second `ul.MenuBarVertical`, which creates the 1-pixel border. In the CSS Styles panel, click the Delete icon to delete the rule.

The second `ul.MenuBarVertical` rule has only one property—the border specification—and can be deleted without impacting the rest of the layout. When the rule creating the border is deleted, `<div.content>` will return to its original position. Let's continue to format the Spry menu to conform to the site design.

10 Double-click the `ul.MenuBarVertical li` rule to edit it. In the Type category, change the Font-size field to **90%**.

11 In the Border category, enter **solid, 1px, #0C0** for the Top border fields.
Enter **solid, 1px, #060** for the Right border fields.
Enter **solid, 1px, #060** for the Bottom border fields.
Enter **solid, 1px, #0C0** for the Left border fields. Click OK.

Adding the 1-pixel border to the menu items may break the layout again. Since you want to keep the border, you'll need to adjust the width of one of the structural elements to compensate, as described earlier. To solve this problem, let's modify the `<div.content>` element instead.

12 In the CSS Styles panel, scroll up to **mygreen_styles.css**.
Expand the style sheet, if necessary, and select the `.content` rule.
In the Box category, change the Width to **765px**. Click OK.

The layout returns to normal. Considering the large size of the `<div>`, reducing its width by 5, or even 10, pixels won't be noticed, but it will go a long way to prevent any further such conflicts in the future.

13 In the CSS Styles panel, scroll down to **SpryMenuBarVertical.css**.
Double-click the `ul.MenuBarVertical a` rule.

14 In the Type category, change the Color field to read **#FFC**.
In the Background category, change the Background-color field to **#090**.
In the Box category, change all Padding fields to **0.5em**.
Click OK.

15 Save all files. Click the Live View button. Position the cursor over each of the Spry menu items and observe the behavior.

The menu is nearly finished. The initial state of the menu looks good, but the `a:hover` state of the hyperlinks doesn't conform to the site color scheme. To investigate the situation, you can access the Code Navigator even in Live view.

16 While hovering over the menu item, right-click the Spry menu. Choose Code Navigator from the context menu. Identify any rules affecting the `a:hover` state of the menu hyperlinks.

There are two rules that apply both text and background colors to the `a:hover` state.

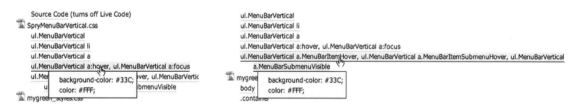

17 Click the Live View button to turn it off.

18 In the CSS Styles panel, click the `ul.MenuBarVertical a:hover,`
`ul.MenuBarVertical a:focus` rule. In the Properties section, change the
Color value to **#FFC** and the Background-color value to **#0C0**.

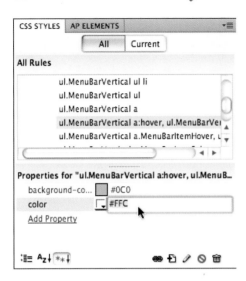

19 In the CSS Styles panel, click the `ul.MenuBarVertical`
`a.MenuBarItemHover, ul.MenuBarVertical`
`a.MenuBarItemSubmenuHover, ul.MenuBarVertical`
`a.MenuBarSubmenuVisible` rule. In the Properties section, change the
Color value to **#FFC** and the Background-color value to **#0C0**. Click OK.

20 Save all files. Test the menu behavior in Live view or the default browser.

The color and behavior matches the menu you tested at the beginning of the lesson.
But, the subitems would look better on one line. How would you correct this problem? Here are two obvious fixes: shorten the text or make the button wider.

Editing CSS using the Code Navigator

The Code Navigator isn't just a tool for examining CSS code, it can also help you to edit it.

Tip: The subitems will remain displayed as long as the Events or Class subitems are selected in the Property inspector. To hide the subitem menu, select a parent element.

1　Click the blue bar above the vertical menu to access the Spry menu interface in the Property inspector. Select the item 2010 Events Calendar in the second column.

The subitems for the Green Events button appear.

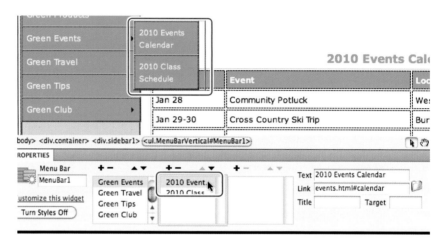

2　Insert the cursor in the subitem 2010 Events Calendar. Press Cmd-Opt-N to activate the Code Navigator. Examine the rules to find the one that formats the width of the subitems.

As with the level-1 items, there are two rules that apply the width to the subitems: `ul.MenuBarVertical ul` and `ul.MenuBarVertical ul li`.

3　In the Code Navigator window, click the rule `ul.MenuBarVertical ul`.

Dreamweaver switches to Split view automatically and loads **SpryMenuBarVertical.css** in the code half and automatically positions the screen at the line in the file for `ul.MenuBarVertical ul`.

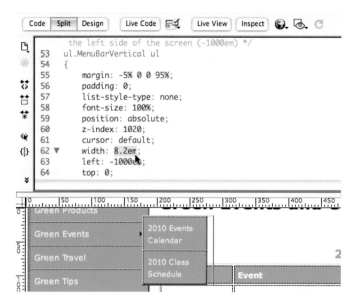

```
             the left side of the screen (-1000em) */
53    ul.MenuBarVertical ul
54    {
55        margin: -5% 0 0 95%;
56        padding: 0;
57        list-style-type: none;
58        font-size: 100%;
59        position: absolute;
60        z-index: 1020;
61        cursor: default;
62 ▼      width: 8.2em;
63        left: -1000em;
64        top: 0;
```

4 Change the Width value to **180px**.

5 Use the Code Navigator as in steps 1 through 3 to access the
   `ul.MenuBarVertical ul li` rule. Change the Width value to **180px**.

6 Save all files.

   You may need to refresh the Design view window to see the results of the
   changes.

7 Click the Refresh Design View (**C**) icon or press F5.

The subitems are wider now, allowing the link text to fit on one line, as desired.
The Spry menu is complete.

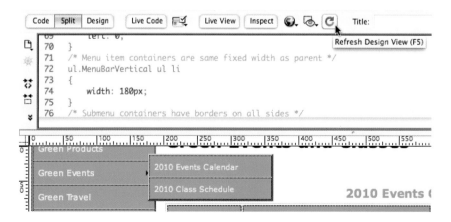

```
69        left: 0;
70    }
71    /* Menu item containers are same fixed width as parent */
72    ul.MenuBarVertical ul li
73    {
74        width: 180px;
75    }
76    /* Submenu containers have borders on all sides */
```

Inserting Spry menus as Library items

Now that the Spry menu is complete, you need to add it to every page in the site. The menu that you're replacing is currently a Library item, so to replace it you'll create a Library item from the Spry menu.

1   Open **events.html**, if necessary. Open the Assets panel. Click the Library (📖) icon.

2   Insert the cursor in the Spry vertical menu. Select the `<ul.MenuBarVertical#MenuBar1>` tag selector.

● **Note:** A dialog box may appear warning that the selection may not appear correctly because of style sheet issues. Remember the styling and behavior of this menu depends on external files. You'll have to attach these files manually. Click OK to close the dialog box.

3   Click the New Library Item icon. Name the new item **SpryMenu**.

A new Library item is created based on the Spry menu. The next step is to replace the original Library item.

4   In the Assets panel, double-click SpryMenu to open it. Switch to Code view and examine the code.

Only the HTML structure of the menu was added to the Library item. No CSS or JavaScript references made it into the file. You could replace the old Library item with this one manually on every page, but there's a simpler method.

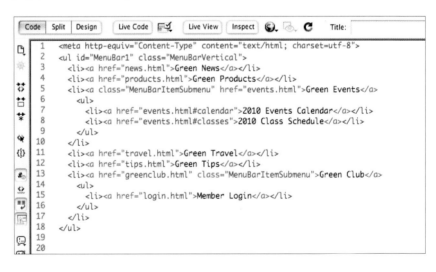

```
1   <meta http-equiv="Content-Type" content="text/html; charset=utf-8">
2   <ul id="MenuBar1" class="MenuBarVertical">
3     <li><a href="news.html">Green News</a></li>
4     <li><a href="products.html">Green Products</a></li>
5     <li><a class="MenuBarItemSubmenu" href="events.html">Green Events</a>
6       <ul>
7         <li><a href="events.html#calendar">2010 Events Calendar</a></li>
8         <li><a href="events.html#classes">2010 Class Schedule</a></li>
9       </ul>
10    </li>
11    <li><a href="travel.html">Green Travel</a></li>
12    <li><a href="tips.html">Green Tips</a></li>
13    <li><a href="greenclub.html" class="MenuBarItemSubmenu">Green Club</a>
14      <ul>
15        <li><a href="login.html">Member Login</a></li>
16      </ul>
17    </li>
18  </ul>
19
20
```

5   Choose File > Save As. Navigate to the Library folder and click **vertical-nav.lbi**. Click Save.

Using this method, the Spry component will replace the original menu stored in the file. You have solved one problem, but there's another. The Spry menu won't work, as is. Spry components require their own CSS and JavaScript files and some specific HTML markup in order to function properly. As you noted in step 4, these files and the needed markup were not included in the Library item.

6 Click the **events.html** tab to bring the document to the front.

7 Switch to Code view and examine the <head> section.

Luckily, the needed files are named in such a way that makes it pretty obvious to what component they belong. In the <head> section, you will find references to a style sheet (SpryMenuBarVertical.css) and a JavaScript (SpryMenuBar.js) file. You need to copy the entire reference code from this file and paste it into the <head> section of the target document. Since the Library item has no <head> section, this means you have to insert the references into the template.

8 Select the link references for SpryMenuBarVertical.css and SpryMenuBar.js. Press Ctrl-X/Cmd-X to cut them.

Note: Cutting this reference will cause the vertical menu to appear as a bulleted list. This will only occur temporarily until the template updates this page in step 18.

```
3   <head>
4   <meta http-equiv="Content-Type" content="text/html; charset=utf-8" />
5   <!-- TemplateBeginEditable name="doctitle" -->
6   <title>Green Start Association - Add TItle Here</title>
7   <!-- TemplateEndEditable -->
8   <link href="../mygreen_styles.css" rel="stylesheet" type="text/css" />
9   <link href="../print_styles.css" rel="stylesheet" type="text/css" media="print" />
10  <!-- TemplateBeginEditable name="head" -->
11  <script src="../SpryAssets/SpryMenuBar.js" type="text/javascript"></script>
12  <link href="../SpryAssets/SpryMenuBarVertical.css" rel="stylesheet" type="text/css">
13  <!-- TemplateEndEditable -->
14  </head>
```

9 Open **mygreen_temp.dwt** from the Template category of the Assets panel. Switch to Code view and locate the CSS references in the <head> section of the file. Insert the cursor at the end of the last reference and press Enter/Return to insert a new line.

10 Press Ctrl-V/Cmd-V to paste the Spry menu references.

Tip: Adding a new line in the code is not necessary for the references to function, it simply makes the markup easier to read.

```
3   <head>
4   <meta http-equiv="Content-Type" content="text/html; charset=utf-8" />
5   <!-- TemplateBeginEditable name="doctitle" -->
6   <title>Green Start Association - Add TItle Here</title>
7   <!-- TemplateEndEditable -->
8   <link href="../mygreen_styles.css" rel="stylesheet" type="text/css" />
9   <link href="../print_styles.css" rel="stylesheet" type="text/css" media="print" />
10
11  <!-- TemplateBeginEditable name="head" -->
12  <!-- TemplateEndEditable -->
13  </head>
```

```
6   <title>Green Start Association - Add TItle Here</title>
7   <!-- TemplateEndEditable -->
8   <link href="../mygreen_styles.css" rel="stylesheet" type="text/css" />
9   <link href="../print_styles.css" rel="stylesheet" type="text/css" media="print" />
10  <script src="../SpryAssets/SpryMenuBar.js" type="text/javascript"></script>
11  <link href="../SpryAssets/SpryMenuBarVertical.css" rel="stylesheet" type="text/css">
12  <!-- TemplateBeginEditable name="head" -->
13  <!-- TemplateEndEditable -->
14  </head>
```

Note: If you're using the method described in the "Jumpstart" section of "Getting Started," preexisting files may display the lesson number, such as mygreen_temp_10.dwt.

You're almost done, but there is one more code section you need to retrieve.

Note: Remember the location of this code entry; you will delete this reference from events.html at the end of the exercise.

11 Click the **events.html** tab to bring the document to the front. Switch to Code view, if necessary. Scroll to the bottom of the code and locate the `<script type="text/javascript">` entry.

```
335    <div class="footer">
336        <p>Copyright 2010 Meridien GreenStart, All rights reserved.</p>
337        <!-- end .footer --></div>
338    <!-- end .container --></div>
339 ▼  <script type="text/javascript">
340 |    var MenuBar1 = new Spry.Widget.MenuBar("MenuBar1", {imgRight:"SpryAssets/SpryMenuBarRightHover.gif"});
341 ▲  </script>
342    </body>
343    </html>
```

Note the reference to `MenuBar1` in the `<script>` element. This entry loads important variables for the Spry menu. Depending on how many you use on a page, this element may include markup for other widgets, as well. For it to work, this entry has to be inserted in the code after all the markup for Spry components, which is why it's at the bottom of the page. If this was the only widget you were going to use on this page, you could insert the `<script>` element at the bottom of the Library item itself. For this example, you'll insert it into the template.

12 Select the entire `<script>`...`</script>` element and its contents. Press Ctrl-X/Cmd-X to cut it.

13 Click the **mygreen_temp.dwt** document tab to bring it to the front. If necessary, switch to Code view. Scroll to the bottom of the code.

14 Insert the cursor in front of the closing `</body>` tag. Press Ctrl-V/Cmd-V to paste.

The `<script>` element is inserted before the closing `</body>` tag. The Spry menu is complete. Before you save the template and update all the files, you should delete the Spry menu from **events.html** and insert the new Library-based menu.

15 Click the **events.html** tab to bring the document to the front. Insert the cursor in the Spry menu. Select the `<mm:libitem>` tag selector. Press Delete.

When Dreamweaver deletes the Spry menu, it also deletes the CSS and JavaScript references from the file.

16 Open the Assets panel. Click the Library (📖) icon, if necessary. Select vertical-nav and click the Insert button.

The Spry menu appears as a bulleted list again. Since the CSS and JavaScript references have not been inserted by the template yet, the menu won't appear, or function, properly.

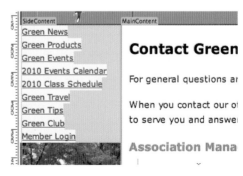

17 Save **events.html**.

18 Click the **mygreen_temp.dwt** tab to bring the document to the front. Save the template and update all files.

The Update Pages dialog box appears and reports how many pages were updated. The template has added the CSS and JavaScript references as requested, but the job isn't finished. The Library item must be updated, separately.

19 Close **mygreen_temp.dwt.** Open **contact_us.html** and switch to Design view, if necessary. Preview the page in Live view.

The old menu is still displayed in **contact_us.html**. Saving over the old Library item in step 5 did not automatically update the affected pages. A Library item won't be updated until the next time you open and make changes to it, or unless you manually invoke the update.

20 Click the Live View button to return to Design view. In the Assets panel, click the Library icon. Right-click vertical-nav and choose Update Site from the context menu. In the Update Pages dialog box, click Start.

The Update Pages dialog box reports how many pages were updated; the report should include all the pages in the current site.

21 Preview **contact_us.html** file in the default browser.

The Spry menu is fully formatted and functions as expected.

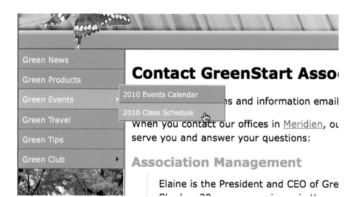

Note: It's important to remember that for this Spry menu to function properly it requires both the Library item markup *and* the CSS references supplied by the template. The Library item is not complete by itself and should not be used outside template-based pages unless you manually add the needed markup as demonstrated in this exercise.

22 Save all pages.

Alternative site design

One downside of storing the menu in a Library item will be losing the support of the cool Spry interface in the Property inspector. From this point forward, you will have to edit the menu entirely by hand. Considering this, it would be worth the time and effort to rework the design of the sidebar to move the Spry menu out of the Library item and entirely into the template file.

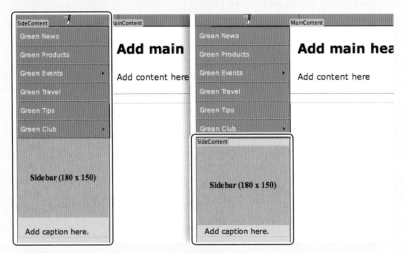

One alternative is to modify the editable region so that it no longer contains the entire sidebar, as in the example on the right.

In a large site, with hundreds, or thousands, of pages, many designers prefer to implement menus as server-side includes (SSI), similar to the one shown in Lesson 7, "Working with Templates." SSIs update automatically each time the page loads in the browser, eliminating the need to update every file on the site whenever the menu is changed.

Checking your page

Dreamweaver will automatically check your page for browser compatibility, accessibility, and broken links. In this exercise, you'll check your links and learn what you can do in case of a browser compatibility problem.

1　If necessary, open **contact_us.html**.

2　Choose File > Check Page > Links.

A Link Checker panel opens. The Link Checker panel reports a broken link to **index.html** and the other links you created for non-existent pages. You'll make these pages later, so there's no need to worry about fixing this broken link now. The Link Checker will also find broken links to external sites, should you have any.

Tip: You can also check links for the entire website by choosing Site > Check Links Sitewide.

SEARCH	REFERENCE	VALIDATION	BROWSER COMPATIBILITY	LINK CHECKER	SITE REPORTS	FTP LOG

Show: Broken Links ▼ (links to files not found on local disk)

Files	Broken Links
/contact_us.html	index.html
/contact_us.html	products.html
/contact_us.html	travel.html

1 Total, 1 HTML 28 All links, 21 OK, 5 Broken, 2 External

3   Right-click the Link Checker tab and choose Close Panel Group.

4   Choose File > Check Page > Browser Compatibility.

The Browser Compatibility report panel opens, listing any identified compatibility problems along with the file that contains the error and a description of it. In the lower-right corner of the panel, you can click the *Learn More* link to receive more information about the issue directly from Adobe.com.

5   Double-click the Browser Compatibility tab to close it.

You've made big changes to the appearance of the pages in this lesson by adding a menu bar and by creating links to specific positions on a page, to e-mail, and to an external site. You also created a link that uses an image as the clickable item and re-created the main navigation menu using a Spry menu bar. Finally, you checked your page for broken links and browser compatibility.

Review questions

1 Describe two ways to insert a link into a page.

2 What information is required to create a link to an external web page?

3 What's the difference between standard page links and e-mail links?

4 What are the benefits of using Spry menu bars?

5 How can you check to see if your links will work properly?

Review answers

1 Select text or a graphic, and then in the Property inspector, select the Browse For File icon next to the Link field and navigate to the desired page. A second method is to drag the Point To File icon to a file within the Files panel.

2 Link to an external page by typing or copying and pasting the full web address (a fully formed URL) in the Link field of the Property inspector.

3 A standard page link opens a new page or moves the view to a position somewhere on the page. An e-mail link opens a blank e-mail message window if the user uses an e-mail application.

4 All the work of setting up the style rules to make a list appear like a horizontal or vertical menu bar has been done for you, and so has the work of writing the JavaScript to make pop-up submenus function.

5 Run the Link Checker to test links on each page or sitewide.

11

ADDING INTERACTIVITY

Lesson Overview

In this lesson, you'll add Web 2.0 functionality to your web pages by doing the following:

- Using Dreamweaver behaviors to create an image rollover effect

- Inserting a Spry Accordion widget

This lesson will take about 60 minutes to complete. Before beginning, make sure you have copied the files for Lesson 11 to your hard drive as described in the "Getting Started" section at the beginning of the book. If you are starting from scratch in this lesson, use the method described in the "Jumpstart" section of "Getting Started."

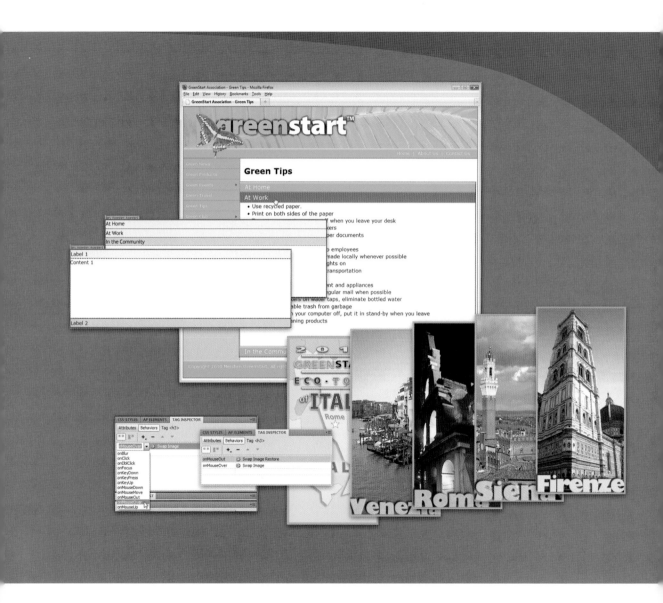

Dreamweaver can create sophisticated interactive
effects with behaviors and Accordion panels using
Adobe's Spry framework.

Learning about Dreamweaver behaviors

A Dreamweaver *behavior* is JavaScript code that performs an action—such as opening a browser window or showing or hiding a page element—when it is triggered by an event, such as a mouse click. Applying a behavior is a three-step process:

1. Create or select the page element that you want to trigger the behavior.

2. Choose the behavior to apply.

3. Specify the settings or parameters of the behavior.

The triggering element often involves a hyperlink applied to a range of text or to an image. In some cases, the behavior is not intended to load a new page, so it will employ a dummy link enabled by the hash (#) sign, similar to ones you used in Lesson 10, "Working with Navigation." The Spry Swap Image behavior you will use in this lesson does not require a link to function, but keep this in mind when you work with other behaviors.

● **Note:** To access the Behaviors panel and menu you must have a file open.

Dreamweaver offers more than 20 built-in behaviors, all accessed from the Tag Inspector panel (Window > Tag Inspector). Hundreds of other useful behaviors can be downloaded from the Internet for free or a small fee. Many are available from the online Dreamweaver Exchange, which you can access by clicking the Add Behavior (**+.**) icon in the Tag Inspector and choosing Get More Behaviors from the pop-up menu. When the Adobe Marketplace & Exchange site loads in the browser, click the link to Dreamweaver for a full list of plug-ins and behaviors.

The Adobe Marketplace and Exchange offers tons of resources for web designers and developers, including both free and paid add-ons to Dreamweaver and other Creative Suite applications.

The following is some of the functionality available to you using the built-in Dreamweaver behaviors:

- Opening a browser window

- Swapping one image for another to create what is called a *rollover effect*

- Fading images or page areas in and out

- Growing or shrinking graphics

- Displaying pop-up messages

- Changing the text or other HTML content within a given area

- Showing or hiding sections of the page

- Calling a custom-defined JavaScript function

Not all behaviors are available all the time. Certain behaviors become available only in the presence, and selection, of certain page elements, such as images or links. For example, you can't use the Swap Image behavior unless an image is present.

Each behavior invokes its own unique dialog box that provides relevant options and specifications. For instance, the dialog box for the Open Browser Window behavior enables you to open a new browser window, set its width, height, and other attributes, and set the URL of the displayed resource. After the behavior is defined, it is listed in the Tag Inspector with its chosen triggering action. As with other behaviors, these specifications can be modified at any time.

Behaviors are extremely flexible, and multiple behaviors can be applied to the same trigger. For example, you could swap one image for another and change the text of the accompanying image caption, and do it all with one click. While effects appear to happen simultaneously, behaviors are actually triggered in sequence. When multiple behaviors are applied, you can choose the order in which the behaviors are processed.

Previewing a completed file

In the first part of the lesson, you'll create a new page for GreenStart's travel services. Let's preview the completed page in the browser.

1 Launch Adobe Dreamweaver CS5.

2 If necessary, press F8 to open the Files panel and choose DW-CIB from the site list.

3 In the Files panel, expand the lesson11 folder. Right-click **travel_finished.html**, choose Preview In Browser from the context menu, and select your primary browser.

The page includes Dreamweaver behaviors.

4 If Microsoft Internet Explorer is your primary browser, a message may appear above the browser window indicating that JavaScript is prevented from running. If so, click Allow Blocked Content.

5 Position the cursor over the heading *Venice: City of Canals*. Observe the image to the right of the text.

The existing image swaps for one of Venice.

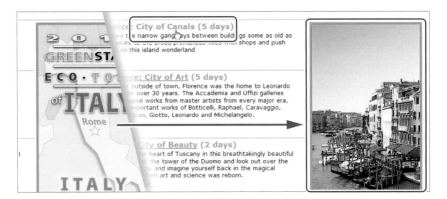

6 Move the pointer to the heading *Florence: City of Art*. Observe the image to the right of the text.

As the pointer moves off the heading, the image swaps back to the Eco-Tour ad until it hovers over the Florence heading. Then, the ad image swaps for one of Florence.

7 Pass the pointer over each of the headings and observe the image behavior.

The image alternates between the Eco-Tour ad and images of each of the cities. This effect is the Swap Image behavior.

8 When you're finished, close the browser window and return to Dreamweaver.

In the next exercise, you will learn how to work with Dreamweaver behaviors.

Working with Dreamweaver behaviors

Adding Dreamweaver behaviors to your layout is a simple point-and-click operation. The travel page has not been created yet.

1 Open the Assets panel and click the Template category icon. Right-click **mygreen_temp** and choose New From Template from the context menu.

   A new document window opens based on the template.

2 Save the new document as **travel.html**.

3 Double-click the image placeholder in the sidebar. Navigate to the site images folder. Select **train.jpg** and click OK/Choose.

   The train image appears in the sidebar.

4 In the Property inspector Alt field, enter **Steam locomotives are not very green** and click OK.

5 Open the Files panel and expand the lesson11 > resources folder. Double-click the **travel-caption.txt** file.

   The caption text opens in Dreamweaver.

6 Press Ctrl-A/Cmd-A to select all the text. Press Ctrl-C/Cmd-C to copy the text. Close **travel-caption.txt**.

7 Select the caption placeholder in the sidebar. Press Ctrl-V/Cmd-V to paste the new caption text.

8 In the Files panel, double-click **travel-text.html**.

   The **travel-text.html** file contains a table and text for the travel page. Note that the text and table are unformatted.

9 In Design view, press Ctrl-A/Cmd-A to select all the text. Press Ctrl-C/Cmd-C to copy the content. Close **travel-text.html**.

10 Insert the cursor in the main heading placeholder *Add main heading here* in **travel.html**. Select the <h1> tag selector. Hold Shift and click at the end of the text *Add content here* to select all the placeholder text in MainContent. Press Ctrl-V/Cmd-V to paste.

Note: Alternative instructions—If you are starting from scratch in this exercise, see the "Jumpstart" instructions in the "Getting Started" section at the beginning of the book. Then, follow the steps in this exercise.

Note: The Image Tag Accessibility Attributes dialog box doesn't appear when you insert an image this way. To add Alt text to this image, use the Alt field in the Property inspector.

Some modes of transportation are more eco-friendly than others. At Meridien GreenStreet we do the research and report on the best ways to get around town.

The content from **travel-text.html** appears. It assumes the default formatting for text and tables applied by the style sheet you created in Lesson 8, "Working with Text, Lists, and Tables."

Let's insert the Eco-Tour ad, which will be the base image for the Swap Image behavior.

11 Double-click the image placeholder. Navigate to the site images folder and select **ecotour.jpg**. Click OK/Choose.

The placeholder is replaced by the Eco-Tour ad. But before you can apply the Swap Image behavior, you have to identify the image you want to swap. You do this by giving the image an ID.

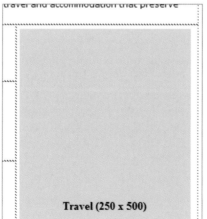

12 If necessary, select **ecotour.jpg** in the layout. Select the existing ID *Travel* in the Property inspector. Type **ecotour** and press Enter/Return.

Tip: Although it takes more time, it's a good practice to give all your images unique IDs.

13 Save the file.

Next, you will create a Swap Image behavior for **ecotour.jpg**.

Applying a behavior

As described earlier, many behaviors are context sensitive, based on the elements or structure present. A Swap Image behavior can be applied to any document text element.

Note: Users of previous versions of Dreamweaver may be looking for the Behaviors panel. It's now called the Tag Inspector.

1 Choose Window > Behaviors to open the Tag Inspector.

2 Insert the cursor in the *Venice: City of Canals* text and select the <h3> tag selector.

3 Click the Add Behavior icon. Choose Swap Image from the behavior list.

The Swap Image dialog box appears, listing any images on the page that are available for this behavior. This behavior can replace one or more of these images at a time.

4 Select the item image "ecotour.jpg" and click Browse.

5 In the Select Image Source dialog box, select **venice.jpg** from the site images folder. Click OK/Choose.

6 In the Swap Image dialog box, select the Preload Images option, if necessary, and click OK.

Note: The Preload Images option forces the browser to download all images necessary for the behavior before the page loads. That way, when the user clicks the trigger, the image swap will occur without any lags or glitches.

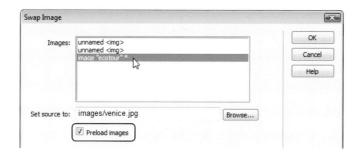

A Swap Image behavior is added to the Tag panel with an attribute of onMouseOver. Attributes can be changed, if desired, using the Tag Inspector.

7   Click the attribute onMouseOver to open the pop-up menu and examine the options.

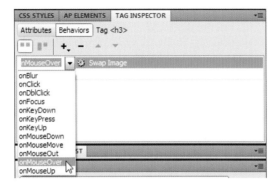

The menu provides a list of trigger events, most of which are self-explanatory.

8   Choose onMouseOver.

9   Save the file and click Live View to test the behavior. Position the cursor over the *Venice: City of Canals* text.

When the cursor passes over the text, the Eco-Tour ad is replaced by the image of Venice. But there is a small problem. When the cursor moves away from the text, the original image doesn't return. That's because you didn't tell it to. To bring back the original image you have to add another command—Swap Image Restore—to the same element.

Applying a Swap Image Restore behavior

In some instances, a specific action requires more than one behavior. To bring back the Eco-Tour ad once the mouse moves off the trigger, you have to add a restore function.

1   Return to Design view. Insert the cursor in the *Venice: City of Canals* text and examine the Tag Inspector.

The inspector displays the currently assigned behavior. You don't need to select the element completely; Dreamweaver assumes you want to modify the entire trigger.

2   Click the Add Behavior icon and choose Swap Image Restore from the pop-up menu. Click OK in the Swap Image Restore dialog box to complete the swap.

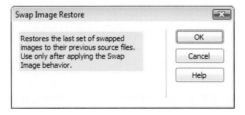

The Swap Image Restore behavior appears in the Tag Inspector with an attribute of onMouseOut.

3   Switch to Code view and examine the markup for the *Venice: City of Canals* text.

The trigger events—onMouseOver and onMouseOut—were added as attributes to the <h3> element. The rest of the JavaScript code was inserted in the document's <head> section.

4   Save the file and click Live View to test the behavior. Test the text trigger *Venice: City of Canals.*

When the pointer passes over the text, the Eco-Tour image is replaced by the one of Venice and then reappears when the pointer is withdrawn. The behavior functions as desired, but there's nothing visibly "different" about the text to indicate that something magical will happen if the user rolls the pointer over the heading. Since most Internet users are familiar with the interactivity provided by hyperlinks, applying a link placeholder on the heading will encourage the visitor to explore the effect.

Removing applied behaviors

Before you can apply a behavior to a hyperlink, you need to remove the current Swap Image and Swap Image Restore behaviors.

1   Open the Tag Inspector, if necessary. Insert the cursor in the *Venice: City of Canals* text.

The Tag Inspector displays the two applied events. It doesn't matter which one you delete first.

2   Select the Swap Image event. In the Tag Inspector, click the Remove Event (**–**) icon. Select the Swap Image Restore event. In the Tag Inspector, click the Remove Event icon.

Both events are removed. Dreamweaver will also remove any unneeded JavaScript code.

3   Save the file and check the text in Live View again.

The text no longer triggers the Swap Image behavior. To apply behaviors to a link, you first have to add a link or link placeholder to the heading.

Adding behaviors to hyperlinks

Behaviors can be added to hyperlinks, even if they don't load a new document.

1   Select the *Venice: City of Canals* text. In the Property inspector Link field, type # and press Enter/Return to create the link placeholder.

2   Insert the cursor in the link. In the Tag Inspector, click the Add Behavior icon and choose Swap Image from the pop-up menu.

As long as the cursor is still inserted anywhere in the link, the behavior will be applied to the entire link markup.

3   In the Swap Image dialog box, select the item `image "ecotour.jpg"`. Browse and select **venice.jpg** from the site images folder. Click OK/Choose.

4   In the Swap Image dialog box, select the Preload Images and Restore Images `onMouseOut` options, and click OK.

The Swap Image event appears in the Tag Inspector along with a Swap Image Restore event. Since the behavior was applied all at once, Dreamweaver provides the restore functionality as a productivity enhancement.

5   Select and apply a link (#) placeholder to the *Florence: City of Art* text.
Apply the Swap Image behavior to the link.
Select the image **florence.jpg** from the site images folder.

6   Repeat step 5 for the *Sienna: City of Beauty* text.
Select the image **sienna.jpg**.

7   Repeat step 5 for the *Rome: City of Magic* text.
Select the image **rome.jpg**.

The link appearance doesn't match the site color scheme. Let's create a custom CSS rule to format it.

8 Insert the cursor in any of the rollover links. Select the `.content h3` rule in the **mygreen_styles.css** style sheet. In the CSS Styles panel, click the New CSS Rule icon.

9 In the rule Name field, enter `.content h3 a`. In the Type category Color field, enter **#090**. Click OK.

10 Save the file and test the behaviors in Live View.

The Swap Image behavior works successfully on all links.

11 Close **travel.html**.

Besides eye-catching effects, Dreamweaver also provides structural components that conserve space and add more interactive flair to your website.

Working with Spry Accordion widgets

The Spry Accordion widget allows you to organize a lot of content into a compact space. In the Accordion widget, the tabs are stacked and when open, they expand vertically rather than side by side. When you click a tab, the panel slides open with a smooth action. The panels are set to a specific height and if the content is taller or wider than the panel itself, scroll bars appear automatically. Let's preview the completed layout.

1 In the Files panel, select **tips_finished.html** from the lesson11 folder and preview it in your primary browser.

The page content is divided among the three panels in the Spry Accordion widget.

2 Click each panel in turn to open and close them.

3 Close your browser and return to Dreamweaver.

Inserting a Spry Accordion widget

In this exercise, you'll incorporate a Spry Accordion widget into your layout.

1 Open **tips.html**.

2 Insert the cursor into the heading *At Home* and select the <h2> tag selector. Press Delete.

3 Insert the cursor in the first bullet *Wash clothes in cold water* and select the <ul> tag selector. Press Ctrl-X/Cmd-X to cut the whole list.

4 Insert the cursor at the end of the heading *Green Tips* and press Enter/Return to insert a new paragraph.

Note: If you are starting from scratch in this exercise, see the "Jumpstart" instructions in the "Getting Started" section at the beginning of the book. Then, follow the steps in this exercise.

5 In the Insert panel Spry category, click the Spry Accordion button.

Dreamweaver inserts the Spry Accordion widget element. The initial element is a two-panel Accordion widget that appears with the top panel open. Like the Spry menu bar, a blue tab entitled Spry Accordion: Accordion1 appears above the new object.

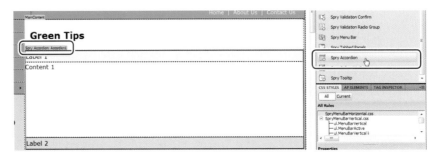

6 Select the placeholder text *Label 1* and type **At Home** to replace the text.

7 Select the text *Content 1* in the top Accordion widget panel. Press Ctrl-V/Cmd-V to paste the bulleted list.

In Design view, you may see only part of the content you added because scrolling isn't active in Design view.

8 To see or edit all the content, double-click the panel, or right-click the tab and choose Element View > Full from the context menu.

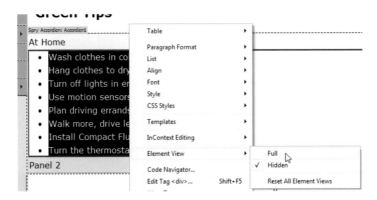

9 Delete the heading *At Work*. Select and cut the subsequent <ul> element containing the "Work" tips.

10 Position the cursor over the bar displaying the text *Label 2*. Click the eye ( ) icon to open panel 2, if necessary.

11 Select the text *Label 2* and type **At Work**.

12 Select the text *Content 2* and paste the `<ul>` element.

Two of the panels are complete, but you need to insert a new panel to complete the Spry Accordion widget.

Adding additional panels

You can add panels or remove panels from the Spry Accordion widget using the Property inspector.

1 Select the blue tab above Accordion1 in the document window.

The Property inspector displays settings for the Accordion widget.

2 In the Property inspector, click the Add Panel icon.

A new panel is added to the Accordion widget.

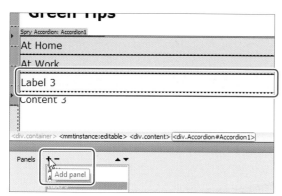

3 In the document window, delete the heading *In the Community*. Select and cut the subsequent `<ul>` element containing the "Community" tips.

4 Change the text *Label 3* to read **In the Community** and paste the bulleted text into the new content area.

5 Save the file and click OK in any additional dialog boxes.

You created a Spry Accordion and added content and additional panels. Although the content added in this exercise was already on the page, you can enter and edit content directly in the Content panels, if desired. You could also copy material from other sources, such as Microsoft Word, TextEdit, and Notepad, among others. In the next exercise, you'll customize the CSS for the Spry Accordion.

Customizing a Spry Accordion

Like other widgets, Spry Accordion widgets are formatted by their own CSS file. In this exercise, you will modify the component and adapt its color scheme to the website. Let's track down the rules that format the horizontal tabs.

1   Insert the cursor into the tab label *At Home* and examine the names and order of the tag selectors.

The tabs are formatted by the `.AccordionPanelTab` class.

2   In the CSS Styles panel, expand the `SpryAccordion.css` style sheet. Double-click `.AccordionPanelTab` to edit it.

3   In the Type category, in the Font-size field, enter **120%**.
    In the Color field, enter **#FFC**.

4   In the Background category, change the Background-color to **#090**.
    In the Background-image field, browse and select **background.jpg**.
    In the Background-repeat field, choose **repeat-x**.

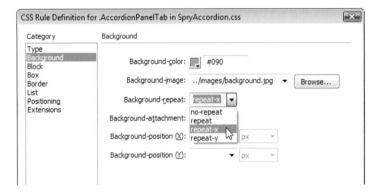

5   In the Box category Left Padding field only, enter **15px**.

6   In the Border category, change the Top Border Color to **#060**.
    Change the Bottom Border Color to **#090**.
    Click OK.

7 Save all files and preview the document in Live view. Test and examine the Accordion behavior.

The horizontal tabs display a hover behavior. The text turns gray, which doesn't look good with the background color.

8 Return to Design view. Examine the Accordion style sheet to find the rule that applies a hover behavior.

Two rules apply a hover effect. One applies when the panel is closed (`.AccordionPanelTabHover`) and one when it is open (`.AccordionPanelOpen .AccordionPanelTabHover`).

9 Double-click `.AccordionPanelTabHover`.
In the Type category, change the Color field to **#FFC**.
In the Background category, apply a Background-color of **#060**.
In the Background-image field, choose **none**.
Click OK.

10 Repeat step 9 with the `.AccordionPanelOpen .AccordionPanelTabHover` rule.

Note the two rules at the bottom of the Accordion style sheet containing the word *focused*, which is a hyperlink behavior identical to hover, except that it's activated when the visitor uses the Tab key or arrow keys instead of the mouse to navigate around the page. These rules may interfere with your hover formatting, so it's a good idea to give them the same settings, too.

11 Repeat step 9 with the `.AccordionFocused .AccordionPanelTab` and `.AccordionFocused .AccordionPanelOpen .AccordionPanelTab` rules.

When open, the panels are not tall enough to display all the bullets at once. You can adjust the height of the panels within the CSS, too.

12 Insert the cursor into the bullet list and examine the names and order of the tag selectors.

The panel content region is formatted by the `.AccordionPanelContent` class.

13 Select the `.AccordionPanelContent` rule in the CSS Styles panel.
In the panel Property section, change the Height value to **450px**.

The new height setting allows most of the content to be visible.

14 Save all files and test the document in the default browser.

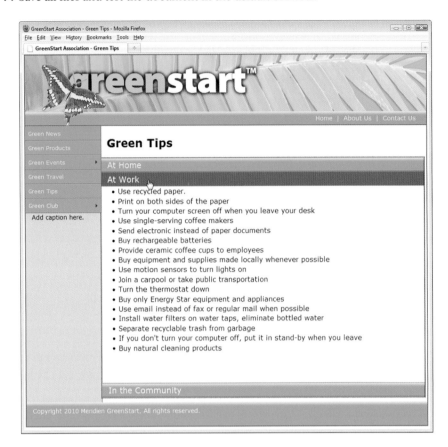

You've successfully applied formatting for the Accordion widget to match the website color scheme and adjusted the component height to allow more content to display. The Spry components allow you to add large amounts of content in a compact and stylish package.

Review questions

1   What is a benefit of using Dreamweaver behaviors?

2   What three steps must be used to create a Dreamweaver behavior?

3   What's the purpose of assigning an ID to an image before applying a behavior?

4   What does a Spry Accordion widget do?

5   How do you add new panels to a Spry Accordion widget?

Review answers

1   Dreamweaver behaviors add interactive functionality to a web page quickly and easily.

2   To create a Dreamweaver behavior, you need to create or select a trigger element, select a desired behavior, and specify the parameters.

3   The ID makes it easier to select the specific image during the process of applying a behavior.

4   A Spry Accordion includes two or more collapsible panels that hide and reveal content in a compact area of the page.

5   Select the panel in the document window and click the Add Panel icon in the Spry interface of the Property inspector.

12

WORKING WITH FLASH

Lesson Overview

In this lesson, you'll incorporate Flash components into your web page and do the following:

- Insert an FLV file

- Insert Flash animation

 This lesson will take about 30 minutes to complete. Before beginning, make sure you have copied the files for Lesson 12 to your hard drive as described in the "Getting Started" section at the beginning of the book. If you are starting from scratch in this lesson, use the method described in the "Jumpstart" section of "Getting Started."

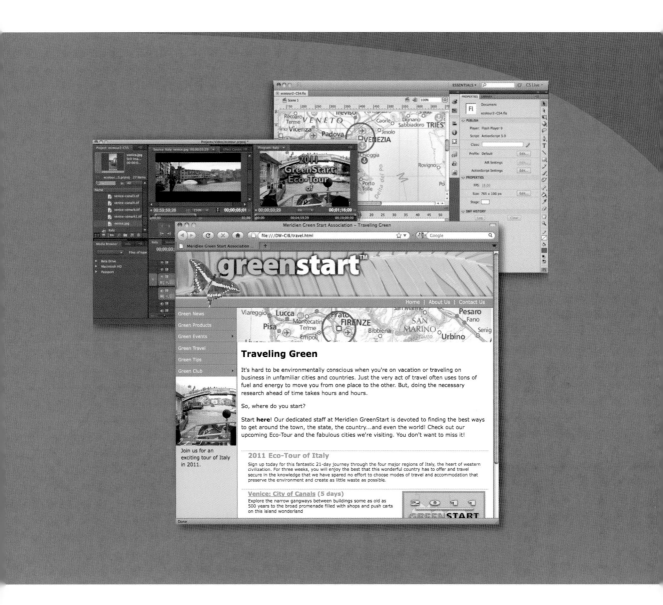

Dreamweaver makes the integration of Flash
for animation and video to a web page as
simple as 1, 2, 3.

Understanding Flash

The web can provide a variety of experiences to the average user. One second, you are downloading and reading a best-selling novel. Next, you're listening to your favorite radio station or performing artist. Then, you're watching live television coverage or a full-length movie. In the past, much of this content was provided in various ways using a hodgepodge of applications, plug-ins, and coder-decoders (codecs) that could transfer data across the Internet to your computer and browser, often with enormous difficulties and incompatibilities. A format that worked in one browser was incompatible with another. Applications that worked in Windows didn't on the Mac. To this mess, entered Flash.

Adobe Flash is renowned for its multimedia functionality. From its humble beginnings as an animation program, Flash has rapidly expanded its realm to include high-end advertisements, interactive content, user interfaces, games, and even video. As befits this popular and versatile authoring tool, Flash Player—the application required to play Flash's SWF and FLV files—enjoys the widest distribution of any browser plug-in.

Dreamweaver seamlessly integrates with Flash. SWF files can be easily inserted and previewed in any document window. Moreover, key properties, such as Autoplay and Loop, are quickly modified in the Property inspector. In many cases, if the source file is available, you can even edit the SWF file in Flash and export it to Dreamweaver.

Previewing a completed file

To see what you will work on in this lesson, preview the completed page in the browser. This is the travel page of the travel site you assembled in the previous lesson.

1 Launch Adobe Dreamweaver CS5.

2 If necessary, press Ctrl-Shift-F/Cmd-Shift-F to open the Files panel and choose DW-CIB from the site list.

3 In the Files panel, expand the lesson12 folder.

4 Select the **travel_finished.html** file and preview it in your primary browser.

    The page includes two Flash elements: the banner animation at the top of the MainContent region and the video inserted in the sidebar.

5   Note that the Flash banner ad plays once, immediately when the page loads completely.

6   To view the video, move your pointer over the video in the sidebar and click the Play button that appears.

    You'll notice that if you move your cursor away from the video, the controls fade, but return once your cursor is positioned over the video again.

7   When you're finished, close your browser and return to Dreamweaver.

Adding Flash animation to a page

As you learned in Lesson 9, "Working with Images," most web graphics are pixel-based. Flash's claim to fame and popularity is based on the fact that it enables you to create vector-based animation for web use. Using vector art drastically reduces file size compared to similar pixel-based animation. And best of all, the objects you animate can be programmed with interactivity and intelligence. In this exercise, you'll insert a vector-based Flash banner animation into the MainContent area of your web page. While creating original Flash animations and videos is beyond the scope of this book, check out the *Adobe Flash Professional CS5 Classroom in a Book* (Adobe Press, 2010) to learn how to create these types of items and much more.

● **Note:** If you are starting from scratch in this exercise, see the "Jumpstart" instructions in the "Getting Started" section at the beginning of the book.

1 Open **travel.html** from the site root folder. Or, if you are starting from scratch in this exercise, see the "Jumpstart" instructions in the "Getting Started" section at the beginning of the book.

The banner needs to be inserted outside any text elements.

2 Insert the cursor in the *Traveling Green* heading text and select the <h1> tag selector. Press the Left Arrow key to move the cursor outside the <h1> element.

3 Select Insert > Media > SWF.

4 When the Select File dialog box appears, navigate to the **movie** folder in the site root folder and select **ecotour.swf**. Click OK/Choose.

The Object Tag Accessibility Attributes dialog box appears.

5 In the Title field, type **2011 Eco-tour of Italy** and click OK.

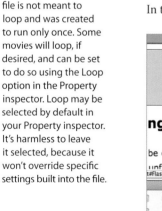

Dreamweaver inserts the Flash code, represented in Design view by a placeholder element. You can preview your newly inserted movie right in Dreamweaver.

● **Note:** This SWF file is not meant to loop and was created to run only once. Some movies will loop, if desired, and can be set to do so using the Loop option in the Property inspector. Loop may be selected by default in your Property inspector. It's harmless to leave it selected, because it won't override specific settings built into the file.

6 If necessary, select Window > Properties to open the Property inspector. In the Property inspector, click Play to preview the movie in Dreamweaver.

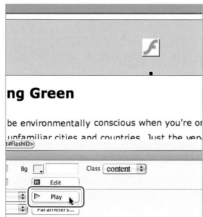

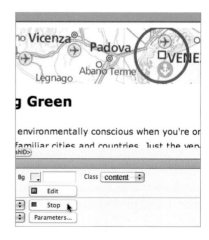

Make sure that Autoplay is selected in the Property inspector so that the movie will play automatically when the page loads into the browser.

7 Save the file.

Code inserted in the page can ensure that viewers are using the latest version of Flash Player.

8 Switch to Code view. Find this block of code; it should appear around line 87:

```
<!-- The browser displays the following alternative content
for users with Flash Player 6.0 and older. -->
<div>
<h4>Content on this page requires a newer version of Adobe
Flash Player.</h4>
<p><a href="http://www.adobe.com/go/getflashplayer">
<img src=
    "http://www.adobe.com/images/shared/download_buttons/
    get_flash_player.gif"
    alt="Get Adobe Flash player" width="112" height="33" />
    </a></p>
</div>
```

If a visitor browses your site using a Flash Player older than version 6.0, they will see the message set in this block of code instead of viewing the movie. You can customize or personalize the message contained within the <h4> tags, as shown in the figure below. The user will be offered the option to download the latest Flash Player.

```
<h4>Sorry, your version of Flash Player can't play the Eco-tour banner.
Click on the following link to download the lastest version.</h4>
<p><a href="http://www.adobe.com/go/getflashplayer">
<img src="http://www.adobe.com/images/shared/download_buttons/get_flash_player.gif"
```

9 Return to Design view.

You can use Flash for something large, as in this banner ad, or something quite small, such as a menu button or animated logo. Although the process was handled totally by Dreamweaver, in CS4 some significant changes were made in the way the program now writes the basic code. To learn more about these changes, see the sidebar "Flash embedding?"

Flash embedding?

From a user's perspective, the way Flash is inserted into Dreamweaver CS5 hasn't changed from previous versions. However, Dreamweaver made significant changes to the underlying code it creates for inserting Flash in Dreamweaver CS4. As a result, Dreamweaver is now in compliance with web standards for <object> elements. The code changes include the following:

- Proprietary <embed> elements and active-content scripts used previously are gone. Instead, a <script> tag points to two dependent files.

- The <object> tag replaced the <embed> tag.

- An in-place Flash Player installation is implemented using Express Installer.

- Alternative content is defined for instances where the Flash Player is missing or is an incorrect version.

For further information, visit www.alistapart.com/articles/flashembedcagematch/.

Before you move on to the next exercise, there's a small aesthetic adjustment you need to make in the layout that involves the Flash banner ad. You may have noticed the extra whitespace that appears above the banner. There's no default margin or padding applied to the Flash object, so the spacing must be the result of some existing rule.

10 Click the Flash banner to select it, if necessary. Examine the tag selectors, and activate Code Navigator by pressing Ctrl-Alt-N/Cmd-Opt-N or by clicking its icon. Examine the rules that affect the banner.

You should quickly identify that the .content rule applies 10 pixels of padding to the top of the <div>. To get rid of the whitespace, you'll have to delete the top-padding specification.

11 In the CSS Styles panel, select the `.content` rule and delete the top padding from the Properties section of the panel.

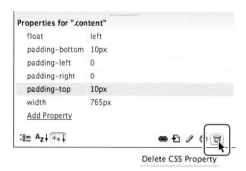

Delete CSS Property

Note: The top padding was a part of the predefined CSS that came with the original layout. Although you did not create it yourself, keep an eye out for any detrimental impact this change may have on your other pages.

The whitespace above the banner disappears. The banner is complete.

Adding an FLV file to a page

Because of the sheer ubiquitousness of Flash Player, the introduction of the FLV file was nothing short of revolutionary. Few technologies have had such a dramatic impact. Overnight, all the hassle and confusion over incompatible video formats and players vanished. With recent releases of Flash Player, video quality has increased, along with its market penetration. The FLV file is now the leading video format on the web.

In some cases, video from cameras, phones, and other portable devices can be converted directly to FLV files or added to a Flash document and then exported using the Adobe Flash CS5 Video Encoder. A native Flash video file has an .f4v file extension and can be played in one of two ways:

- Progressive download—Video begins playing after a brief delay during which the first segment is received by the browser. The video continues to download during playback. Progressive download FLV files can be hosted on any standard web server.

- Streaming—Video starts playing immediately and offers advantages over progressive download such as *seek*ability, which means the video playhead can be moved to any position to instantly begin playing at that point. However, streaming FLV files must be hosted on a web host using Flash Media Server.

In this exercise, you'll place an FLV file in progressive download format on your page.

1 If necessary, open **travel.html**.

2 Select the image placeholder Sidebar 180 x 150 and press Delete.

3 Choose Insert > Media > FLV.

4 When the Insert FLV dialog box appears, make sure the Video Type pop-up menu is set to Progressive Download Video.

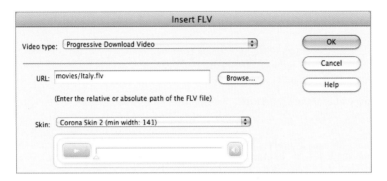

5 Click Browse and navigate to the **movie** folder in the site root. Choose **italy.flv**, and click OK/Choose.

6 From the Skin pop-up menu, choose Corona Skin 2.

7 Click the Detect Size button to enter the Width and Height of the video automatically. Select the Constrain and Auto Rewind options. Click OK.

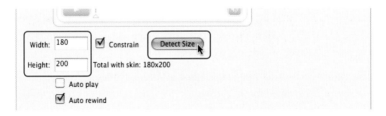

The Corona Skin 2 will easily fit the limited width of the sidebar, and it interactively appears and disappears when the visitor moves his cursor over the video.

As with the SWF file, Dreamweaver inserts a placeholder, which can be customized somewhat with the Property inspector. Unlike SWF files, however, FLV files cannot be previewed within Design view and must be viewed in Live view or a browser.

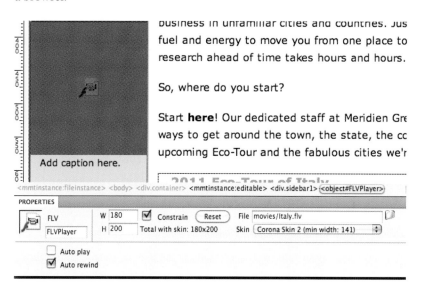

8   Select the caption placeholder and type **Join us for an exciting tour of Italy in 2011. Click here to sign up.**

9   Save the file.

When you save the file, the Copy Dependent Files dialog box may appear displaying a message explaining that the dependent files **expressInstall.swf** and **swfobject_modified.js** will be placed into a new Scripts folder. These files are essential for running an FLV file in the browser and must be uploaded to your web server to support Flash functionality. If and when this dialog box appears, click OK.

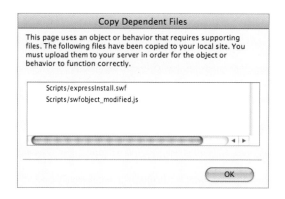

Note: The Travel page now contains two notices prompting users to sign up for the Eco-Tour. In Lesson 13, "Working with Forms," you will create a new page with the sign-up form and link this text to it.

Note: The Copy Dependent Files dialog box may not appear for users following the jumpstart method in this lesson. The files already exist in your site folder and Dreamweaver doesn't need to copy them.

10 Preview the page in Live view, or preview the page in the browser. If the video controls are not visible, move your cursor over the still image to display them. Click the Play button to view the movie.

There is no sound in this movie, but the controls include a speaker button to turn the sound off and on.

11 When you're finished, switch back to Design view.

You've added an FLV file and controls that allow the user to start and stop the video, and to turn the sound off and on. You also detected the size of the video automatically.

Review questions

1   What is the difference between Flash animation and other types of web-compatible animation?

2   What is the advantage of using FLV files?

3   Identify two methods for delivering an FLV file. Which format does not require a specialized web server?

4   What is alternative content?

5   What role do "dependent files" play in the operation of an FLV file?

Review answers

1   Flash animation can be built with vector-based graphics, which dramatically reduces file size and allows for intelligence and interactivity.

2   FLV files allow you to play video directly through Flash Player, eliminating the worry about incompatible codecs and plug-ins.

3   The two FLV file playback methods are "progressive download" and "streaming." Progressive download files do not require a specialized server, while streaming files require the Flash Media Server.

4   Alternative content is text or other data that displays automatically if the user does not have Flash Player, or if his or her version of Flash Player is outdated.

5   Dependent files provide essential functionality on the Internet for playing Flash components and must be uploaded to your server along with the relevant HTML and video.

13 WORKING WITH FORMS

Lesson Overview

In this lesson, you'll create forms for your web page and do the following:

- Insert a form
- Include text fields
- Work with Spry Form widgets
- Insert radio buttons
- Insert check boxes
- Insert list menus
- Add form buttons
- Incorporate field sets and legends
- Create an email solution for processing data
- Style your form with CSS

 This lesson will take about 1 hour and 45 minutes to complete. Before beginning, make sure you have copied the files for Lesson 13 to your hard drive as described in the "Getting Started" section at the beginning of the book. If you are starting from scratch in this lesson, use the method described in the "Jumpstart" section of "Getting Started."

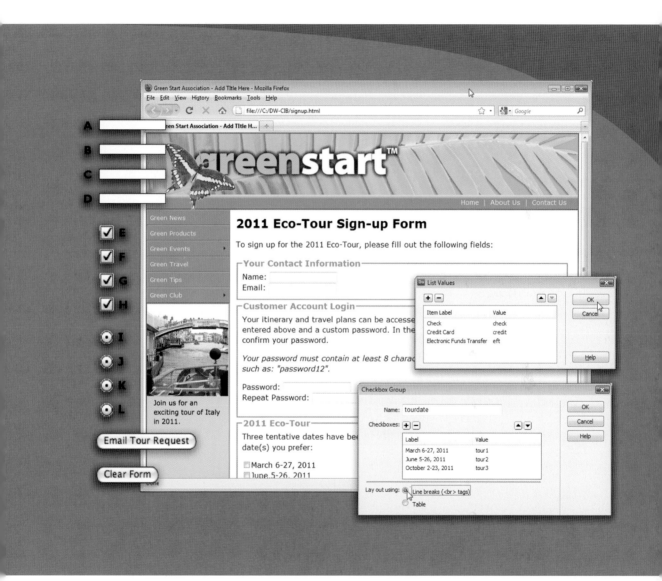

For many people, the first time they encounter interactivity on the web is when they fill out a form. Forms are an essential tool on the modern Internet, allowing you to capture important information and feedback.

Previewing a completed file

To understand the project you will work on in this lesson, you can preview the completed 2011 Eco-Tour page in the browser.

1 Launch Dreamweaver CS5.

2 If necessary, open the Files panel and select DW-CIB from the site list. Expand the lesson13 folder.

3 Select **signup_finished.html**, and preview it in your primary browser.

   The page includes several form elements. Try them out to observe their behaviors.

4 Click in the Name field and type a name. Press Tab.

   The name appears in the data field.

○ **Note:** If Microsoft Internet Explorer is your primary browser and a message appears at the top of the browser window indicating that scripts are prevented from running, click the message bar and choose Allow Blocked Content from the menu that appears.

5 Click in the Email field, and then press Tab without entering an email address.

   A Spry Form widget provides validation for this field and displays an error message if the field is left empty.

   ┌─**Your Contact Information**──────────
   │ Name: John Doe
   │ Email: [   ]   Please enter a valid email address.
   └

6 In the Email field, type **jdoe@mycompany**. Press Tab.

   Because you left off the *.com*, the Spry Form widget displays an error message prompting you to correct the entry.

   ┌─**Your Contact Information**──────────
   │ Name: John Doe
   │ Email: jdoe@mycompany   Invalid format.
   └

7 At the end of the *jdoe@mycompany* entry, type **.com**. Press Tab.

   Now that the entry represents a complete email address, the error message disappears.

8 In the Password field, type **mypassword**. Press Tab.

   An error message appears, saying that the password entered doesn't meet the minimum requirements described.

   Password: ●●●●●●●●●   The password doesn't meet the specified strength.
   Repeat Password:

9 In the Password field, type **mypassword12**.
Press Tab.

10 In the Repeat Password field, type **mypass12**.
Press Tab.

The Spry Validation Confirm widget detects that the two passwords do not
match and displays an error message.

11 In the Repeat Password field, type **mypassword12**.
Press Tab.

12 Select one or more options to indicate when you plan to travel.

13 Use the radio buttons to choose a number of travelers.

14 Click in the Restrictions And Limitations field.
Type **I prefer window seats.**
Press Tab.

If this form were loaded on your web server, you would normally click the Email
Tour Request button to submit the form. A thank-you page like the one pictured
below would take the place of the signup page.

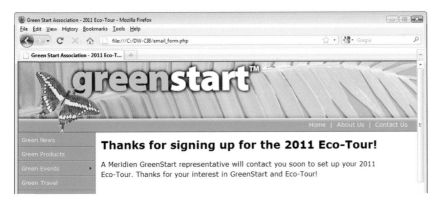

15 When you're finished, close all browser windows and return to Dreamweaver.

Before you construct your own form with its various form elements, let's take a
look at how forms work.

Learning about forms

Forms, on paper or on the web, are tools for gathering information. In both cases, the information is entered into designated data areas, or *fields*, to make it easier to find and understand. Forms should be clearly delineated: Paper forms often use a separate page or graphical borders to distinguish them, while web forms use the `<form>` tag and other specific HTML elements to designate and contain the desired data.

Online forms have decided advantages over paper forms because the user enters the data in a way that can then be automatically transferred into spreadsheets or databases, reducing the labor costs and error rates associated with paper forms.

Web-based forms are composed of one or more HTML elements, each used for a specific purpose:

- Text field—Permits the entry of text and digits, up to a specific number of characters. Text fields designated as password fields mask or obscure characters as they are typed.

- Text area—Identical to text fields, but intended for larger amounts of text, such as multiple sentences or paragraphs.

- Checkbox—A graphical element that permits users to designate a yes or no selection. Checkboxes can be grouped together; however, unlike radio buttons, they allow multiple items to be chosen within the group. Also unlike radio buttons, checkboxes can be deselected, if desired.

- Radio button—A graphical element that permits users to select one option from a group of items. Only one item in the group can be chosen. The selection of a new item in the group deselects any currently selected item. And once one item is selected, it can't be deselected.

- List/menu—Displays entries in a pop-up menu format. Lists (also called select lists) may enforce the selection of a single element or allow the choice of multiple items.

- Hidden—A predefined data field that conveys information to the form-processing mechanism that is unseen by the user. Hidden form elements are used extensively in dynamic page applications.

- Button—Submits the form or performs some other single-purpose interaction, such as clearing or printing the form.

Paper forms, when completed, are mailed or passed along for processing. Web forms are electronically mailed or processed. The `<form>` tag includes an *action* attribute, and the value of the action attribute is triggered when the form is submitted. Often, the action is the web address for another page or server-side script that actually processes the form.

Adding a form to a page

For this exercise, you will create a new page for signing up participants for the 2011 Eco-Tour described in the travel page completed in Lesson 12, "Working with Flash."

1 Open the Assets panel and click the Template category icon. Right-click **mygreen_temp** and choose New From Template from the context menu.

Note: If you are starting from scratch in this exercise, see the "Jumpstart" instructions in the "Getting Started" section at the beginning of the book. Then, follow the steps in this exercise.

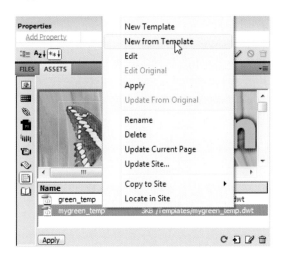

2 Save the file as **signup.html** in the site root folder.

3 In the MainContent region, select the placeholder heading *Add main heading here* and type **2011 Eco-Tour Sign-up Form** to replace the text.

4 Select the placeholder paragraph *Add content here*.
Type **To sign up for the 2011 Eco-Tour, please fill out the following fields:** Press Enter/Return to create a new paragraph.

All form fields must be contained within a `<form>` element, so it's typically best to add it to the page before inserting any field elements. Any field inserted outside the `<form>` element will be ignored when the form is submitted and processed.

Note: If you try to insert a form element without a `<form>` tag, Dreamweaver will prompt you to add one.

5 Open the Insert panel and select Forms from the category list.
In the Forms category, click the Form (□) icon.

Dreamweaver inserts the `<form>` element at the insertion point, which is indicated visually by a red outline. Forms should always feature a unique ID. If you don't create your own, Dreamweaver will add one.

Note: Dreamweaver will add unique IDs to forms and all form elements if you forget to.

One tag to control them all

Text fields, checkboxes, radio buttons, list menus, and text areas have at least one thing in common: They are all created using the HTML `<input>` tag. Just change the `type` attribute, and/or one or more other settings, and you can convert a checkbox into a radio button, a text field, or a list menu. No other HTML element is so flexible and powerful. As you insert form fields in this lesson, feel free to peek in the code to see how this magic is accomplished.

You may see something like the following examples:

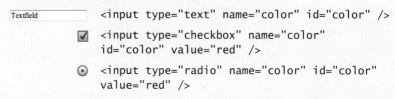

```
<input type="text" name="color" id="color" />

<input type="checkbox" name="color"
id="color" value="red" />

<input type="radio" name="color" id="color"
value="red" />
```

6   If necessary, select the `<form#form1>` tag selector.
Select the *form1* text that appears in the ID field of the Property inspector.
Type **ecotour** and press Enter/Return to create a custom ID.

The `<form#ecotour>` element extends left and right to the edges of `<div.content>`. As is, fields and labels within the form will also hug the sides of the container unless you add some custom padding or margins.

7   Open the CSS Styles panel, if necessary.
Select the `.content` rule in the **mygreen_styles.css** style sheet.
In the CSS Styles panel, click the New CSS Rule icon.

8   Choose Compound and name the new rule `.content #ecotour`. Click OK.

9   In the Box category, enter **15px** only in the Left and Right margin fields.
Click OK.

A new rule—`.content #ecotour`—will appear in the CSS Styles panel. The red outline of the form indents 15 pixels away from the left and right edges of MainContent.

2011 Eco-Tour Sign-up Form

To sign up for the 2011 Eco-Tour, please fill out the following fields:

10 Save all files.

You created a form element; next, you'll insert some form fields.

Inserting text form elements

Text fields are the workhorses of all the form elements. Text fields are the basic vehicles for gathering unstructured text and numeric data, and it's hard to imagine a form without them. In fact, many forms are composed exclusively of text-input fields.

In the upcoming exercises, you'll insert basic text fields, Spry text fields, password text fields, password-confirmation text fields, and text areas. Before you can start, however, confirm that Dreamweaver is configured to add form elements in their most accessible format.

Setting preferences for accessible forms

Accessibility technologies place special requirements on form elements. Assistive technology devices, such as screen readers, require precise code that allows them to correctly read forms and individual form elements. Dreamweaver provides an option that outputs form code in the proper format. These preferences may be set as the default configuration; if so, merely confirm that the options for accessible forms are set.

1 Choose Edit > Preferences (Windows) or Dreamweaver > Preferences (Mac).

2 When the Preferences dialog box appears, select the Accessibility category.

3 In the Accessibility category, make sure that the Form Objects option is selected. Click OK.

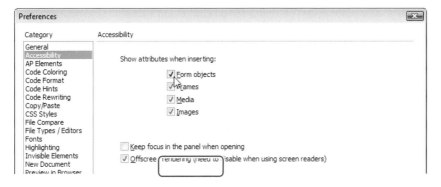

As you'll see in the following exercises, when accessibility for form objects is enabled, a dialog box appears before the form element is inserted. This dialog box has a number of options for including a form element label, as well as other special attributes. You'll learn more about these attributes later.

Using text fields

Text fields accept alphanumeric characters—letters and numbers. Unless otherwise specified, a text field can display around 20 characters. If you type more characters than will fit, the text will scroll within the field. To show more or fewer characters on the screen, set a specific field size in the Width field in the Property inspector. Although there's no built-in limit to the amount of text you can enter into a text field element, you're more likely to run into limits imposed by your chosen data application.

Spreadsheet and database fields frequently limit the amount of data that can be entered. If you enter too much data into a field and submit it, the data application usually just ignores, or dumps, whatever exceeds its maximum capacity. To prevent this from happening, you can restrict HTML text fields to a specific number of characters, if desired, by using the Max Chars attribute field in the Property inspector.

1 If necessary, open **signup.html** from the site root folder.

2 Insert the cursor in the red form outline.

3 In the Forms category of the Insert panel, click the Text Field ⬛ icon.

   The Input Tag Accessibility Attributes dialog box appears. The dialog box enables you to designate specific attributes and markup for the <input> element. When a form field is inserted, Dreamweaver makes it easy to define some of these options immediately.

   For example, the most important attribute is id, because it gives the field a unique name that assists in processing the form data later. If you don't give each form field a unique ID, Dreamweaver will create generic ones for you, like *textfield*, *textfield2*, *textfield3*, and so on. Since generic IDs will be difficult to work with, it's important to create descriptive custom names yourself.

4 In the ID field, type **name**.
   Press Tab.

   Text fields can also include HTML markup for a descriptive label that will appear in the web page. Such markup is optional, and if you select the No Label Tag option in the dialog box, Dreamweaver will leave off the <label> markup entirely.

   On the other hand, if you wish to use the <label> element, Dreamweaver inserts the HTML markup for you and provides two methods for inserting it: by wrapping the label around the text field element or by inserting it as a separate element that uses a "for" attribute. In most cases, the "for" option provides the most flexibility for form design.

5 In the Label field, type **Name:**
Press Tab.

The ID is in lowercase, because it appears only in the code. The label is capitalized because it actually displays in the form, before or after the text field element.

6 Select the Attach Label Tag Using 'for' Attribute option.
Select the Before Form Item option, if necessary.
Click OK.

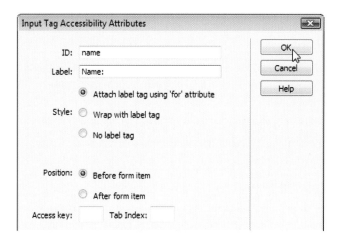

When the Attach Label Tag Using 'for' Attribute option is selected, Dreamweaver inserts code like this:

```
<label for="name">Name</label><input type="text" id="name" />
```

This code arrangement allows for maximum flexibility in your form design. For example, you can keep the two elements on the same line, put them on two lines, or format each separately using CSS.

7 Save the file.

The first of your form objects is now in place. Inserting other standard text fields is a similar operation. In the next exercise, you'll add a Spry Validation Text Field, which is a specialized version of the text field that has been customized with Ajax functionality.

Including Spry Text fields

In Lesson 11, "Adding Interactivity," you learned about the Adobe Spry Framework for Ajax and worked with the Spry Accordion panel. Dreamweaver also includes a range of Spry objects for forms. Each Spry Form widget combines form elements with sophisticated JavaScript to create easy-to-use form fields with built-in *validation*.

Validation is the process of verifying that appropriate data has been entered into a form element. This maintains the integrity and quality of the data entered into the form and passed to your data application. For example, if a site visitor enters an incomplete or invalid email address into an email text field, the form data becomes worthless. Validation can also ensure that all required fields are completed before the form can be submitted.

Spry Form widgets are available for several kinds of form elements, including text fields, text areas, checkboxes, passwords and password confirmation, radio groups, and select lists. Each widget works basically the same way: You insert the widget and then specify its properties using the Spry interface in the Property inspector.

In this exercise, you'll insert a Spry Validation Text Field to make sure that the user submits a properly structured email address.

1 If necessary, open **signup.html**.

2 Insert the cursor at the end of the Name text field inserted in the previous exercise and press Shift-Enter/Shift-Return to insert a forced line break.

3 In the Forms category of the Insert panel, click the Spry Validation Text Field (⌶) icon.

The Input Tag Accessibility Attributes dialog box appears.

> ▶ **Tip:** Press Tab to move quickly from field to field.

4 In the ID field, type **email**.
In the Label field, type **Email:**
Select the Attach Label Tag Using 'for' Attribute option.
Select the Before Form Item option.
Click OK.

5 Save the file. If Dreamweaver alerts you of the external JavaScript files used, click OK.

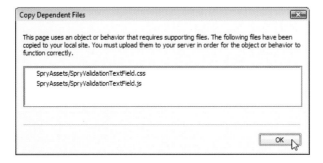

Once the element is inserted on the page, you can customize its Spry functionality.

6 If the blue Spry TextField tab isn't visible, position your mouse pointer over the email text field and wait until it appears. Click the tab to select the element. If necessary, open the Property inspector.

The Property inspector displays attributes and settings for a generic Spry text field.

7 In the Property inspector, choose **Email Address** from the Type pop-up menu.

The Email Address field type checks to see that the entry contains an @ character followed by a domain name. Examine the available triggers in the Property inspector. The Blur option is a trigger activated when a user tabs from one field to the next in a form. The Change option activates when data is entered or altered in the field. The Submit option is activated when the form is processed by the browser and the web application.

8 In the Property inspector, select Validate On Blur and make sure that the Required option is selected.

By default, all validations occur when the form is submitted, but as in the Email field, you can add triggers to check validation sooner. This type of interactivity provides a more immediate response and a better user experience. The user doesn't have to wait until they are finished filling out the entire form before being notified that they missed a field or entered incorrect data. Dreamweaver makes it easy to customize the error messages using the Spry interface in the Property inspector.

Note that the Preview States menu displays the text *Initial*.

9 From the Preview States menu, choose Required.

The warning text *A value is required* appears to the right of the Spry Email field. Let's make the warning a bit less cryptic.

Note: When a field is required, the user must complete it before the form will submit.

10 Select the text *A value is required* and type **An email address is required.**

This message will appear when an invalid email address is entered in the field.

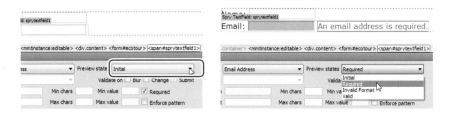

11 From the Preview States menu, choose Invalid Format.

The warning text *Invalid Format* appears to the right of the Spry Email field.

12 Select the text *Invalid Format* and type **Please enter a valid email address.**

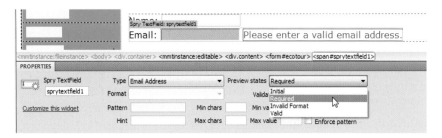

13 Save the file.

Creating a field set

One way to make forms more user friendly is to organize fields into logical group-ings, called field sets. The HTML <fieldset> element was designed for this purpose and even features a helpful description element called *legend*.

1 If necessary, open **signup.html**.

2 Insert the cursor in the Email label. Click the blue tab to select the Spry text field. Press the Right Arrow key to move the cursor after the Spry component. Press Enter/Return to create a new paragraph.

3 Insert the cursor into the Name label and select the <label> tag selector. Hold the Shift key and click at the end of the Email text field to select both fields and their associated markup.

Selecting the relevant code can be a bit tricky in Design view. To make sure you are selecting everything you need, switch to Code or Split view.

4 Ensure that you've selected this entire code block.

```
50    <form id="ecotour" name="ecotour" method="post" action="">
51        <label for="name">Name:</label>
52        <input type="text" name="name" id="name" />
53        <br />
54        <span id="sprytextfield1">
55        <label for="email">Email:</label>
56        <input type="text" name="email" id="email" />
57        <span class="textfieldRequiredMsg">Please enter a valid email address.</span><span class=
      "textfieldInvalidFormatMsg">Invalid format.</span></span>
58        <p> </p>
```

5 In the Forms category of the Insert panel, click the Fieldset (⬚) icon.

The selected code is inserted into a `<fieldset>` element.

6 In the Legend field, type **Your Contact Information**.
Click OK.

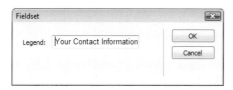

7 Switch to Design view.

The field set is not rendered accurately in Design view; however, it does clearly display the legend.

8 Save All and preview the page in Live view.

The field set neatly encloses the two fields in a labeled container.

```
┌─Your Contact Information────────────────────────────┐
│ Name: [                    ]                        │
│ Email: [                    ]                       │
└─────────────────────────────────────────────────────┘
```

9 Switch back to Design view.

In the next exercise, you'll create password and password confirmation fields.

Creating password text fields

The password field is a common sight on the web. Normally, a text field displays the characters entered into it, but this wouldn't be desirable for a password field. Instead, password fields mask the characters as they're typed, displaying a series of asterisks or bullets, depending on the browser. Designed as a security measure, it prevents a casual passerby from observing your password as you type.

1 Insert the cursor anywhere in the field set you just created and select the <fieldset> tag selector. Press the Right Arrow key to move the cursor after the element. Press Enter/Return to create a new paragraph.

2 Type the following text:

Your itinerary and travel plans can be accessed online using the email address you entered above and a custom password. In the following fields you can set up and confirm your password.

3 Press Enter/Return to create a new paragraph.
Click the I button in the Property inspector to begin the <em> tag.
Type *Your password must contain at least 8 characters, at least two of them numbers, such as "password12."*

4 Press Enter/Return to create a new paragraph. In the Forms category of the Insert panel, click the Spry Validation Password (⊠ˣˣˣ) icon.

The Input Tag Accessibility Attributes dialog box appears.

5 In the ID field, type **password**.
In the Label field, type **Password:**
Select the Attach Label Tag Using 'for' Attribute and Before Form Item options. Click OK.

6 Click the blue Spry Password tab.

The Property inspector displays the settings and attributes for the Spry Password field.

● **Note:** If you don't want the default error message to show in your design window, in the Property inspector, choose Initial from the Preview States menu.

7 Select the Required and Validate On Blur options.
In the Min Letters field, enter **8**.
In the Min Numbers field, enter **2**.

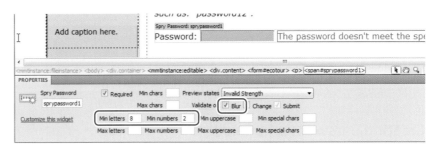

8 Press the Right Arrow key to move the cursor after the password field. Then, press Shift-Enter/Shift-Return to create a line break after the password field.

9 In the Forms category of the Insert panel, click the Spry Validation Confirm (⊠✓) icon to create a password confirmation text field.

The Input Tag Accessibility Attributes dialog box appears.

10 In the ID field, type **confirm_pw**.

In the Label field, type **Repeat Password**.

Select the Attach Label Tag Using 'for' Attribute and the Before Form Item options.
Click OK.

11 Click the blue Spry Confirm tab.

Select the Required and Validate On Blur options.

From the Validate Against pop-up menu, choose "Password" In Form "Ecotour."

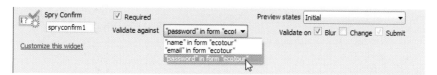

The instructions created in step 2 and the three new text fields can be enclosed in their own field set at this point.

12 Select the instructional paragraph and the two Spry fields.

13 In the Insert panel, click the Fieldset button.

In the Legend field, type **Customer Account Login**.
Click OK.

Note how the text and password fields in the second field set are indented more than the fields in the first. The indent is being applied by one of the preexisting CSS rules from the original layout. You'll correct this inconsistency and apply additional styling by creating a custom CSS style sheet just for forms at the end of the lesson.

▶ **Tip:** Although you may not need to use Code view or Split view to help you select the desired code this time, don't hesitate to use these valuable tools whenever necessary.

14 Save all files.

The password field you added allows a website user to create a password within rules you set. The password-confirm field requires that the password be retyped in exactly the same form. This will help website users to detect typos so they don't unintentionally submit a password that is not what they intended.

Inserting checkboxes

Checkboxes provide a series of options that can be chosen in any combination. Like text fields, each checkbox has its own unique ID and value attributes. Dreamweaver provides two methods for adding checkboxes to your page. You can either insert each checkbox individually or insert an entire group at once. You can also choose between normal HTML checkboxes and ones powered by Spry. The Spry check-boxes allow you to add customized error messages and other functionality. In this exercise you will insert a Checkbox Group.

1 If necessary, open **signup.html**.

2 Insert the cursor in the Online Account Login field set and select the `<fieldset>` tag selector. Press the Right Arrow key to move the cursor outside the element. Press Enter/Return to insert new paragraph.

3 Type **Three tentative dates have been selected for the 2011 Eco-Tour. Please select any date(s) you prefer:** in the field.

4 Press Enter/Return to insert a new paragraph.

5 In the Forms category of the Insert panel, click the Checkbox Group (▦) icon.

The Checkbox Group dialog box appears, displaying two predefined options.

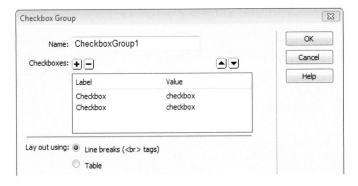

6 Change the Name field to **tourdate**.

Note how the dialog box offers two columns: Label and Value. Unlike text fields, checkboxes provide predefined options where the label can be different from the value actually submitted. This method offers several advantages over user-*fillable* fields.

First, the predefined options can deliver specific desired values that may not make any sense to the user. For example, the label can display the name of a product, while the value can pass along the stock-keeping unit, or SKU, number. Secondly, checkboxes and other predefined fields greatly reduce user-entry errors common in many forms.

7 In the Checkbox Group dialog box, click the Add (+) button next to the word *Checkboxes* to create a third item in the list.

8 Change the first label to **March 6-27, 2011**.
Change the first value to **tour1**.
Change the second label to **June 5-26, 2011**.
Change the second value to **tour2**.
Change the third label to **October 2-23, 2011**.
Change the third value to **tour3**.

Tip: Press Tab to move quickly between labels and values to fill out the entire list.

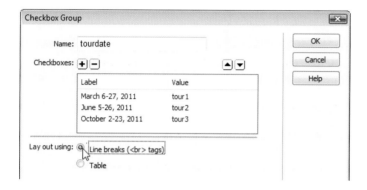

9 For the Lay Out Using option, select Line Breaks (
 Tags). Click OK.

Note: Labels for checkboxes and radio buttons appear after the element, by default.

The checkbox group appears in the document below the text typed in step 3. Using the checkbox group eliminates the need to enter any settings in the Property inspector. A quick glance at the code reveals the advantages of using the checkbox group.

10 Insert the cursor in any of the checkbox labels and switch to Split view. Examine the code for the related `<input>` element.

Each checkbox in the group displays the `name="tourdate"` attribute. Note how the ID attributes have been automatically incremented as `tourdate_0`, `tourdate_1`, and `tourdate_2`. By using the checkbox group, Dreamweaver has saved you time by automating the process of adding multiple checkbox elements.

```
<label><input type="checkbox" name="tourdate" value="tour1" id="tourdate_0" />March 6-27, 2011</label><br />
<label><input type="checkbox" name="tourdate" value="tour2" id="tourdate_1" />June 5-26, 2011</label><br />
<label><input type="checkbox" name="tourdate" value="tour3" id="tourdate_2" />October 2-23, 2011</label><br />
```

11 Save the file.

You've created a group of checkboxes. More than one checkbox can be selected in a group. In the next exercise, you will learn how to work with radio buttons.

Creating radio buttons

Sometimes you want users to select one option from an array of choices. The element of choice in that case is the radio button. Radio buttons differ from checkboxes in two ways. When a radio button is selected, it can't be deselected, except by clicking one of the other buttons in the group. Then, when you click one radio button, any other option in the same group is deselected automatically.

The enabling mechanism behind this behavior is simple but effective. Unlike other form elements, each radio button does not have a unique name and ID; rather, all radio buttons in a group have the same name and ID. Radio buttons are differentiated by giving each distinctive values, instead.

As with checkboxes, you can add radio buttons to your page using two methods. You can insert each radio button individually, or insert an entire group at once. You can also choose between normal HTML radio buttons and ones powered by Spry. If you choose HTML radio buttons, you'll be totally responsible for inserting and naming each manually. If you choose the Spry Validation Radio Group, Dreamweaver will take care of all the naming logistics, as well as the associated JavaScript and CSS files needed for the customized error messages and styling. In this exercise, you'll insert the Spry Validation Radio Group.

1   If necessary, open **signup.html** and switch to Design view.

2   Insert the cursor in the last checkbox label. Select the <label> tag selector and press the Right Arrow key to move the cursor after the element. Press Enter/Return to insert a new paragraph.

3   Type **How many people will be traveling?**
Press Enter/Return to create a new paragraph.

4   In the Insert panel, click the Spry Validation Radio Group (icon) icon.

5   Change the Name field to **travelers**.

6   Click the Add (+) button for Radio Buttons three times to create a total of five radio buttons.

As with checkboxes, you can enter values that are different than the labels.

7   Change the first label to **One**.
Change the first value to **1**.
Change the second label to **Two**.
Change the second value to **2**.
Change the third label to **Three**.
Change the third value to **3**.
Change the fourth label to **Four**.
Change the fourth value to **4**.
Change the fifth label to **More**.
Change the fifth value to **contact**.

Note: Checkboxes and radio buttons basically use identical code markup. To convert a radio button to a checkbox, simply give each item a unique ID and name. To change a checkbox to a radio button, give each item the same name and ID.

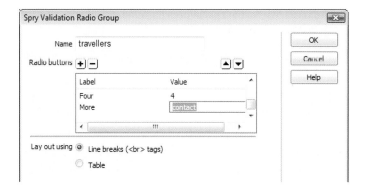

Tip: If you want to re-order the radio buttons in this dialog box, use the up and down arrows.

8 From the Lay Out Using options, choose Line Breaks (
 Tags). Click OK.

The Spry Radio Group appears below the text entered in step 3.

9 If necessary, click the blue tab to select the Spry Radio Group widget. In the Property inspector, select the Required option.

10 From the Preview States menu, choose Required. Examine the Spry error text.

Let's customize the generic error text.

11 Select the Spry error text *Please make a selection.* Type **Please choose the number of travelers.**

12 Save all files.

You've created a set of radio buttons. By using the Spry Validation Radio Group interface, you easily made this element a required form field and customized the error text. If the user does not select one of the radio buttons, the error message will appear when the form is submitted.

Incorporating text areas

Every now and then you may want to give users an opportunity to enter a larger amount of information. Text areas provide a vehicle to enable this goal. Text areas permit multiple-line entry and word wrapping. If the entered text exceeds the physical space of the text area on the page, scroll bars automatically appear.

Dreamweaver offers both HTML and Spry text area components. The Spry-based text area component allows you to include a customized user prompt, so we'll use it in this exercise.

1   If necessary, open **signup.html** and switch to Design view.

2   Click the blue tab to select the Spry radio group. Press the Right Arrow key to move the cursor after the element. Press Enter/Return to create a new paragraph.

3   In the Forms category of the Insert panel, click the Spry Validation Textarea (🖳) icon.

    The Input Tag Accessibility Attributes dialog box appears.

4   In the ID field, type **requirements**.
    In the Label field, type **Requirements and Limitations:**
    If necessary, select the Attach Label Tag Using 'for' Attribute and the Before Form Item options.
    Click OK.

The comment text area appears displaying inline with the label, which doesn't look very attractive. So, let's move the text area to its own line.

5   Insert the cursor in the text area label *Requirements and Limitations*.
    Select the `<label>` tag selector and press the Right Arrow key.
    Press Shift-Enter/Shift-Return to create a line break.

    The text area label *Requirements and Limitations* is sufficiently vague that it requires a bit more description to generate the desired response. In an HTML-based text area you can insert some default text, or an *initial value*, to request the proper data.

    Basically, it works this way: You enter text in the Initial Val field of the Property inspector and save the page. When the browser renders the form, this text appears automatically in the text area.

    Unfortunately, the text in the initial value field will be passed to the data application if the user doesn't enter his or her own response. This can clog your database with lots of repetitive and useless data. Since many users won't have special travel requirements, this field will be skipped over frequently. That's where the Spry Validation Textarea comes in. It provides a different technique to supply the initial value that doesn't pass the unwanted data.

6 Click the blue tab to select the Spry Textarea. In the Property inspector Hint field, type **Please enter any personal travel requirements or limitations**.

When the website user begins to type in this field, the initial value will disappear automatically, but since the hint text is not stored in the field itself it can't be passed to your data application.

The Spry Textarea is formatted to be a required field, by default. Since this will be an optional field, you need to deselect this checkbox.

7 Click the Required option to deselect it.

The default text area is quite small and should have more space.

8 Click the text area to select it. In the Property inspector Char Width field, enter **60**.
Press Enter/Return.

▶ **Warning:** Design view doesn't render text fields accurately. Always test widths in Live view or a browser.

9 Save all files.

The text area you added allows the website user to type comments that aren't limited to a single line or checkbox. Another important form element also allows you to present multiple choices to the visitor, but in a more compact space.

Working with lists

List and menu form elements offer a flexible method for presenting multiple options in two different formats. When displayed as a menu, the element functions like radio buttons. When displayed as a list, the element behaves like checkboxes. In this exercise, you'll insert a menu element with three options.

1 If necessary, open **signup.html** and switch to Design view.

2 Select the Spry Textarea and press the Right Arrow key. Press Enter/Return.

3 Type **How would you like to pay?** and press Enter/Return.

4 In the Insert panel, click the Select (List/Menu) (⊞) icon.

The Input Tag Accessibility Attributes dialog box appears.

5 In the ID field, type **payment**.
Leave the Label field empty.
Select the No Label Tag option.
Click OK.

There is no need for a label tag because the text in the form element serves as label text for this form element.

An empty menu element appears in the document. Now you're ready to add the list entries. Dreamweaver provides a separate dialog box for this task, accessible from the Property inspector.

6 In the Property inspector, click the List Values button.

The List Values dialog box appears. Note that the first label field is selected automatically.

▶ Tip: Lists don't have to be in alphabetical order, but it makes the options easier to read and find, especially in longer lists.

7 In the first Label field, type **Check**.
In the first Value field, type **check**.
For the second label, type **Credit Card**.
For the second value, type **credit**.
For the third label, type **Electronic Funds Transfer**.
For the third value, type **eft**.
Click OK.

The options appear in the Initially Selected field of the Property inspector. Once the list menu is complete, you can select the item that's displayed by default.

8 In the Property inspector, from the Initially Selected list, select Credit Card. If necessary, in the Type area, select the Menu option.

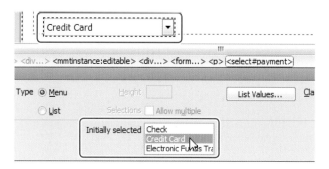

► **Tip:** One strategy favored by some developers is to select your most preferred option to display by default. In other words, if you like the convenience and security offered by credit cards, the credit card option should be the option displayed.

When the List/Menu element is formatted as a Menu, multiple selections are not allowed. To allow multiple selections, change the attribute to List, and then select the Allow Multiple option.

In some browsers, to select multiple options you first have to hold the Ctrl/Cmd key. If this is the case with your menu, you should add a note that explains how to make multiple selections.

Let's enclose the last four components in their own field set.

9 Select the last four components you created using the appropriate tag selector and keyboard and mouse actions. In the Insert panel, click the Fieldset button. Name the new field set **2011 Eco-Tour**.

10 Save all files.

Menus can contain numerous choices—like all 50 states—and so they provide a powerful tool to the website designer and developer, while requiring only a tiny amount of space on the web page itself. Using a database connection, the list options can also be populated dynamically, and even updated instantly as new entries are made by administrators, or other users.

Your form is almost complete—the last step is to add a button to submit the entered information for processing.

Adding a submit button

Every form needs a control to invoke the dynamic process, or *action*, desired. This job typically falls to the *submit* button that when clicked sends the entire form for processing. By default, buttons inserted by Dreamweaver are set to Submit, although they can also be assigned the options Reset or None. Although many buttons used on the Internet feature the text *Submit*, it's not required and may not clearly reflect what action will be performed.

1 Insert the cursor in any form element in the last field set and select the `<fieldset>` tag selector.

You'll insert the Submit button outside the last field set.

2 Press the Right Arrow key to move the cursor after the selected field set. Then press Enter/Return to create a new paragraph for the button.

3 In the Insert panel, click the Button (▢) icon.

The Input Tag Accessibility Attributes dialog box appears.

4 In the ID field, type **submit**.
If necessary, select the checkbox No Label Tag.
Click OK.

The Submit button appears in the document at the bottom of the form. The Property inspector displays the settings specific to this element. Note that the Button Name and Value fields show the text *submit* and the Action radio button for Submit Form is selected. Let's change the text in the button to better reflect what's going to happen.

5 In the Property inspector, change the Value field to **Email Tour Request**.

Some users may change their minds while filling out a form and want to start over or clear the form. In this case, you need to add a Reset button to the form, too.

6 Insert a space after the Submit button.
Repeat steps 2–5 to create a Reset button.
In the ID field, type **reset**.
In the Value field, type **Clear Form**.
Select the Reset Form option.

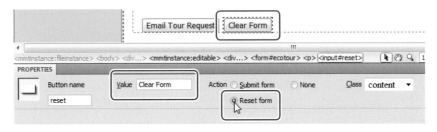

7 Save the file.

The form elements are all in place and ready to be accessed and filled in, but the form itself won't be complete until you add an action to specify how the data will be processed. Typical actions include sending the data by email, passing it to another web page, or inserting it into a web-hosted database. In the next exercise, you will apply an action and create the supporting code to email the form data.

Tabbing tantrums

When filling out forms online, have you ever pressed the Tab key to move from one form field to the next and nothing happened? Or, worse yet, the focus moved to some other field out of the expected order? The ability to tab through forms is a default process that you should support on your website. It may even be required, in some cases, under Section 508 accessibility mandates.

Tabbing to the various form fields you have created should happen automatically in most browsers. But some browsers may not support every field type automatically. So, to enforce the tabbing order, you can add a `tabindex` attribute to each field, like this:

```
<input type="text" name="name" id="name" tabindex="1" />
<input type="text" name="address" id="add1" tabindex="2" />
```

When inserting certain form fields, you may notice a Tab Index field in the dialog box. Enter the desired tab order number here. If the field isn't available, you can insert the attribute manually in Code view. By inserting this code attribute into each form element, you will codify the tabbing order and make your form more accessible to all users, as well as comply with web standards.

Specifying a form action

As described in the exercise "Setting up e-mail links" in Lesson 10, "Working with Navigation," sending email is not as simple as inserting the mailto command into the Action field and adding your email address. Many of your web visitors don't use email programs installed on their computers; they use web-hosted systems like AOL, Gmail, and Hotmail. To guarantee that you receive the form responses, you need to use a server-based application like the one you'll create in this exercise. The first step is to set the form action that passes the data to generate the email.

1 If necessary, open **signup.html**.

2 Insert the cursor anywhere in the form and select the `<form>` tag selector.

The Property inspector displays the settings and specifications for the form.

3 In the Property inspector Action field, type **email_form.php**.
If necessary, from the Method field menu, select POST.

Note: In this exercise, we're using PHP-based code to generate the email form. To set up the action for ASP or ColdFusion coding, you simply add the appropriate extension (.asp or .cf) for the target application.

4 Save all files.

HTML provides two built-in methods—GET and POST—for processing form data. The GET method transfers data by appending it to the URL. You see this method used most in search engines, like Google and Yahoo. The next time you conduct a web search, examine the URL on the results page and you will see your search term tucked away somewhere after the domain name, usually bracketed by special characters. There are a couple of disadvantages to using the GET method. First, the search term is visible in the URL, which means other people can see what you're searching for and will be able to retrieve your search from the browser cache. Second, URLs have a maximum size of 255 characters (including the filename and path information), which drastically limits the total amount of data you can pass.

The POST method doesn't use the URL. Instead it passes the data behind the scenes and places no limits concerning the amount of data. The POST method doesn't cache the data, so no one can recover sensitive information, like your credit card or driver's license numbers, from the browser history. This method is used by most high-end data applications and online stores. The only disadvantage to using the POST method is that you can't see how the data is being passed to the next page—as you can using GET—which helps when you are troubleshooting application errors.

By selecting POST in step 3, the data entered into the form by the user in **signup.html** will be passed to the file **email_form.php** when you click the Email Tour Request (submit) button. As with most hyperlinks, the process loads the new page in the window and resets **signup.html**, deleting the user data from the form. If you navigate back to that page using the site menus, or hyperlinks, the form will be blank. In some instances, you can reload the form page with the data by clicking the Back button in the browser. However, security-conscious developers sometimes add code to their form pages that deletes form data automatically when the page is submitted to prevent this very situation. But, no matter how you set up your form, closing the browser will delete the data irrevocably from the local computer.

Emailing form data

The **email_form.php** file targeted by the form action doesn't exist, so you need to create it from scratch. Although the GreenStart template is an HTML file, you can use it to create a PHP form mailer.

1   Open the Assets panel. Select the Template category. Right-click **mygreen_temp** and choose New From Template from the context menu.

2   Save the page as **email_form.php**.

The file extension .php is used for dynamic pages that use the server-based scripting language PHP. The extension informs the browser that the page needs to be processed differently than basic HTML. Some browsers may ignore ASP, ColdFusion, and PHP scripting if the files don't use the appropriate extensions.

3   Select the text *Add main heading here.*
Type **Thanks for signing up for the 2011 Eco-Tour!**

4   Select the text *Add content here.*
Type **A Meridien GreenStart representative will contact you soon to set up your 2011 Eco-Tour. Thanks for your interest in GreenStart and Eco-Tour!**

5   Switch to Code view.

The page currently is identical to the HTML-based template and has no PHP markup. The scripting that will process the data and generate the server-based email will be inserted before all other code on the page, even before the <DOCTYPE> declaration that starts the HTML code.

6   Insert the cursor at the beginning of line 1 in Code view.
Type **<?php** and press Enter/Return to create a new paragraph.

```
1   <?php
2   <!DOCTYPE html PUBLIC "-//W3C//DTD XHTML 1.0 Transitional//EN"
    "http://www.w3.org/TR/xhtml1/DTD/xhtml1-transitional.dtd">
```

Dreamweaver's Code Hinting feature starts to help you to enter the code, but you'll quickly realize that this feature doesn't support PHP as it does HTML and JavaScript, so if you like to hand-code PHP you'll be on your own.

▶ **Warning:** Typing code is tedious and exacting work. PHP—as all scripting languages, like ASP, ColdFusion, JavaScript, and so on—is not as forgiving of errors as is HTML. While a web page may function and display in the browser with a broken or incomplete code element, in many cases, a PHP script will fail completely if you miss even a single needed character or punctuation mark. So, type carefully.

Note: This email address is for the fictitious GreenStart Association. For your own website insert an email address supported by your server.

7   Type **$to = "info@green-start.org";** and press Enter/Return to create a new line.

The dollar sign ($) declares a variable in PHP. A variable is a piece of data that will be created within the code or received from another source, such as your form. In this case, the **$to** variable is declaring the email address to which all the form data will be sent. If you want to experiment with PHP, feel free to substitute the sample address with your own personal email.

8   Type **$subject = "2011 Eco-Tour Sign Up Form";** and press Enter/Return to create a new line.

```
1  <?php
2  $to = "info@green-start.org";
3  $subject = "2011 Eco-Tour Sign Up Form";
4  <!DOCTYPE html PUBLIC "-//W3C//DTD XHTML 1.0 Transitional//EN"
   "http://www.w3.org/TR/xhtml1/DTD/xhtml1-transitional.dtd">
```

This line creates the variable for the email subject. A **$subject** variable is required in the PHP code, but it can be left blank (" "), if desired, although subjects help you organize and filter emails quickly.

9   Type **$message =**

This variable begins the body of the email. The next code elements you enter will list all the form fields you wish to collect, as well as a bit of structural trickery to make the email easier to read. Although you can list the fields in any order you want (and more than once), in this exercise you will type them in the same order they are in the form. If you recall, the first field in the sign-up form was Name.

10 Type **"Customer name: " . $_POST['name'] . "\r\n" .**

The first part of this entry is part of the "trickery" we just mentioned. The text **"Customer name: "** has nothing to do with the form. You are adding it to the email simply to identify the raw customer data that's being inserted by the **$_POST['name']** variable. The period (.) character concatenates, or combines, the text and the data variable into one string. The code element **"\r\n"** inserts a new paragraph after the customer name. Insert this code after each form variable to put each piece of data on its own line.

11 Complete the email body by typing the following code. Insert spaces after the colon (:) to indent the variable statements so that they align to the same position. (Some lines will get more spaces than others.)

```
"Email:            " . $_POST['email'] . "\r\n" .
"Password:         " . $_POST['password'] . "\r\n" .
"\r\n" .
"Requested tour:   " . $_POST['tourdate_0'] . "\r\n" .
"Requested tour:   " . $_POST['tourdate_1'] . "\r\n" .
"Requested tour:   " . $_POST['tourdate_2'] . "\r\n" .
"Total travellers: " . $_POST['travellers'] . "\r\n" ."\r\n" .
"Restrictions:     " . $_POST['restrictions'] . "\r\n" ."\r\n" .
"Payment type:     " . $_POST['payment'];
```

When you are finished, the code should look like the following figure.

```
 4  $message = "Customer name:    " . $_POST['name'] . "\r\n" .
 5  "Email:            " . $_POST['email'] . "\r\n" .
 6  "Password:         " . $_POST['password'] . "\r\n" . "\r\n" .
 7  "Requested tour:   " . $_POST['tourdate_0'] . "\r\n" .
 8  "Requested tour:   " . $_POST['tourdate_1'] . "\r\n" .
 9  "Requested tour:   " . $_POST['tourdate_2'] . "\r\n" .
10  "Total Travellers: " . $_POST['travellers'] . "\r\n" . "\r\n" .
11  "Restrictions:     " . $_POST['restrictions'] . "\r\n" . "\r\n" .
12  "Payment type:     " . $_POST['payment'];
13  <!DOCTYPE html PUBLIC "-//W3C//DTD XHTML 1.0 Transitional//EN"
    "http://www.w3.org/TR/xhtml1/DTD/xhtml1-transitional.dtd">
```

Adding spaces before the variables should align the form data when inserted into the message. Note how certain lines show code for two paragraph returns ("\r\n" . "\r\n"). Putting extra lines between specific data elements can help make the email easier to read.

12 Press Enter/Return.

Type **$from = $_POST['email'];**
and press Enter/Return.

This variable creates a variable that will be used to populate the *from* email address using the information the customer entered in the form.

13 Type **$headers = "From: $from" . "\r\n";**
Press Enter/Return.

This line creates the email "From" header using the variable from step 12.

14 Type `$headers .= "Bcc: lin@green-start.org" . "\r\n";`
Press Enter/Return.

This line is optional. It generates a blind carbon copy of the email to Lin, the transportation expert at GreenStart. Feel free to customize the code by adding your own email here or the email of a co-worker.

15 Type `mail($to,$subject,$message,$headers);`
Press Enter/Return.

This line creates the email and sends it using a PHP-enabled server.

16 Type `?>` to close and complete PHP form email function.

```
11  "Restrictions:       " . $_POST['restrictions'] . "\r\n" . "\r\n"
12  "Payment type:       " . $_POST['payment'];
13  $_POST['ecotour']; $from = $_POST['email'];
14  $headers = "From: $from" . "\r\n;
15  $headers = "Bcc: lin@green-start.org" . "\r\n;
16  mail($to,$subject,$message,$headers);
17  ?>
18  <!DOCTYPE html PUBLIC "-//W3C//DTD XHTML 1.0 Transitional//EN"
```

17 Press Enter/Return to insert one last paragraph return. Save all files.

Supporting other scripting languages

The server-based functionality you just created is also available in every major scripting language. Although Dreamweaver doesn't provide this functionality out of the box, frequently you can find the exact code structure you need by a quick search of the Internet. Just type the phrase *form data to email* or *web form mail* and you'll get thousands of options. Add your favorite scripting language to the search phrase (like *form data to email+ASP*) to target or narrow the results.

Here are a few examples:

- **ASP:** tinyurl.com/yalqnby
- **ColdFusion:** tinyurl.com/yep6br9
- **PHP:** tinyurl.com/ybxq5uk

You may also find these books good resources:

- *Adobe Dreamweaver CS3 with ASP, ColdFusion, and PHP: Training from the Source,* Jeffrey Bardzell and Bob Flynn, Adobe Press (2007)
- *The Essential Guide to Dreamweaver CS4 with CSS, Ajax, and PHP,* David Powers, friends of ED (2008)
- *Foundation Flex for Developers: Data-Driven Applications with PHP, ASP.NET, ColdFusion, and LCDS,* Sas Jacobs, friends of ED (2007)

Styling forms

Although the form and the email application you've been working on in this lesson are now functional, it's mostly *un*-styled. Good styling can enhance form readability and comprehension and can make it easier to use. In the following exercise, you'll style your form by creating a new custom style sheet.

1 If necessary, open or switch to **signup.html**.

2 Open the CSS Styles panel.

You'll create a new style sheet just for forms; that way it can be attached to this and other form pages but not to the entire site. Separating the CSS rules for forms from the master style sheet limits the amount of code that must be downloaded and creates a more efficient site overall. Less code means faster downloads and a better user experience.

3 At the bottom of the CSS Styles panel, click the Attach Style Sheet ( ) icon.

The Attach External Style Sheet dialog box appears

4 In the File/URL field, type **forms.css**. Select the Link and Screen options. Click OK.

Dreamweaver alerts you that the named style sheet does not exist.

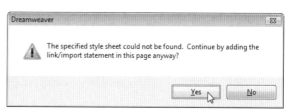

5 Click Yes to link to the new style sheet.

6 Insert the cursor in the legend text *Your Contact Information*. Click the New CSS Rule icon.

The New CSS Rule dialog box appears.

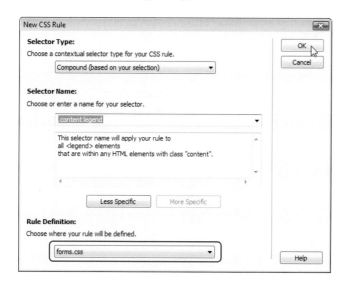

7 At the bottom of the dialog box, select the **forms.css** style sheet from the pop-up menu. This tells Dreamweaver to define your new rule in the **forms.css** page.
Choose Compound from the Selector Type menu.
Edit the Selector Name to read `.content legend`.
Click OK.

Dreamweaver asks if you want to create the **forms.css** style sheet.

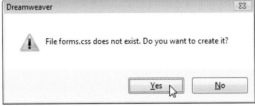

8 Click Yes to create the style sheet.

9 In the Type category Font-size field, enter **110%**.
In the Font-weight menu, choose bold.
In the Color field, type **#090**.
Click OK.

10 Create a new compound CSS rule in **forms.css**.
Name the rule `.content fieldset`.

11 In the Box category, set all padding fields to **10px**.

12 In the Border category, enter these settings in all fields: **solid**, **2px**, and **#090**.
Click OK.

Now, let's reset the paragraph indents in the field sets.

13 Insert the cursor in one of the <p> elements in the second field set.
In the CSS Styles panel, click the New CSS Rule icon.

14 In the Selector Type menu, choose Compound.
Edit the selector name to be `.content fieldset p`.
Click OK.

15 In the Box category, set the Left and Right padding to **0**.
Click OK.

The text is no longer indented.

16 Save all files.

17 Preview the page in the primary browser.

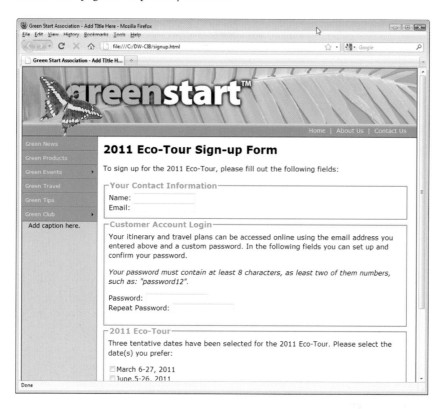

In this lesson, you built a user-fillable form with a variety of HTML and Spry form elements. You created and attached a custom style sheet to liven up its appearance. In the browser, you will be able to test all the form fields. When you click the Email Tour Request button, the form data will be passed to the file **email_form.php**. If the page is previewed in a PHP-enabled system, an email will be generated and sent to the email address targeted in the PHP code.

At the moment, this form simply collects the data and processes it as a standard, text-based email. The recipient still has to access and further process the data manually going forward. To take this process to the next level of automation, you can use Dreamweaver to modify **signup.html** so that it will insert the information directly into a web-hosted database.

● **Note:** If you to try submit the form you will probably receive an error message. That's because the code you created is designed to work on the fictitious GreenStart website running a PHP server. For your own website, insert email addresses supported by your server and modify the code as necessary.

Review questions

1 What is the purpose of the `<form>` tag?

2 What does selecting the Attach Label Tag Using 'for' Attribute option do?

3 What advantages do the Spry Form widgets have over standard form objects?

4 What's the difference between a standard text field and a text area?

5 What's the main difference between radio buttons and checkboxes?

6 How do you specify that separate radio buttons belong to a group?

7 What is the purpose of the `<fieldset>` element?

Review answers

1 The `<form>` tag wraps around all the form elements and includes an action attribute that defines the file or script to handle the form processing.

2 It connects the `<label>` tag to the form element, which has a matching ID value.

3 Spry Form widgets make it easier to create form elements. They include built-in validation to ensure that the data submitted is properly formatted and, if required, completed.

4 A standard text field is intended for short character strings, whereas a text area can hold multiple paragraphs.

5 Radio buttons only allow for mutually exclusive choices, whereas checkboxes permit the user to select as many items as desired.

6 All radio buttons with the same name will be in the same radio button group.

7 A `<fieldset>` element is used to group related form fields together with an accompanying `<legend>` element that identifies the group. It helps to organize a form and clarify the purpose of the various form fields.

14 WORKING WITH ONLINE DATA

Lesson Overview

In this lesson, you will learn how to work with information stored in tables and databases to do the following:

- Create dynamic content based on HTML tables and XML data sets

- Select a server model

- Set up a testing server

- Connect to a data source

 This lesson will take about 90 minutes to complete. Before beginning, make sure you have copied the files for Lesson 14 to your hard drive as described in the "Getting Started" section at the beginning of the book. If you are starting from scratch in this lesson, use the method described in the "Jumpstart" section of "Getting Started."

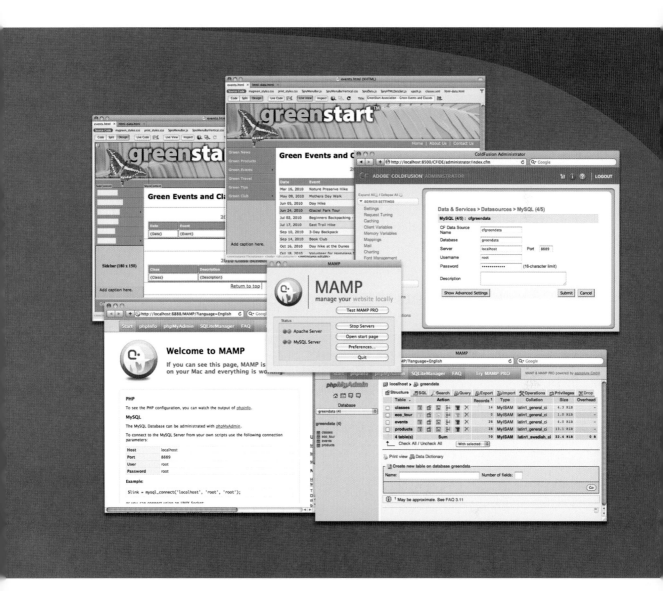

By its very nature, the web is a dynamic environment.
Get the most out of your website by connecting it to
live data using Spry, ASP, ColdFusion, or PHP.

Working with dynamic content

Except for a few interactive Spry components and a little Flash animation and video, the pages you have built in this training have been mostly static, like text and pictures on paper. Yet, the web is a dynamic environment. The live connection to the Internet makes the delivery of text, pictures, animation, and video only a click away.

Many of the most popular websites today supply content through two-way interactions with their visitors. This "query and response" method of content delivery can't be accomplished by HTML alone. It requires scripting and a variety of server-based applications that are supported by languages like Ajax, ASP, ColdFusion, JavaScript, and PHP, among others. This technique also requires information stored on the Internet, usually in the form of a table or database.

Until a few years ago, HTML tables were static containers. But now the lowly table has been liberated through the intervention of Ajax. Dreamweaver can easily harness all the power of Ajax through Adobe's Spry framework and some surprisingly powerful widgets. At the moment, you may lack the ability to develop more sophisticated applications, but there's no longer any excuse for putting static tables on your website.

Previewing the completed file

● **Note:** If you are starting from scratch in this lesson, see the "Jumpstart" instructions in the "Getting Started" section at the beginning of the book.

To see what Ajax can do for HTML-based tables, let's preview the completed file.

1   Launch Dreamweaver, if necessary.
    Open **events_finished.html** in the lesson14 folder.
    Examine the Events Calendar and Class Schedule tables.

    The Events Calendar and Class Schedule are Spry widgets that generate the tables dynamically. Note the placeholder text in the second row of each table, such as: {Date} and {Event}.

2   Preview the page in Live view.

    The placeholders are replaced by data from external sources, and additional rows are automatically generated. Note how the text in the Events table is sorted by date.

3   Click the header cell for the Events column.

The table sorts based on the names of the events.

4   Move the cursor over each row in the table.

As the cursor passes over each row, it changes color momentarily.

5   Click any row in the table, and then move the cursor away from that row.

The selected row changes color completely and remains highlighted as the cursor moves away.

6   Repeat steps 3–5 for the Class table.

The Class table exhibits the same behaviors as the Events table. The functionality for sorting tables interactively and creating the *hover* and *select* effects are all produced by Ajax scripting.

In the next exercise, you'll learn how to tap into the power of Ajax by using Spry to liberate data stored in HTML tables and XML files, and you will produce these same effects.

Using HTML and XML data

Before you can display data on your web pages, you'll need to establish a proper data source. In years past, this meant working with proprietary programming languages like ASP, ColdFusion, and PHP. These are powerful languages that are still used in thousands of websites today, and you'll learn more about them later in this lesson. But Ajax has revolutionized the role of data within many sites. As powerful as they are, the traditional languages can only display data changes after they reload the entire page. On the other hand, Ajax can update data in real time.

This capability is enabled through the use of HTML and XML data sets. In HTML, the data is stored in tables. XML (Extensible Markup Language) data is stored in a plain-text file using a standardized specification for marking up text. In the following exercises, you'll work with both HTML and XML data sets.

HTML (left) and XML (right) store information in different ways, but both are accessible to Dreamweaver.

```
<table>
    <tr>
        <td>May 09, 2010</td>
        <td>Mothers Day Walk</td>
        <td>Meridian Park</td>
        <td class="cost">Free</td>
    </tr>
</table>
```

```
<?xml version="1.0" encoding="UTF-8"?>
<dataroot xmlns:od="urn:schemas-microsoft-com:officedata"
generated="2010-03-23T15:34:13">
    <events>
        <event_ID>1</event_ID>
        <event_date>2010-05-09T00:00:00</event_date>
        <event_name>Mothers Day Walk</event_name>
        <event_location>Meridian Park</event_location>
        <event_cost>0</event_cost>
    </events>
</dataroot>
```

Working with HTML data

Until the advent of Ajax, data stored in HTML tables was static and unusable by the rest of the website. In other words, the data in a table on page A could not be used by page B unless you copied and pasted part or all of the data onto that page, too. The problem with this workflow is obvious. Once you paste the data onto multiple pages, you have to constantly update every page manually when the data changes, creating a lot more work and possibilities for error. Using the Adobe Spry framework, Dreamweaver can now tap into HTML table-based data in a new, dynamic way.

▶ **Tip:** HTML tables can be created quickly and easily from spreadsheet and database files. See Lesson 15, "Building Dynamic Pages with Data," for more information.

1   If necessary, launch Dreamweaver and switch to Design view. Open **events.html** from the site root folder.

This page contains two HTML-based tables filled with data. At the moment, the data here is static, but using Ajax via the Spry framework you'll be able to tap into this data for a variety of purposes. The first step is to move the table into a separate document.

2   Insert the cursor into the Events table and select the `<table#calendar>` tag selector. Press Ctrl-X/Cmd-X to cut the table.

3   Select File > New.
    Choose Blank Page > HTML > <none>.
    Click OK/Create.

    A new, blank document is created.

4 If necessary, insert the cursor in the Design view window.
Press Ctrl-V/Cmd-V to paste the table.
Insert a new, empty paragraph after the table.

Before a table can be used as a Spry data set, it must have a unique ID.

5 Insert the cursor into the table. Examine the tag selectors.

The tag selector displays `<table#calendar>`.

6 Select the `<table#calendar>` tag selector and examine the Property inspector.

Note: You may notice that none of the attached style sheets contain a `#calendar` rule. Although IDs are frequently used to create styling, no CSS rule has to be created to use the ID for this purpose.

Note that the ID field displays the text *calendar*. You applied IDs to both tables in Lesson 10, "Working with Navigation," and the ID was preserved when you copied and pasted into this file.

7 Save the file as **html-data.html** in the site root folder.

There's no limit to how many tables one file can hold, but don't go crazy; files containing lots of tables can take longer to download from the Internet and can detract from a user's overall experience.

8 Click the **events.html** document tab to bring it to the front.
Repeat step 2 to cut the Class table.
Switch to **html-data.html**.
Paste the Class table in the empty paragraph below the Events table.

Note: The order of the tables does not affect how you must use them.

9 Save and close the file.

10 If necessary, click the tab for **events.html** to bring the document to the front.
Insert the cursor at the end of the *Green Events and Classes* heading and press Enter/Return to create a new, empty paragraph.

11 Open the Insert panel.
Choose Spry from the Category menu.
Click the Spry Data Set button.

The Spry Data Set dialog box appears.

12 In the Select Data Type menu, choose HTML.
In the Data Set Name field, enter **ds_events**.
In the Detect field menu, choose Tables.
Click Browse and, from the site root folder, select **html-data.html** and click Open/Choose.

A preview of the data sources in **html-data.html** appears in the Data Preview window.

Spry data types

The proper data type is necessary for sorting operations. The available data types are:

- string—Alphanumeric data
- number—Numeric data only
- date—A full date, such as 1/1/2011 or January 1, 2011 or Jan 1, 2011
- html—Marked-up text, such as the lists in this example

  You may notice that the Cost column of the Events table contains text and non-text characters. If a field contains characters other than those accepted by that type of data, you should choose *string* from the Type menu.

13 In the Data Containers menu in the upper right, choose Calendar. Click the Next button at the bottom of the dialog box.

The Spry Data Set dialog box now displays a window to set data options. In this window you can identify specific types of data, such as text (string), numbers, dates, and HTML code. Identifying the data type is important if you want to sort data by certain values, such as date or cost, or use the data for other special purposes.

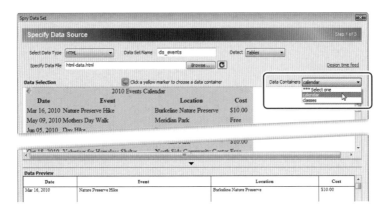

14 Choose Date from the Column Name menu.

In the Type menu, choose *string*.

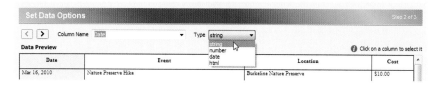

Note how the Use First Row As Header option is selected. If you use a table that doesn't contain a header row, this option should be deselected.

15 In the Sort Column field, choose Date.

Examine the order of the data in the Data Preview window.

Note how the column sorts incorrectly, based on the spelling of the month. You can correct this problem by changing its data type.

16 Click the first row of the Date column. In the Type menu, choose *date*.

The column is now sorted correctly, based on the event date.

For Spry applications, dates can be entered in two basic formats: by spelling out the month, day, and year—typically Jan (or January) 1, 2011—or by standard numeric notation, such as 1/1/2011. However, the Spry Data Set dialog box will not recognize dates written like this: 1-1-2011.

17 Click the first row in the Event column.

In the Type menu, choose *string*.

Select the Location column. In the Type menu, choose *string*.

Select the Cost column. In the Type menu, choose *number*.

Click Next.

The Spry Data Set dialog box now displays the insert options for the data set.

18 Click the Set Up button beside the Insert Table option.

The Spry Data Set–Insert Table dialog box appears. This dialog box allows you to specify what data will be displayed and how it will appear. Feel free to experiment by removing or changing the order of the data columns, and by specifying whether they are *sortable* or not.

Note: Choosing Numeric for the Cost column will cause an error when the data is rendered because the column currently contains non-numeric data. Before you can test the file successfully, you will have to remove the dollar sign ($) and any other non-numeric characters.

19 Enable the Sort Column When Header Is Clicked option, if necessary.

In the Odd Row Class field, enter **odd**.

In the Even Row Class field, enter **even**.

In the Hover Class field, enter **rowhover**.

In the Select Class field, enter **rowselect**.

Click OK.

This dialog box assigns CSS classes to style the table interactively, powered by JavaScript. These classes don't exist yet, otherwise you could select them from the menus.

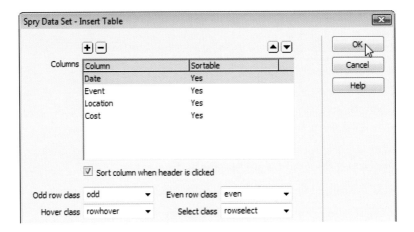

20 Click Done.

A two-row Spry data table placeholder is inserted in the layout. Some of the formatting on the placeholder should match the default table styling you created in Lesson 8, "Working with Text, Lists, and Tables." The Spry component is nearly complete; but it still needs custom CSS rules for the classes you assigned in step 19.

Styling Spry tables

The odd/even, hover, and select effects are styled using CSS rules invoked by JavaScript. These rules don't exist yet. You will also have to reapply some of the table styles you created in Lesson 8.

1   In the CSS Styles panel, select the last rule in **mygreen_styles.css**.
    Click the New CSS Rule icon in the CSS Styles panel.

    The new rule will be inserted at the end of the style sheet.

2   In the Selector Type menu, choose Class.
    In the Selector Name field, enter **odd**.
    Click OK.

3   In the Background category, enter **#FFC** and click OK.

4   Create a new CSS class for **even**.
    Assign it a background color of **#CFC**.

5   Create a new CSS class for **rowhover**.
    Assign it a background color of **#9C6**.

6   Create a new CSS class for **rowselect**.
    In the Type category Color field, enter **#FFF**.
    Assign it a background color of **#990**.

7   Save all files.

    A dialog box may appear indicating that files are being added to the SpryAssets folder to enable the Spry functionality. Before you test the Spry functionality, let's reapply the styling for the Date and Cost columns.

8   If necessary, click OK.

9   Insert the cursor in the header for the Date column.
    Select the <th> tag selector.
    From the Class menu in the Property inspector, choose w100.

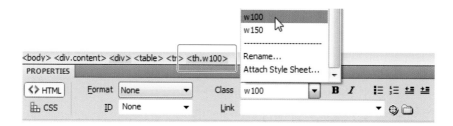

10 Select the cells in both rows of the Cost column.
From the Class menu, choose Cost.

The last step is to re-create the table caption. Tag selectors can help you locate specific markup when you work in Code view.

11 Insert the cursor in the table. Click the `<table>` tag selector. Switch to Code view.
Insert the cursor directly after the opening table tag.
Type **`<caption>2010 Event Calendar</caption>`**.

```
<table><caption>2010 Event Calendar</caption>
   <tr>
```

12 Switch to Design view. Save all files.

13 Preview the page in Live view and test the table behaviors.

When you click the header fields, the table sorts based on the data content. When you move the cursor over the rows, they change color. When you click any individual data row, the color of the row changes completely and the text appears in white.

The only problem seems to be coming from the Cost column, which is displaying an error message, NaN, that stands for "Not a Number." The original table was not designed for this use, and the data contains non-numeric characters. You'll have to remove these characters from the data table to complete the component.

2010 Event Calendar

Date	Event	Location	Cost
Mar 16, 2010	Nature Preserve Hike	Burkeline Nature Preserve	NaN
May 09, 2010	Mothers Day Walk	Meridian Park	NaN
Jun 05, 2010	Day Hike	East Side Park	NaN

Updating HTML data

You can correct the data table manually, or you can use Dreamweaver's Find/Replace command.

1 Open **html-data.html** from the site root folder. Select the dollar sign ($) in the first row of the Events table. Press Ctrl-F/Cmd-F.

The Find and Replace dialog box appears. The dollar sign ($) is entered in the Find window automatically.

2 Leave the Replace window empty. Confirm that the Current Document and Text options are selected, and click Replace.

The selected dollar sign is removed and Dreamweaver automatically selects the next dollar sign in the file.

3 Continue to click Replace to remove the dollar signs one at a time, or click Replace All to remove them all at once.

Clicking Replace All will close the Find and Replace dialog box. To perform the next step you will have to press Ctrl-F/Cmd-F to re-open the Find and Replace dialog box.

4 Replace the text *Free* with the number **0** (zero).
Delete the word *Donation* and leave the cell blank.

5 Close the Find and Replace dialog box.
Save and close **html-data.html**.

6 Click the tab for **events.html** to bring it to the front.
If necessary, preview the page in Live view.

Now that you have removed the non-numeric characters, the HTML-based data displays properly. But users may be confused by prices appearing without dollar signs. Although the dollar sign is incompatible in the data file, there's a simple trick that will allow you to use it in the final display.

7 Switch back to Design view. Insert the cursor before the data placeholder {cost}. Type **$**.

The placeholder now appears as ${cost}

8 Preview the document in Live view.

By adding the dollar sign before the data placeholder, Dreamweaver clones it automatically for each data row. You can use this method for all sorts of introductory characters and text.

9 Save all files.

Spry data sets can also be based on XML data.

Working with XML data

XML is a markup language closely related to HTML. They both use the same tag-based method for marking up text. The reason XML is called *extensible* is because, unlike HTML, you create your own tag names.

The language was invented directly in response to HTML's limitations in dealing with data in web applications. The simplest way to explain their different roles is this: HTML was designed to *display* data; XML was designed to *define* it.

In XML, data elements are placed between opening and closing tag pairs, like this:

```
<company>Meridien GreenStart</company>
```

XML can be written by hand or it can be exported from a number of data applications, such as MS Access, MS Excel, FileMaker Pro, and large-scale databases like Oracle and SQL Server. Non-proprietary databases—such as MySQL—are very popular on the web and are also compatible with XML. You will learn about other types of web-based database applications later in this lesson.

Spry data sets can use XML data and HTML data tables interchangeably.

1 If necessary, open **events.html**. In Design view, insert a new paragraph after the *Return to top* hyperlink.

The XML-based data set must be inserted outside the <div> element containing the HTML data set. Nested Spry data sets are not allowed in Dreamweaver.

2 In the Insert panel, click the Spry Data Set button.

The Spry Data Set dialog box appears.

3 From the Select Data Type menu, choose XML.
In the Data Set Name field, enter **ds_classes**.
Browse and select **classes.xml** from the lesson14 > resources folder.

4 Select the classes tag and note the Data Preview window. Click Next.

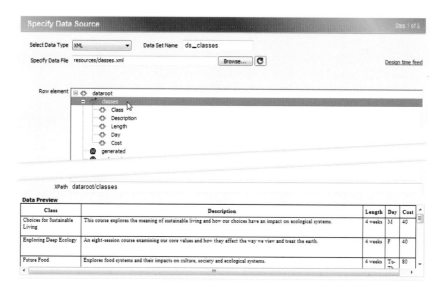

The Set Data Options screen appears.

5 For the data type for the first four columns, choose *string*.
For the Cost column, choose Number.
In the Sort Column menu, choose Class.

This file doesn't contain date data; the entire contents can be treated as text or numbers.

6 Click Next. For the Insert Table option, click Set Up.

7 Make sure the Sort Column When Header Is Clicked option is selected.
In the Odd Row Class field, enter or select **odd**.
In the Even Row Class field, enter or select **even**.
In the Hover Class field, enter or select **rowhover**.
In the Select Class field, enter or select **rowselect**.
Click OK.

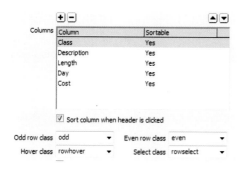

Selecting the class names from the menus can prevent you from typing the names incorrectly. Since the CSS classes already exist, the new table should be ready to function.

8 Click Done.

The XML-based Spry table is inserted in the page.

9 Save all files and preview the page in Live View.

Both tables display the appropriate data and behave just like the sample you previewed at the beginning of the lesson.

Spry data sets provide a powerful option for importing and displaying HTML and XML source materials dynamically, but it's not a perfect solution. Although Ajax makes the data *display* dynamic, the data *files* are anything but. For one thing, there's no native method for updating HTML and XML data that changes quickly, like sports scores and weather forecasts.

Instead, developers store data in traditional databases and then, using custom scripting, generate HTML and XML data files periodically or interactively upon a user request. This type of hybrid system brings together the benefits of both techniques, and many sites are following this model today. Although many sites have switched over to Ajax completely, quite a few are still using ASP, ColdFusion, and PHP. In upcoming exercises, you'll explore how some of these powerful tools and capabilities work.

Choosing a server model

If you decide to build dynamic web applications, one of the first choices you have to make before you write a single line of code is the server model you'll use for your site. Many factors go into this decision, including the purpose of the site, the type of applications you wish to develop, the cost of the server model, and even the type of database you wish to use. In some cases, the choice of database will select the server; in others, the reverse will be true.

For example, the MS Access database favors the ASP server model, which runs on Windows Server operating systems. On the other hand, the MySQL database, which is typically combined with either ColdFusion or PHP, runs equally well on all servers. Here's a quick overview of the major server models that you should keep in mind while you are making your choice:

ASP (Active Server Pages) is a Microsoft technology that runs natively in Windows. Dreamweaver provides server behaviors for ASP in Visual Basic (VBScript) but not in JavaScript. While some think it's difficult to learn and use, it's included for free with Microsoft's Internet Information Services (IIS), which means that all Windows users can immediately create applications with little extra setup. Also available is ASP.NET, the successor to ASP, developed to correct some of ASP's limitations and increase the speed and power of the resulting web applications. Dreamweaver no longer provides server behaviors for ASP JavaScript and ASP.NET, although you will still be able to hand-code and test these pages in the program.

ColdFusion is an Adobe server technology that uses a tag-based syntax that some feel is easier to learn and use than ASP or PHP. For many processes, ColdFusion requires fewer lines of code, which provides advantages during development and deployment of web applications. Unlike the other server technologies described here, ColdFusion is not free, although some feel that the productivity gains are worth the extra cost. ColdFusion can run on Windows, Linux/Unix, and Macintosh servers. To get a head start, you can download and install the free Developer's Edition of ColdFusion that enables you to build a fully workable dynamic site locally, before you upload it to the Internet.

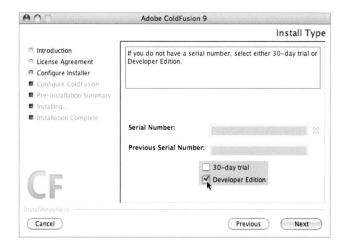

PHP (PHP Hypertext Processor), originally known as Personal Home Page, is now one of the most popular languages used on the web. It is free and works well with a variety of databases and other services. It offers a similar level of difficulty as ASP, but because of its popularity there are plenty of resources available to obtain code examples as well as support, which is also free, for the most part.

Configuring a local web server

There are two ways to test dynamic pages. You can upload them to your web host and test them live on the Internet; or, you can test the files *before* you upload them on your own personal computer. While nothing beats the authenticity of the actual Internet servers that will host your site, a local server offers advantages of both speed and security. It also allows you to work offline, without a live connection to the Internet.

Before you can test any of the dynamic web pages that you will build in the next lesson, you must install the applications and components needed for a local web server. This process is tedious and prone to error. It consists of numerous critical steps for loading and configuring all aspects of your chosen environment. As such, it is outside the scope of this book. Luckily, there are many sources both in print and online that can assist you in this endeavor. Here are a few:

In Print:

*   *Adobe Dreamweaver CS3 with ASP, ColdFusion, and PHP: Training from the Source*, Jeffrey Bardzell and Bob Flynn, Adobe Press (2007)

Online:

*   ASP and IIS—tinyurl.com/2yx46y *or* tinyurl.com/ybhfaef
*   ColdFusion—tinyurl.com/2h8hey
*   PHP—tinyurl.com/39p3gh

Setting up a testing server

Note: Internet-based servers usually require authentication using a user name and password, which you should obtain in advance from your server administrator.

At this point, you should have chosen your server model and successfully installed a local testing server. To preview and test dynamic pages, you need to connect to a testing server in Dreamweaver. You may also use the actual web server where you intend to upload your website.

When you choose to test a particular page, Dreamweaver copies the necessary files to the testing server and then loads the document in a browser or in Live view. The testing server is configured in Dreamweaver's Site Setup dialog box.

1   Select Site > Manage Sites.

2   Select DW-CIB from the Manage Sites dialog box. Click Edit.

3 Select the Servers category.

If you have an existing server configured, you can click the check box under the Testing column in the server list to identify it as your testing server. For the purpose of the following exercises, we're assuming you have chosen and configured PHP/MySQL as your server model and will use an Apache local web server to test pages on your computer.

● **Note:** The MAMP server is free, easy to set up, and compatible with both Windows- and Mac OS X-based computers.

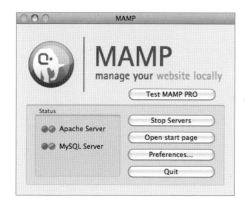

The specific examples shown in this book are based on the Windows/Macintosh Apache MySQL PHP (WAMP/MAMP) web servers, available for download at **tinyurl.com/crxqfs**.

4 Click the Add New Server button at the bottom of the server list.

5 Name the server **Local-PHP**.
From the Connect Using menu, choose Local/Network.

6 Click the Browse button to the right of the Server Folder field.
Navigate to the **MAMP/htdocs** folder (In Windows, this folder will probably be named **WAMP/www**).

● **Note:** The htdocs folder is created by MAMP automatically. Your computer will treat this folder as if it's a live web server and all sites located within it as if they're on the Internet.

7 Create a new folder in htdocs and name it **DWCIB-Test**.
If necessary, double-click the new folder to open it.
Click Select/Choose.

For Mac users, the Server Folder field displays the path **Applications/MAMP/htdocs/DWCIB-Test**. For Windows users, the path will be **C:\wamp\www**.

▶ **Tip:** Windows servers are not case-sensitive, so the capitalization of your file and folder names is not critical. Linux/Unix servers are case-sensitive. It's a good idea to write down file and folder names or use only lowercase characters to prevent server errors when loading test pages and content.

8 Enter the path to the testing site in the Web URL field.

For the MAMP PHP testing server, the default URL will probably be **http://Localhost:8888/DWCIB-Test**, but for other types of server models, the URL may be different. Enter the URL appropriate for your server. Without the correct URL, the page may not load correctly in your local server.

9 Click the Advanced button.

The dialog box displays the Advanced configuration options.

10 From the Server Model menu, choose PHP MySQL.

11 Click Save.

12 Click the Testing option in the Servers category to enable the testing server.

13 Click Save to dismiss the Site Setup dialog box. Dreamweaver will probably prompt you to rebuild the cache. Click OK.

14 Click Done to close the Manage Sites dialog box.

Your testing server for PHP is now configured. Although the server is intended for one specific language, other scripting languages may still be supported, depending on your server setup. As you may have noticed from the menu in step 10, Dreamweaver supports all the major server models. The importance of what server model you select can't be overstated. Changing server models once you start to build pages would probably require you to scrap all your work and start over.

Building database applications

One thing ties all of these applications together. They all require a database of some sort. Database applications come in two basic categories: stand-alone and server-based. Stand-alone applications like MS Access and Apple FileMaker Pro are usually accessible by one user at a time in a desktop environment. In some cases, multiple users can be allowed to access the data, but the total number of simultaneous users is typically small. Server-based databases—like IBM DB2, Oracle, and SQL Server—are much more robust and can easily host thousands of simultaneous requests for information. But with this power comes a hefty price tag. Between these two tiers exists a popular alternative: MySQL, which offers server-based capabilities at a great price—free. A more robust *enterprise* version of MySQL is also available, but it's not free. Check it out at tinyurl.com/235onn.

For the purposes of creating dynamic applications on the Internet, both types of databases can be used effectively. Which one you will use depends primarily on the type of data and how much of it you need to store, how many users will access the data at any particular time, and cost. If you expect the number of simultaneous users to be from 1 to 1000, then a stand-alone database application may work for you. If you're trying to build the next Amazon.com, then you need to focus exclusively on server-based applications.

Luckily for the purposes of this lesson, Dreamweaver interfaces with stand-alone and server-based databases in an almost identical fashion.

Database design basics

A database is similar to a spreadsheet. Data is stored in a series of columns and rows. Spreadsheets typically supply the names of the columns and rows for you, using letters (A, B, C) for the columns and numbers (1, 2, 3) for the rows. Databases differ in this area by requiring you to supply the column, or *field*, names. Rows, or *records*, are usually delineated with unique numbers or IDs. Some databases refer to these as *unique keys*, or just keys. The key allows you or your data application to retrieve a specific record or set of records.

Spreadsheets (left) and databases (right) have common roots and can perform similar tasks.

Simple databases store all the information being gathered in a single table, usually called a *flat* file. Using a single table for everything often leads to the duplication of data when certain types of information are entered multiple times, as when you take new orders from repeat customers. For example, the customer's name, address, and phone number are entered in the same table for each order they place. This type of redundant data bloats the size of the database unnecessarily and can cause errors over time. For example, if an order is shipped to an address listed in a previous order.

One way to prevent duplication is to separate certain types of data into their own tables and then link the various tables together. This process of linking multiple tables creates what is called a *relational* database and makes for a much more efficient system.

Relational databases typically store the *customer* and *product* information as separate functions, and then bring them together in an *orders* table that keeps track of what products are ordered by each customer. That way, if any changes need to be made to a customer or product record, it only has to be made in one place, where it will instantly update all other instances. All the popular databases in use today support these types of relationships.

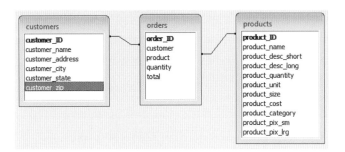

Relational databases store information in separate tables and connect them together in logical relationships. This prevents data duplication and makes the database function more efficiently.

An online database is typically stored within a subfolder of the target website, where it can be accessed by any page on the site. Databases can provide a variety of different types of information, from product descriptions and pricing, to customer names and addresses, to complete site editorial content. While some databases are configured to be read-only, where data is served in only one direction, most online databases are capable of both serving and capturing data, providing the utmost power and flexibility.

Connecting to a database

Once your database is created, properly uploaded, and configured, you need to connect each dynamic page to it before the data can be accessed. Each server model features specific methods for connecting to a database. For our exercises, we will concentrate on the PHP/MySQL using the WAMP/MAMP environment as noted earlier.

Note: In some situations, the database will be stored within your own site. In others, the database may be hosted by the server itself and stored in a location to which you may not have access. Check with your IS/IT manager or your hosting provider for specific details about your configuration.

Connecting to MySQL

In a PHP/MySQL environment, database connections are handled by custom scripts or by configuration files located on your hard drive or on the server. These scripts and configuration files handle the connection and any required user authentication.

There are numerous ways to write the code for these items, depending on the server model and specific database, so it's best to consult your server administrator or support staff to obtain the proper syntax. Many times, Dreamweaver can help you create the needed files and write the necessary code. In this exercise, you will connect to a MySQL database on a PHP server model.

1 Before attempting to complete this exercise, you first have to install and configure the necessary files and components for a PHP server and MySQL database.

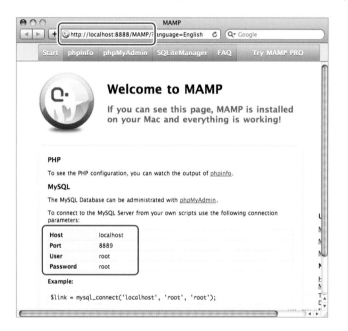

Here is a sample start page for a MAMP installation. The URL of this start page and displays the port: **8888** for the MAMP Apache server and the page displays the port: **8889** for the MySQL database server. Note the host name, ports, and other configuration settings in your own start page. You will need these specifications to connect to your servers and databases.

▶ **Tip:** In OS X, the *greendata* database folder located on the CD-ROM typically would be copied to the **MAMP > db > mysql** or in Windows to **wamp > bin > mysql5.1.36 > data > mysql** folder. However, your installation may be different.

The master Lessons folder on the disc that came with this book contains a MySQL folder holding the *greendata* database intended for this training. Copy this database to the testing server as required under your PHP/MySQL server installation.

If the *greendata* MySQL database is installed correctly, it will appear in the database list displayed on the phpAdmin page.

● **Note:** To find more information about setting up an all-in-one PHP server and MySQL database environment called MAMP, check out tinyurl.com/255l6n.

2 Configure a testing server in Dreamweaver for PHP/MySQL.

The PHP/MySQL configuration should point to the folder on your hard drive that will eventually hold your web content on the testing server. In Windows, it's typically named *www*; on the Mac it's called *htdocs*. However, the name on your server may be different.

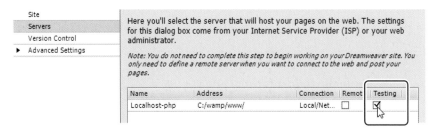

Note: You can't connect to a MySQL database until you set up (and launch) the compatible PHP testing server.

To learn more about setting up a testing server, check out the Dreamweaver Help file or tinyurl.com/ybn4hul.

Although you wouldn't normally develop applications for ASP and PHP at the same time for a single site, it's possible to install and configure both servers to run concurrently, if desired. Check out tinyurl.com/y9at5ab to learn how.

3 If necessary, launch Dreamweaver.
Create a new page based on the site template.
Save the page into the root folder as **products.php**.

MySQL databases can be used by all major server models. In this exercise, you'll use PHP.

4 Click the plus (✚) icon in the Databases panel and choose MySQL Connection.

The MySQL Connection dialog box opens.

Note: The Databases panel's appearance and function change slightly depending on what type of server model you choose.

5 When the MySQL Connection dialog box opens, create a connection name and enter your server name, your user name and password, and the database name. If you have multiple databases available or if you are unsure of the exact name of the database, you can click the Select button and choose it from a list.

▶ **Tip:** If the plus icon is not selectable, you may need to select a document type as described in the sidebar "Testing server testiness" that appears later in this lesson.

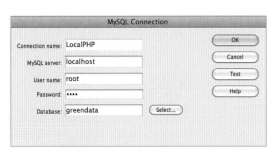

Extension tension

When you try to save a new document, Dreamweaver will often add the .html extension by default. If you use the wrong extension, you won't be able to connect to your data source. Although you can always add the appropriate extension manually, there's a way to force Dreamweaver to add the correct one for your server model automatically.

1 Create a new document from the site template.

2 Before you save, open the Databases panel.

3 Click the *document type* link that appears in the panel.

4 When the Choose Document Type dialog box opens, choose PHP or other appropriate document type from the pop-up menu and click OK.

5 Select File > Save.

When the Save As dialog box appears, Dreamweaver will prompt you for a name for the new document and will have added the appropriate extension automatically.

6 Click Test.

Dreamweaver reports a successful connection to the database.

7 Click OK. Examine the Databases panel.

The Databases panel displays the name of your database connection.

▶ **Tip:** If you receive an error message after this step, check if the MAMP server is running. If it is, check if you have the correct user name and password for the database.

8 Expand the database listing.

The listing displays the stored procedures, tables, and views contained within the database.

9 Save all files.

In this lesson, you learned how to work with HTML and XML data. Then, you selected a server model, configured a testing server, and created a database connection. You have developed the foundation for a dynamic website using PHP. In the next lesson, you will use this environment to build dynamic pages.

Testing server testiness

After you save your new files with the .php extension, Dreamweaver may still not enable the new database connection icon. Note the text in the Databases panel. It provides three or more steps that you need to accomplish before you can create or access your database connection.

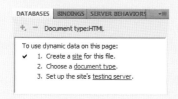

1   Note any checked items listed under the text *To use dynamic data on this page*. These have already been accomplished to Dreamweaver's satisfaction. Note the items that haven't been checked. These items must still be accomplished before you can make the connection.

2   Click the link in the first item that is not checked, and perform the requested task. It may require you to save the file with the proper extension or to choose the appropriate testing server.

3   Complete any remaining tasks.

Once you complete the tasks successfully, you should be able to make a database connection or access any connection that has already been made.

Review questions

1 What advantage does Ajax/Spry have over traditional data applications?

2 True or False: XML is a method for storing data in a plain-text file for use in web applications.

3 What is a server model?

4 What is a testing server?

5 You have a file compatible with your server model (.asp, .cfm, or .php), but your database doesn't appear in the Databases panel. How can you make the connection appear in the panel again?

6 True or False: The MySQL database can be used only on Linux/Unix and OS X server platforms.

Review answers

1 Ajax/Spry applications don't have to reload an entire page; they can update data in real time.

2 True. XML is similar to HTML and is used to identify data.

3 A server model is the basic environment used to build dynamic web applications. It also encompasses specific programming languages and scripting models, such as ASP, ColdFusion, and PHP.

4 A testing server is a server where dynamic pages are tested using a compatible server model. It is set up in the Site Setup dialog box.

5 Examine the Databases panel and the displayed steps for connecting to your data source. Complete any steps that are not checked. The data source should then be displayed again.

6 False. MySQL can be used on any web server.

15

BUILDING DYNAMIC PAGES WITH DATA

Lesson Overview

In this lesson, you will learn how to dynamically create web page content using information stored in tables and databases to do the following:

- Create a recordset from online data
- Insert data on a web page dynamically
- Create a master/detail page set
- Collect data from an online form and insert it into a database

 This lesson will take about 90 minutes to complete. Before beginning, make sure you have copied the files for Lesson 15 to your hard drive as described in the "Getting Started" section at the beginning of the book. If you are starting from scratch in this lesson, use the method described in the "Jumpstart" section of "Getting Started."

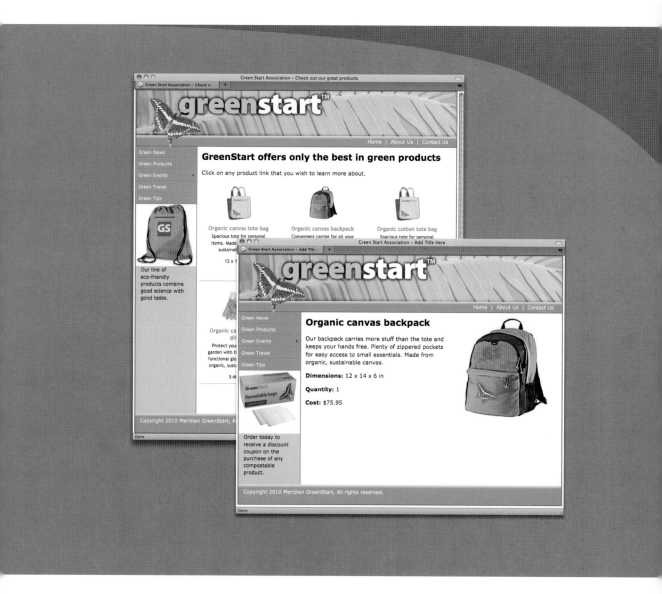

Dreamweaver has built in features to help you build rich, dynamic, data-driven web pages, using simple point-and-click tools.

Building pages with ASP, ColdFusion, or PHP

Note: Developing dynamic applications is an exacting chore that can fail for the simplest reasons. Read and follow every step in this lesson carefully.

In Lesson 14, "Working with Online Data," you learned how to select a server model, set up a testing server, and connect to an online database. Once connected, Dreamweaver makes it easy to access this data to create dynamic content.

Creating a recordset

The next step in the process of generating dynamic content is to create a recordset. A recordset is an array of information pulled from one or more tables in your database in response to a question posed by code in the web page written in Structured Query Language (SQL).

Warning: This exercise can only be completed if you have successfully configured a testing server and connected to the greendata database as you were instructed in Lesson 14, "Working with Online Data."

The question, or *query*, can be as simple as "Show me all the events in the Events table," or as complex as "Show me the events in the table that occur after May 1st that cost less than $10 and list them in descending alphabetical order." Frequently, the query is also dynamic—created by the user by clicking on checkboxes or radio buttons, choosing from menus, or typing into a text field (as you do on Google and Yahoo).

Note: If you were using the jumpstart method in Lesson 14, you may continue to use the same site setup, files, and folder for Lesson 15.

Like ASP, ColdFusion, and PHP, SQL is a robust language with its own terms, structure, and syntax. Dreamweaver can help you write most of the statements you'll ever need, but to perform complex data routines you may need to hire a professional or learn some SQL yourself. Adobe provides a good SQL primer at tinyurl.com/yk5xnag, or you can check out tinyurl.com/6l43z for the SQL tutorial offered by W3Schools.

In this exercise, you'll create the 2010 event calendar dynamically by using a table from your current database connection.

1 Open **events.html** from the site root folder. Examine the Databases panel.

The database connection you created earlier is not visible and the plus icon is grayed out, indicating that you can't create a database connection even if you wanted to. The Events page uses the extension .html, which is not compatible with any dynamic server model other than Ajax.

Tip: If the database connection doesn't appear, check the Databases panel to see what steps need to be completed before you can connect. In most cases, you will only have to click the link to select a document type, as described in Lesson 14.

2 Select File > Save As.
   Change the name to **events.php**.

For ASP you should use the extension .asp and for ColdFusion you should use the extension .cfm, or as appropriate for your server model.

The database connection should appear in the Databases panel. Dreamweaver provides the database connection automatically (if you made one already) as soon as you open or save a page with a compatible extension.

3 Select Window > Bindings.

The Bindings panel appears or comes to the front in its panel group. It is typically grouped with the Databases and Server Behaviors panels.

4 Click the plus (+) icon at the top of the Bindings panel.
Choose Recordset (Query) from the pop-up menu.

The Recordset dialog box appears. The current database connection should appear in the Connection menu, by default. If you have more than one database connection, the dialog box may not display the one you desire.

5 Select the desired database connection from the Connection menu and click the Simple button, if necessary.

By selecting options within this dialog box, Dreamweaver enables you to write sophisticated SQL statements without having to know a single line of the SQL language. The Advanced version of the Recordset dialog box allows you to create more complex SQL statements.

6 In the Name field, enter **rs_events**.

This field creates the name of the recordset that will be referenced in the query.

7 From the Table menu, choose **events**.

This selection identifies the table from which the data will be retrieved.

8 If necessary, click the All option for the Columns radio button.

This option indicates that you want to retrieve data from all columns in the table.

9 In the Filter section, choose event_date from the first menu.
Choose >= from the drop-down beside the first menu.
Choose Entered Value from the second menu.
Then in the subsequent field, enter the current date in the yyyy/m/d format.

▶ **Tip:** If the greendata database doesn't appear in the Databases panel, you may need to click the Define button and enter your login information again.

● **Note:** In the MySQL database, the year is entered first.

The Filter section refines the search by targeting specific data and excluding others. These selections are requesting a list of events from the table that take place today or in the future. Events scheduled prior to today's date will be ignored and should not appear in the results.

10 In the Sort menu, choose event_date.
   In the subsequent menu, choose Ascending.

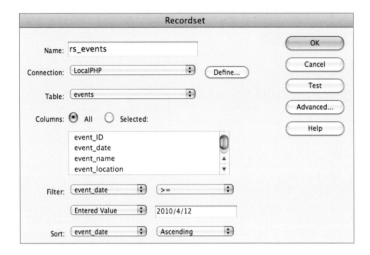

The Sort section allows you to display the data in ascending or descending alphanumeric order.

11 Click the Test button.

If everything works properly, the Test SQL Statement dialog box will appear displaying the results from the query you just constructed. If you don't see any data or if an error message appears, it could mean that the table has no records that meet your search criteria or that you have to troubleshoot your database, database connection, or testing server configuration.

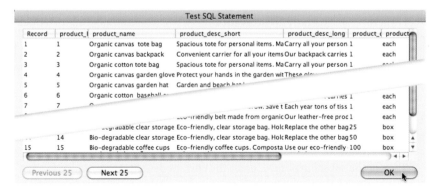

12 Click OK to return to the Recordset dialog box.
Click the Advanced button.

The Recordset dialog box provides advanced options for creating an SQL statement. You should notice that the SQL statement you created is displayed in the SQL field of the dialog box. If you already know how to write SQL statements, you can enter them directly into this field. Note the sections in the dialog box that are devoted to variables and database items. These built-in point-and-click productivity enhancements help to speed up the process of writing statements by hand by giving you quick access to your data resources and specific SQL commands.

Note the date text displayed in the SQL window. This is the date you entered in step 9. Entering a date in this fashion is fine if the date doesn't change. The problem here is that you want the table to show only current and future events. By tomorrow, the filter you created will be out of date. Instead, you need to enter a special SQL function that will always remain valid.

13 Select and delete the date.

14 Type **now()** in the field.

The now() function obtains the current time and date from the server to use for the data filter. The manually entered date is no longer needed.

15 Click the Test button.

The Test SQL Statement dialog box appears displaying the query result. It should look identical to the test you performed in step 11.

16 Click OK to complete the recordset.

Recordset (rs_events) appears in the Bindings panel.

● **Note:** Many times you can copy and paste SQL statements from other programs, like Microsoft Access, into this dialog and they will work just fine.

● **Note:** The table contains dates up to 12/31/2011. If the date you enter in the dialog box is after 12/31/2011, your recordset will be empty.

17 Expand Recordset (rs_events) and examine the items displayed.

The recordset contains items for all five data columns in the Events table.

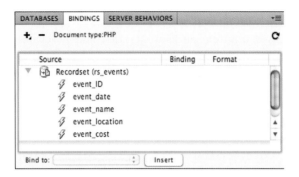

18 Save all files.

You are now ready to create a dynamic web page. In the next exercise, you will learn how to display data generated by a recordset.

Displaying data from a database

Now that you have all the cogs installed, the only thing left to do is put the machinery into action. As with most of the other steps, displaying data in Dreamweaver is a simple point-and-click process.

1 If necessary, open **events.php** or the file you created in the previous exercise.

The file's extension should be compatible with your server model now, and it should feature the database connection and recordset you created previously. But the page also displays two Spry-based recordsets. You're not going to use the Spry data, but that doesn't mean you have to start completely from scratch. You will discard the Spry data sets and support code, but reuse the table placeholder.

2 Insert the cursor in the Events table placeholder. Select the tag selector for the <table> placeholder. Press Ctrl-X/Cmd-X to cut the table.

The Spry table was contained in a <div> element that contains a reference to the Spry data set and is no longer needed. If you haven't moved your cursor, the <div> element is still displayed in the tag selectors.

3 Select the <div> tag selector. Press Delete.

Although they probably won't cause any trouble, you should also delete the unneeded Spry code references.

4 Switch to Code view. In the <head> section you will find approximately 12 lines of code specific to the Spry data tables within the `<!-InstanceBeginEditable name="head" -->`... `<!InstanceEndEditable -->` tags.

5 Select the code between these tags and delete it.

```
12  <!-- InstanceBeginEditable name="head" -->
13  <script src="SpryAssets/SpryData.js" type="text/javascript"></script>
14  <script src="SpryAssets/SpryHTMLDataSet.js" type="text/javascript"></script>
15  <script src="SpryAssets/xpath.js" type="text/javascript"></script>
16  <script type="text/javascript">
17  var ds_events = new Spry.Data.HTMLDataSet("html-data.html", "calendar", {sortOnLoad: "Date",
    sortOrderOnLoad: "ascending"});
18  ds_events.setColumnType("Date", "date");
19  ds_events.setColumnType("Cost", "number");
20  var ds_classes = new Spry.Data.XMLDataSet("lesson08/resources/classes.xml",
    "dataroot/classes", {sortOnLoad: "Class", sortOrderOnLoad: "ascending"});
21  ds_classes.setColumnType("Cost", "number");
22  </script>
23  <!-- InstanceEndEditable -->
```

You won't be able to delete the tags themselves because they are part of the template markup and locked.

● **Note:** Deleting this code will also disable the Spry features of the Class table.

6 Switch to Design view.

7 Insert the cursor at the end of the *Green Events and Classes* heading. Press Ctrl-V/Cmd-V to paste the table placeholder.

The table placeholder appears below the heading. It contains Spry code residue that should also be deleted.

8 Insert the cursor in the table header row. Switch to Code view and examine the header row elements.

Each of the <th> elements contains a `spry:sort="..."` attribute.

9 Delete the `spry:sort="..."` attributes from each of the <th> elements. Be careful not to delete any `class="..."` attributes.

Note the other Spry attributes in the data row.

```
<table><caption>2010 Event Calendar</caption>
  <tr>
    <th class="w100" spry:sort="Date">Date</th>
    <th spry:sort="Event">Event</th>
    <th spry:sort="Location">Location</th>
    <th class="cost" spry:sort="Cost">Cost</th>
  </tr>
  <tr spry:repeat="ds_events" spry:odd="odd" spry:even="even" spry:hover="rowhover" spry:select="rowselect">
```

10 Delete all Spry references in the data row.

All Spry references in the Events table are gone.

11 Switch to Design view and save all files.

Converting the Spry data placeholders for the current workflow is a simple process.

12 In the table, select the {Date} placeholder.

13 Open the Bindings panel, if necessary.
Expand the rs_events recordset.

14 In the Bindings panel, select the event_date field.
Click the Insert button at the bottom of the Bindings panel.

A new {rs_events.event_date} placeholder appears in the table cell, replacing the Spry placeholder.

15 Select the {Event} placeholder.
Replace it with the event_name field.

16 Select the {Location} placeholder.
Replace it with the event_location field.

17 Select the {Cost} placeholder.
Replace it with the event_cost field.

Date	Event	Location	Cost
{rs_events.event_date}	{rs_events.event_name}	{rs_events.event_location}	{rs_events.event_cost}

18 Save all files.

When working on dynamic pages, it's essential to test the functionality frequently. But unlike the Spry data structure, certain files must be uploaded to the testing server before you can preview the current dynamic layout.

Staging files on the testing server

● **Note:** You won't be able to test this page until you have successfully installed and configured a local testing server for PHP and MySQL. See Lesson 14 for more details.

You won't be able to test this file in Live view or in a browser until you upload specific files that connect the page to the database to the local testing server. So, what files need to be uploaded? Luckily, Dreamweaver will handle the logistics for you.

1 Select Live view.

Dreamweaver prompts you to update the file on the testing server.

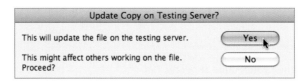

2 Click Yes to update the file on the testing server.

Dreamweaver should prompt you to upload dependent files. If this is the first time you have tested this file, click Yes. This will upload whatever files are needed to display this page properly. Once the dependent files are uploaded, there's probably no need to upload the dependent files again unless you make significant changes to this page.

If Dreamweaver didn't prompt you to upload dependent files, you probably have to modify a setting in Dreamweaver Preferences. Under the Site category, select the Dependent Files option for both the Get and Put operations.

3 Click Yes to upload dependent files.

The table displays one row of data. To display more data, you have to add a *repeat region* behavior.

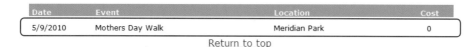

Date	Event	Location	Cost
5/9/2010	Mothers Day Walk	Meridian Park	0

Return to top

Adding a repeat region

Data placeholders can only display one record at a time. To see more than one record, you have to wrap the placeholders in a server behavior called a repeat region.

1 Position the cursor at the beginning of the data row of the table and select the entire row. Select the `<tr>` tag selector.

2 Select Window > Server Behaviors.
In the Server Behaviors panel, click the plus (✚) icon, and choose Repeat Region from the pop-up menu.

The Repeat Region dialog box appears. The Recordset menu displays rs_events as the current recordset. By default, the behavior will display ten records at a time. You can specify a different number or display all the records at once.

When you choose to display fewer than all the records, you will also have to insert a *record paging* behavior to permit the user to view the remaining data. For this table, let's keep things simple and display all the records.

Note: The proposed workflow for this exercise includes a local web server. The MySQL database is currently loaded on your own hard drive and hosted by this server. You may also configure this site to use an Internet-based PHP/MySQL web server. In that case, you will have to upload and configure the included MySQL database before proceeding.

Note: For the dynamic content to work properly, you'll need to upload the dependent files to the testing server at least once for this exercise.

Note: When you preview a file in Live view, Dreamweaver uploads any needed files to the testing server before displaying the content.

3 Select the radio button for All Records. Click OK.

A gray tab displaying the word *Repeat* appears above the data row of the table.

	Event	Location	Cost
{rs_events.event_date}	{rs_events.event_name}	{rs_events.event_location}	{rs_events.event_cost}

⬤ **Note:** Except for
the date filtering, the
steps needed to replace
the remaining Spry
Class table with a PHP
equivalent are identical
to the ones described in
this exercise. If you have
the time, put your new
skills to the test and try
replacing the remaining
Spry widget on your
own.

4 Save all files. Preview the page in Live view.

The table displays all the upcoming events from today's date into the future. As you may have guessed, you have only scratched the surface of the possibilities you can achieve with dynamic web pages. In the next exercise, you will build one of the most common dynamic applications: a master/detail set. In the next exercise, you will build one of the most common dynamic applications: a master/detail set.

Bonus Exercise:
Creating a dynamic table for classes and seminars

Before you move on to the next exercise, use the skills and understanding you have learned so far to rebuild the Spry table for the classes and seminars. The steps to recreate this table are simple and straightforward:

⬤ **Note:** You may
need to click the Simple
button to return to
the simple recordset
dialog box.

1 Create a recordset that returns data from all fields of the *classes* table in the database. Unlike the events recordset, there's no need to filter or sort the class data by date.

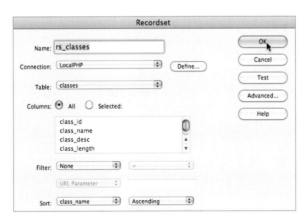

2 Select the Spry table and cut it into memory. Delete the Spry `<div>` element and paste the table back into the layout at the same position.

3 Clean up any residual Spry code left in the table.

4 Insert data placeholders from the new recordset into the appropriate data row cells.

5 Apply a repeat region server behavior on the data row.

6 Test the results.

7 Save all files.

Displaying data dynamically is a huge improvement over static lists and tables. Allowing users to interact with data engages them in the process in a way that can't be done otherwise. That's where the concept of the master/detail page set comes from.

It's a common scenario on many websites: a page displays a list of several products or events and you click on the one that interests you most; then the website loads a new page with specific details about the item you clicked. But what you didn't see, or notice, is how the first, or *master,* page, passed your request to the second, or *detail,* page. In the next exercise, you'll learn how to create a master/detail page set.

Creating a master/detail page set

The master/detail page set is used frequently on data-driven websites. By adding a hyperlink to the displayed data, you allow visitors to navigate to a new page that will display information specific to the selected item. Master/detail page sets can be created using ASP, ColdFusion, PHP, or Spry. The steps and procedures are similar for each server model. ASP provides a built-in server behavior to link to the detail page, while ColdFusion and PHP require you to build the dynamic link by hand.

Creating the master page

In this exercise, you will create a master/detail page set using your existing database connection.

1 Launch Dreamweaver, if necessary, and open the **products.php** page you created in Lesson 14.

You'll use this page as the master.

2 Select the text *Add main heading here.*
Type **GreenStart offers only the best in green products** to replace the text.

3 Select the text *Add content here.*
Type **Click on any product link you wish to learn more about** to replace the text.

4 Press Enter/Return to insert a new paragraph.

5 Open the Databases panel to ensure that the connection is still available.

6 Click the Bindings tab to bring the panel to the front, or select Window > Bindings. Click the plus (➕) icon and choose New Recordset from the Bindings panel pop-up menu.

> ⬤ **Note:** You created the **products.php** page in Lesson 14. If you skipped that lesson, you will need to create the file now and connect it to your database. See Lesson 14 for more details.

7 Name the recordset **rs_products**.

From the Connection menu, choose LocalPHP.

From the Table menu, choose products.

In the Sort menus, select product_category and Ascending.

Click Test.

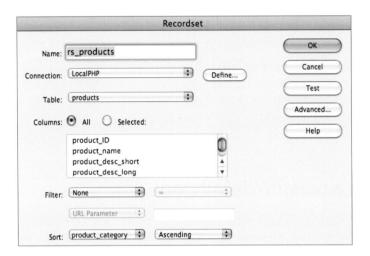

The Test SQL Statement dialog box displays a list of product data from the greendata database.

8 Click OK in all dialog boxes to return to the document window.

The rs_products recordset appears in the Bindings panel. There's no restriction on how you use the data fields in the recordset. You can insert them once, multiple times, or not at all. They can also be displayed in any order on the page.

9 If necessary, insert the cursor in the empty paragraph you created in step 4.

10 Open the Insert panel.

Click Insert Div Tag.

If necessary, choose At Insertion Point.

In the Class field, type **productmaster**.

Click OK.

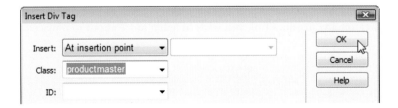

The new <div> element appears with the placeholder text selected. If you insert a field from the recordset, it will automatically replace the placeholder text.

11 In the Bindings panel, select the product_name field.
Click Insert.

The text {rs_products:product name} replaces the placeholder text in `<div.productmaster>`.

12 Format {rs_products:product_name} as a Heading 3.
Insert a new paragraph after the placeholder.

13 In the next line, insert the product_desc_short field.
Create a new paragraph and insert the product_size field.

```
{rs_products.product_name}

{rs_products.product_desc_short}

{rs_products.product_size}
```

14 Save all files. Preview the page in Live view. If prompted to Put Dependent Files, choose Yes.

● **Note:** If you try to preview the page in a browser, it will show you only the raw HTML page unless you upload all the dependent files to the testing server. But Live view should work fine.

If your testing server is properly configured, Dreamweaver will display the selected three fields of the first record of the database in the document window. But dynamic content isn't limited to text; you can display images dynamically, too.

Displaying images dynamically

What would a product page be without pictures of the products? Adding images to the product description is no more difficult than inserting text. In this exercise, you'll learn how to insert dynamic images into your layout.

1 Switch back to Design view.

2 Create a new paragraph before the `<h3>` element in `<div.productmaster>`.

3 Insert the cursor in the new paragraph. In the HTML mode of the Property inspector, select Paragraph from the Format menu, if necessary.

4 Select Insert > Image.

The Select Image Source dialog box appears. Normally, you would select the desired image and simply click OK. But to insert a dynamic image, you have a few extra steps.

5 Click the Data Sources button.

The dialog box changes from a file browser to a display of the data fields from the rs_products recordset.

6 Select the product_pix_sm field.

The URL field in the dialog box displays a complex piece of code that will insert a picture based on the filename stored in the database field—in this case, product_pix_sm. But the field contains only the filename of the picture.

Since folder names and locations can change over time, it doesn't make sense to insert path information into a database field. Instead, you can simply build the image path statement in the dynamic code at the time you need it. That way, if you move pictures from one folder to another on the site, you only have to make one small edit in the code to adapt to the change.

7   Insert the cursor at the beginning of the Code field.
    In the field, type **products/**.
    Click OK.

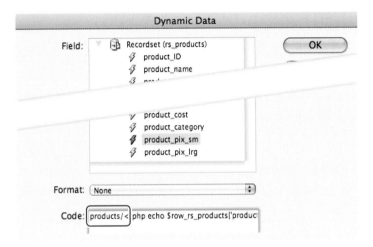

By inserting the folder name into the URL field, Dreamweaver will append the text *products/* to the image name to pull the desired image from that subfolder of your site, like this: **products/1-lrg.jpg**.

8   In the Image Tag Accessibility Attributes dialog box, select <empty> from the Alternate Text field menu. Click OK.

9   Save all files and preview the page in Live view.

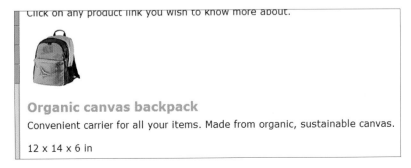

The small image of the sample product now appears on the screen. Now that you have one product displayed successfully, it's a simple matter to show multiple products as you did with the Event and Class tables earlier.

Displaying multiple items

To display more than one record, you need to add a repeat region as you did before. Although there's no table row as in the previous example, you can assign the behavior to the element `<div.productmaster>` instead.

1   Switch back to Design view and select the `<div.productmaster>` tag selector.

2   Click the Server Behaviors tab to bring the panel to the front, or select Window > Server Behaviors.

3   In the Server Behaviors panel, click the plus (➕) icon, and choose Repeat Region.

4   If necessary, choose rs_products from the Recordset menu.
     Select the radio button beside the Show field.
     In the Show field, enter **6**.
     Click OK.

A gray tab displaying the word *Repeat* appears above `<div.productmaster>`.

5   Save all files. Preview the page in Live view.
     Click Yes to update the page on the testing server.
     Click Yes to upload dependent files.

Dreamweaver now displays six records from the *products* table. Since `<div.productmaster>` defaults to 100 percent of the width of the main content area, the records stack one atop the other. To display the next set of six records, you have to add a paging behavior.

Creating a record paging behavior

Paging controls are usually inserted outside the repeat region so that they appear only once per page. In this exercise, you will create a record paging behavior for the rs_products recordset.

1 Click the Repeat tab to select the repeat region. Press the Right Arrow key to move the cursor outside the code for the `<div>` element and the repeat region.

The paging controls can be inserted as text or graphical elements on the page. Frequently, tables are used to control their presentation.

2 Insert a table with 2 rows and 4 columns.
Delete all other field entries.

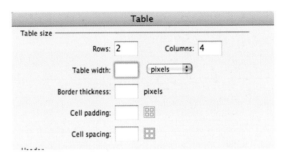

3 In the Table ID field, enter **master_paging**.

4 Enter the following text in the first row of the table:
Cell 1: << **First**
Cell 2: < **Previous**
Cell 3: **Next** >
Cell 4: **Last** >>

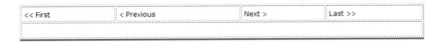

The angle brackets provide a visual cue to the user for the results of the paging behavior.

5 Select the text << *First*.
Select Insert > Data Objects > Recordset Paging > Move To First Page.

The Move To First Page dialog box appears. The Link field displays the item *Selection: "<< First"* and the Recordset field menu displays *rs_products.*

6   In the Move To First Page dialog box, click OK.

A hyperlink behavior is applied to the text that will load the first record of the *products* table.

7   Apply the following paging behaviors to the other words:
< Previous: Move To Previous Page.
Next >:   Move To Next Page.
Last >>:   Move To Last Page.

8   Save all files. Preview the page in Live view.

The first six records appear. If you click the paging controls nothing happens. To invoke the paging controls, you have to use a modifier key.

9   Hold down the Ctrl/Cmd key and click the *Next* paging link.

The Live view loads the next six records.

10 Hold down the Ctrl/Cmd key and click the *Last* paging link.

Live view loads the last set of records.

11 Test the *Previous* and *First* paging links.

All the paging controls work as desired, but there's a small problem. When you are on the first set of records, the *First* and *Previous* paging links are still visible although they don't do anything. This is potentially confusing to a user and is just poor interface design. Luckily, there's a server behavior intended just for this situation.

Hiding unneeded paging controls

Visibility is a common property that can be controlled by HTML and CSS. It's relatively easy to set an element's visibility and then invoke a behavior or scripted action to change it for a specific purpose. In this exercise, you will apply a dynamic server behavior that will modify the paging link's visibility based on the results of the recordset. In effect, it will hide certain controls when they are invalid.

1 Insert the cursor in the *First* link and select the `<a>` tag selector.

To hide all traces of the link, you have to select all the markup for the record paging element. The Show behavior can be accessed from the Insert menu or from the Server Behaviors panel.

2 In the Server Behaviors panel, click the plus (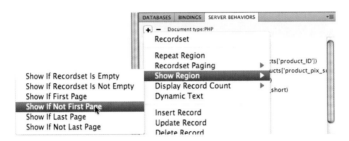) icon and select Show Region > Show Region If Not First Page.

The Show Region If Not First Page dialog box appears displaying rs_products in the Recordset menu.

3 Click OK.

A gray tab displaying the words *Show If* appears above the *First* link.

4 Select the *Previous* link, as in step 1.
Apply the Show Region If Not First Page server behavior.

5 Select the *Next* link and then the *Last* link, and apply to each the Show Region If Not Last Page server behavior.

6 Save all files and preview the page in Live view.

The first six records are displayed. Examine the paging links. The *Last* and *First* links don't appear.

7 Hold down the Ctrl/Cmd key and click the *Last* link.

The last set of records is displayed. Note that the *Next* and *Last* links are no longer displayed. The Show Region behaviors will automatically hide and display the paging links based on whether the page shows the first or last set of records, or somewhere in between. Dreamweaver offers over two dozen pre-built server behaviors that allow you to customize all aspects of the records display.

Displaying the record count

When you have lots of records to view, it's easy to lose track of what record you're looking at. It's a good idea to give the user a status report. In this exercise, you'll insert a behavior that will display the total number of records and pages in the set.

1   Switch to Design view.
    Select all four cells in the second row.
    Right-click the selection and choose Table > Merge Cells from the context menu.

2   Select Insert > Data Objects > Display Record Count > Recordset Navigation Status.

    The Recordset Navigation Status dialog box appears.

3   If necessary, select the rs_products recordset. Click OK.

    A complete block of code and placeholder text is inserted into the second row.

> Records {rs_products_first} to {rs_products_last} of {rs_products_total}

4   Save all files and preview the page in Live view.

    The status report displays the text *Records 1 to 6 of 28*.

> Records 1 to 6 of 28

5   Hold down the Ctrl/Cmd key and click the *Next* link.
    Examine the status report.

    The status report displays the text *Records 7 to 12 of 28*.

6   Switch back to Design view.

The page is nearly complete, but before you create the detail page and the behaviors that are needed to connect the two pages together, let's add a bit of style to the product display.

Styling dynamic data

Adding style and flair to dynamic data is no different than styling static pages. In this exercise, you will create CSS rules to format the text and structure of your dynamic data. Let's start by changing the way the products are arranged on the page.

1   Open the Products page you created in the previous exercises and switch to Design view, if necessary.

2 Open the CSS Styles panel.

Select the last rule in the **mygreen_styles.css** style sheet.

3 Create a new compound CSS class named `.content .productmaster` and apply the following styling:

Properties for ".content .productmaster"	
border-bottom... ▢	#090
border-bottom...	solid
border-bottom...	1px
float	left
font-family	"Trebuchet MS", Arial, Helvetic...
height	300px
line-height	120%
margin	10px
text-align	center
width	30%

4 Create a rule named `.content .productmaster h3` and apply the following styling:

Properties for ".content .productmaster h3"	
color	▢ #090
font-size	100%

5 Create a rule named `.content .productmaster p` and apply the following styling:

Properties for ".content .productmaster p"	
font-size	85%

● **Note:** Remember that the border-collapse option has to be entered manually. See Lesson 6, "Working with Cascading Style Sheets," for details.

6 Create a rule named `.content #master-paging` and apply the following styling:

Properties for ".content #master-paging"	
border	none
border-collapse	collapse
clear	both
font-family	"Trebuchet MS", Arial, Helvetica, sans-serif
margin-left	auto
margin-right	auto
margin-top	20px
text-align	center
width	50%

7 Create a rule named `.content #master-paging td` and apply the following styling:

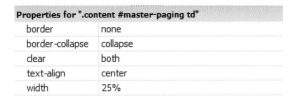

Properties for ".content #master-paging td"	
border	none
border-collapse	collapse
clear	both
text-align	center
width	25%

8 Create a rule named `.content #master-paging a` and apply the following styling:

Properties for ".content #master-paging a"	
color	#060
font-weight	bold
text-decoration	none

9 Create a rule named `.content #master-paging a:hover` and apply the following styling:

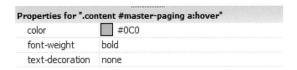

Properties for ".content #master-paging a:hover"	
color	#0C0
font-weight	bold
text-decoration	none

10 Save all files. Preview the page in Live view.

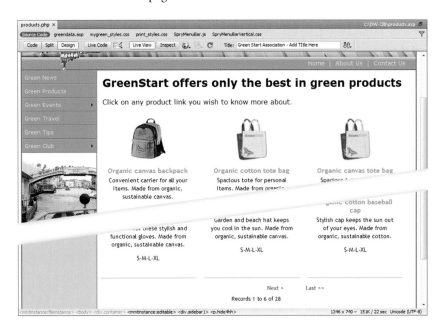

The new styling displays the products side by side in two convenient rows—taking up less space and permitting the user to see more products without scrolling. The paging controls enable the user to flip through the whole catalog simply by clicking. In the next exercise, you will learn how to add a special hyperlink to the master elements that will load a detailed view of a specific product.

Inserting a go-to-detail-page behavior

By keeping the product picture and descriptions small on the master page, you allow the customer to browse quickly through your entire catalog. The more products you can show comfortably in one place, the more likely it is that the customer will find something that interests them. Then, usually they want to learn more about one product. That's where the detail page comes in. In this exercise, you'll insert a special behavior in the dynamic placeholders that will load a detail page for any item clicked on the master page.

1   Open **products.php** and switch to Design view, if necessary.

A dynamic link can be added to text or pictures to take the user to a detail page. Although ASP provides a custom behavior for this purpose, you have to create this link yourself in ColdFusion and PHP.

2   Select the image placeholder in `<div.productmaster>`.

A dynamic link is added using the Link dialog box.

3   Click the Browse icon next to the Link field in the Property inspector.

4   When the Select File dialog box opens, click the Data Sources button.

5   Select the product_ID field.

When you select product_ID, the following code is inserted in the URL field.

```php
<?php echo $row_rs_products['product_ID']; ?>
```

6   Insert the cursor at the beginning of the text in the URL field.

7   Type **product_detail.php?product_ID=** and click OK.

The code you entered will pass the product_ID of the selected element to the detail page, where it should then be displayed.

8   Save all files.

Before you can test the functionality, you first need to create the detail page.

Creating a detail page

The detail page is almost identical to the master page in construction. Both create a recordset and display placeholders for specific fields. The major difference lies in that the master page can display all the records, while the detail page will show only one. In this exercise, you will create a detail page so that it will show information about only the product selected by the user.

1   Create a new page based on the site template.
    Save it as **product_detail.php**.

▶ **Tip:** If you're not using PHP, add the extension appropriate for your server model.

2   If the Databases panel doesn't display your current data connection, click the *document type* link and choose PHP or the appropriate server model for your workflow.

3   In the Bindings panel, create a new recordset named **rs_product_detail**.

    The Recordset dialog box appears. The previous recordsets you have created have shown all the records in a table. For a detail page, you have to add a filter to show only the record selected by the user on the master page.

4   Enter the following specifications in the Recordset dialog box:

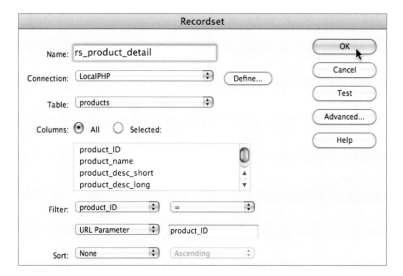

5   Click Test.

    A dialog box appears requesting a test value. You have to enter a value that would be pertinent to the specific field, such as the SKU or ISBN number of the product. The values in the current *products* table are simple digits from 1 to 28.

6   Enter **1** and click OK.

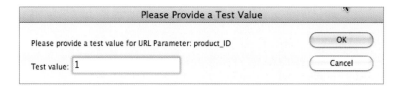

The Test SQL Statement dialog box appears displaying one record.

7 Click OK in all dialog boxes to return to Design view.

Now you're ready to build the detail page data display.

8 Select the text *Add main heading here.*
In the Bindings panel, select the product_name field.
Click the Insert button.

9 Select the text *Add content here.*
Insert the product_desc_long field.

10 Create a new paragraph.
Type **Dimensions:** in the new paragraph.
Insert the product_size field.

11 Create a new paragraph.
Type **Quantity:** in the new paragraph.
Insert the product_quantity field.
Press Ctrl-Shift-Spacebar/Cmd-Shift-Spacebar to insert a non-breaking space.
Insert the product_unit field.

12 Create a new paragraph.
Type **Cost: $** in the new paragraph.
Insert the product_cost field.

13 Insert the cursor at the beginning of the placeholder
{rs_products.product_name}.
Select Insert > Image.

14 Select the Data Sources button.
Select the product_pix_lrg field.
Type **products/** at the beginning of the Code field.
Click OK.

15 In the Image Tag Accessibility Attributes dialog box, select <empty> from the
Alternate Text field menu. Click OK.

16 Select the new image placeholder.
From the Class menu, choose fltrt.
In the Width and Height fields, enter **300**.

17 Save all files.

Before you upload the pages to the remote site, you should test the go to detail page behavior locally.

18 Open the products page. Preview the page in Live view.
Hold down Ctrl/Cmd and click one of the product names or pictures.

Live view loads the selected product data into **product_detail.php**.

You have completed the rudimentary steps for building a full-fledged online store. The design and construction of an online store, shopping cart, and payment gateway is complex and well beyond the scope of this book.

Prebuilt shopping cart and store solutions are available for all server models supported by Dreamweaver. They vary in cost and complexity to suit any need and budget. Some of the most economical solutions are offered by Google, Yahoo, and PayPal, among others, and they even simplify the method of receiving electronic payments by credit card and bank transfer.

In this lesson, you have created dynamic pages using live data. You've generated page content from an online database and built a complete master/detail page set. But, after all that, you've barely looked under the hood of what Dreamweaver can do with dynamic data.

Review questions

1 What is a recordset?

2 Why would you need to use a repeat region?

3 What is a master/detail page set?

4 For what purpose would you use record paging behavior?

5 How can you hide paging controls when there are no more records to display?

Review answers

1 A recordset is an array of information pulled from one or more tables in a database by a query created in Dreamweaver.

2 A repeat region allows the data application to display more than one record at a time.

3 The master/detail page set is a common feature of data-driven websites. The master page displays multiple records and provides dynamic links within each record, which allows you to load specific information about the selected item on the detail page.

4 A record paging behavior is used to load the results of a recordset, when only a limited number of records are displayed at one time.

5 Select the paging control link and apply a "Show" behavior pertinent to the recordset.

16

WORKING WITH CODE

Lesson Overview

In this lesson, you'll learn how to work with code and do the following:

- Select code elements in new ways

- Collapse and expand code entries

- Write code using code hinting

- Use Code Navigator to identify and edit CSS code

- Use Live Code to test and trouble-shoot dynamic code

- Use the Inspect feature to identify HTML elements and associated styling

- Access and edit attached files using the Related Files interface

 This lesson will take about 1 hour to complete. Before beginning, make sure you have copied the files for Lesson 16 to your hard drive as described in the "Getting Started" section at the beginning of the book. If you are starting from scratch in this lesson, use the method described in the "Jumpstart" section of "Getting Started."

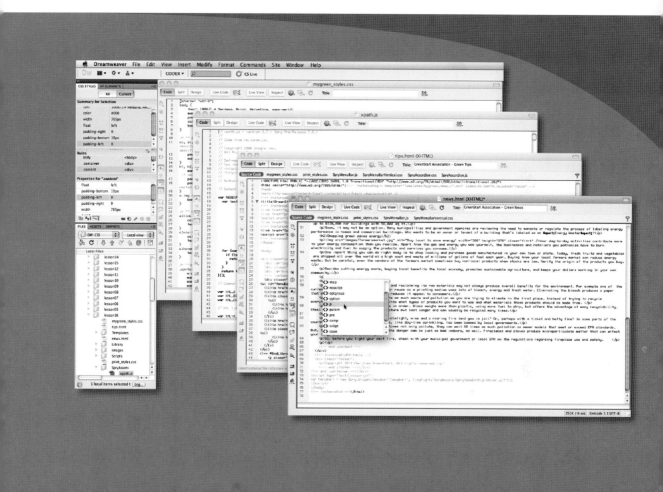

Dreamweaver's claim to fame is as a visually based
HTML editor, but its code-editing features don't take
a back seat to its graphical interface and offer no
compromises to professional coders and developers.

Code tools overview

As the leading WYSIWYG HTML editor, Dreamweaver allows users to create elaborate web pages and applications without touching or even seeing the code that does all the work behind the scenes. But for many designers, working with the code is not only a desire but a necessity.

That's why it's important to know that Dreamweaver makes it as easy to work with a page in Code view as in Design view. While the program is geared toward visual designers, Dreamweaver offers significant productivity tools for coders and developers, too. In fact, it helps to unify the entire web development team by providing a single platform that can handle almost any needed task.

You'll find that often a specific task is actually easier to accomplish in Code view than in Design view alone. In this exercise, you'll learn more about how Dreamweaver makes working with the code an effortless task.

1   In Dreamweaver, open **tips.html** from the site root folder.

2   Switch to Code view.

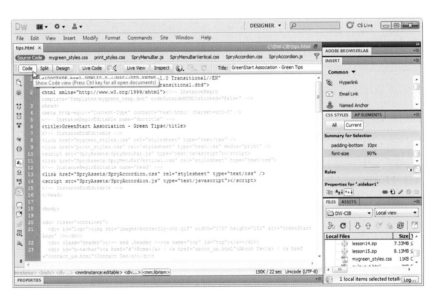

Note: The Code view options are only selectable when Code view is active.

3   Choose View > Code View Options, and examine the options available.

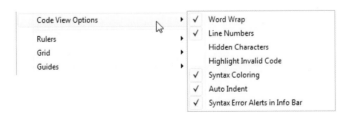

These seven options help to simplify code editing and improve productivity when working in the code. Note any check marks appearing beside the options, indicating that they are already selected.

Code view options

Word Wrap—Wraps long lines of code to fit them in the code window, making the code easier to read and edit.

Line Numbers—Displays numbers at the left margin of the code window to help quickly identify specific lines of code.

Hidden Characters—Displays icons representing spacing and breaks within the code that are normally invisible. An invaluable option in certain applications where line breaks and whitespace can affect the way the code operates.

Highlight Invalid Code—Visually marks code that is improperly constructed.

Syntax Coloring—Formats specific types of code to display in color to help you quickly distinguish tags and other markup from content.

Auto Indent—Automatically indents child code elements to make the markup easier to read.

Syntax Error Alerts in Info Bar—Displays a warning at the top of the Code view window identifying any structural errors in the code and pointing to the line on which the error occurs.

4 Select Word Wrap, Line Numbers, Syntax Coloring, and Syntax Error Alerts in Info Bar, if necessary.

For most purposes, these options should always be selected.

Code view and Design view are closely integrated, and many of Dreamweaver's features work identically in both. For example, you can use tag selectors in Code view to help quickly and easily select entire code elements.

Selecting code

Dreamweaver provides several methods for selecting code elements in Code view. One of the easiest ways is to use the tag selectors, as you have frequently done in previous lessons.

1 Scroll down the code and locate `<h1>Green Tips</h1>`.

2 Insert the cursor anywhere in the `<h1>` element. Examine the tag selectors at the bottom of the document window.

The tag selectors in Code view display the <h1> tag and all its parent elements, the same way as they do in Design view. Note how some elements are grayed out, indicating that they are part of the template and therefore locked.

3   Select the <h1> tag selector.

The entire <h1> element, including its content, is highlighted in Code view. It can now be copied, cut, moved, or collapsed. The <h1> element is a child of <div.content>. It would be difficult to manually select the entire <div> element within the Code view window, but the tag selectors make the chore simple. To select the parent element, you can click the <div.content> tag selector.

4   Select the <div.content> tag selector.

The entire <div> element is selected. But you'll notice that tag selectors for <div.content> are grayed out and *un*selectable. This is where Code view shines with a few of its own tricks.

5   Select View > Toolbars > Coding to display the Coding toolbar, if necessary.

6   Insert the cursor anywhere in the text *Green Tips* in the <h1> element.

7   Click the Select Parent Tag (🔖) icon in the Coding toolbar.

The <h1> element is highlighted.

```
47        <div class="content">
48  ⊟       <h1>Green Tips</h1>
49          <div id="Accordion1" class="Accordion" tabindex="0">
            [Select Parent Tag] div class="AccordionPanel">
51              <div class="AccordionPanelTab">At Home</div>
```

8   Click the Select Parent Tag icon again.

The entire <div.content> element is selected.

9   Click the Select Parent Tag icon again.

The entire <div.container> element is selected. It doesn't matter whether the elements are locked or not. Each time you click the button, Dreamweaver selects the parent element of the current selection.

Working with long sections of code can be unwieldy. But Code view offers a handy option to collapse long sections and make them easier to work with.

Collapsing code

Collapsing code is a productivity tool that makes it a simple process to copy or move large sections of code. Code sections are also collapsed when developers are looking for a particular element or section of a page and they want to temporarily hide unneeded code sections from view. Code can be collapsed either by selection or by logical element. Use the collapse and expand icons on the toolbar to the left to collapse or expand sections of code.

1 Select the first three items in the unordered list starting with: `<li>Wash clothes in cold water.</li>`.

These items are part of a long list of tips that are within an unordered list within a panel of the Spry Accordion. Note the selection markers near the line numbers on the left. The minus/vertical arrow icons indicate that the selection is currently expanded.

2 Click one of the minus/vertical arrow icons on the left or the Collapse Selection (⊟) icon in the Coding toolbar to collapse the selection.

The selection collapses, showing only the `<li>` code element and a snippet of text from the collapsed code.

You can also collapse code based on logical elements, like `<ul>` or `<div>`.

3 Insert the cursor in the `<ul>` tag. Click the Collapse Full Tag (⟡) icon.

The entire `<ul>` element collapses in the Code window, showing only the `<ul>` element and a portion of the next element. In either case, the code hasn't been deleted or damaged in any way. It still functions and operates as expected. Also, the collapse functionality only appears in Dreamweaver Code view; on the web or in another application, the code will appear normally. To expand the code, just reverse the process.

Expanding code

When the code is collapsed, you can copy, cut, or move it like you would any other selected element. You can expand elements one at a time, or all at once.

1 If necessary, insert the cursor in the collapsed `<ul>` element. Note the icon displayed on the left edge of the Code view window.

A plus/horizontal arrow is displayed, indicating that the code has been collapsed. To expand the code, you can click the plus/horizontal arrow icon.

2 Click the plus/horizontal arrow icon to expand the code.

The `<ul>` element expands, but the three `<li>` elements that were collapsed earlier are still collapsed. Dreamweaver provides a method to expand all elements at once.

3 Click the Expand All button in the Coding toolbar.

All collapsed elements are now expanded. Code can be added, edited, or deleted in Code view.

Adding new code

Code view isn't just for tweaking or troubleshooting the code, it's a fully functioning code-writing environment with numerous productivity enhancements for code writers. Besides the fact that Code view can color-code the tags and markup to make them easier to read, Dreamweaver offers code hinting for 10 different web development languages, including but not limited to HTML, CSS, JavaScript, ColdFusion, and PHP.

Code hinting for HTML markup is extensive and includes support for CSS. In this exercise, you will create a hyperlink to jump to the top of the page, as in Lesson 10, "Working with Navigation."

1 Open **news.html**. Switch to Code view, if necessary.

2 Scroll down and insert the cursor before
`<h2>Shopping green saves energy</h2>`.

3 Type **<** at the cursor position.

The code-hints menu appears, showing you a list of HTML-compatible codes that you can select from.

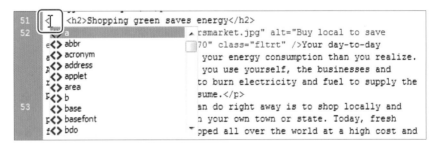

▶ **Tip:** You may also use the keyboard arrow keys to select the desired menu option and press the Tab key to insert it.

4 Type or select **p**.
Press the spacebar to insert a space.

The code-hints menu opens again; this time it displays compatible HTML attributes for the <p> element.

5 Double-click the `class` attribute.

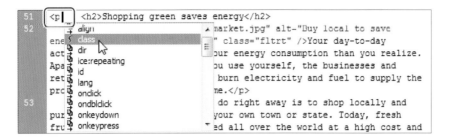

The code-hints menu now shows a list of available CSS classes.

6 Double-click the CSS `ctr` class.

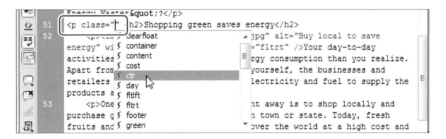

Dreamweaver inserts the `ctr` class within the quote ("...") marks and moves the insertion point outside the closing quote mark.

7 Type **>** at the cursor position.

The opening <p> tag is complete. Now you can build the hyperlink.

8 Type **<a** at the cursor position.
Press the spacebar to insert a space.

Code hinting offers a list of compatible attributes for the anchor element.

9 Double-click the `href` attribute.

Dreamweaver automatically creates the attribute and adds the proper structure, moving the insertion point between two quotation marks. A Browse link appears, enabling you to navigate to a file on the hard drive, if desired. In this case, the link is an internal reference to the named anchor *top* that you created in Lesson 10 and added to the template.

10 Type **#top** at the cursor position.

When you enter code manually, you have to move the cursor manually outside the element before you can continue.

11 Press the Right Arrow key to move the cursor outside the closing quote (") mark.

12 Type **>Return to top** at the cursor position.

This closes the opening <a> tag and creates the link text.

```
<p class="ctr"><a href="#top">Return to Top</a>| <h2>Shopping green saves
```

13 Type **</** to close the <a> tag.

Dreamweaver automatically closes the appropriate tag, in this case using the closing </a> tag. You can now close the <p> element, too.

14 Type **</** to close the <p> tag.

Press Enter/Return to insert a new paragraph.

The </p> is closed automatically by Dreamweaver, and the element and link are complete.

```
<p class="ctr"><a href="#top">Return to Top</a></p>
|h2>Shopping green saves energy</h2>
```

15 Copy the entire <p> element, with the hyperlink, and paste copies after each of the news items.

16 Save all files.

As you can see, Dreamweaver simplifies the task of writing code by providing a variety of productivity enhancements including code hinting and automatic code completion. These features work in a similar fashion for all the supported languages.

Some tools work in Code view the same way they work in Design view. Code Navigator is a good example of one.

Using Code Navigator

Code Navigator is an essential tool for troubleshooting CSS problems and identifying pertinent CSS rules for specific markup. It works identically in Design, Code, or Live view.

1 Click the document tab for **tips.html** to bring it to the front, or open it from the site root folder. Switch to Split view.

This document window splits, showing both Code and Design view. The document features a Spry Accordion containing the three sections for green tips.

2 In the Design view side, right-click the text *Green Tips* and select Code Navigator. Note the names and order of the CSS rules displayed in the pop-up Code Navigator window.

3 Repeat step 2 in the Code view side with the `<h1>Green Tips</h1>` code.

The names and order of the rules in Design and Code view are identical. But there is a limit to what Code Navigator can do by itself.

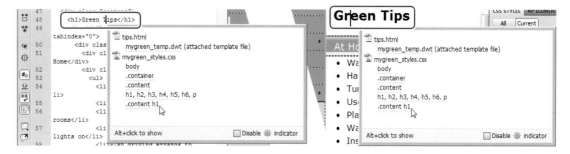

4 Click the Live View button. Test the functionality of the Accordion panels on the Design view side of the split.

The Accordion panels open and close interactively. Note how each panel displays a hover effect when the cursor passes over the panel tab. You can use Code Navigator to identify the CSS rules that format the Accordion structure.

Code Navigator can be accessed in any view of Dreamweaver.

5 Position the cursor over the *At Home* tab. Right-click the tab and choose Code Navigator from the context menu.

Note how the tab changes color when the cursor passes over it. Examine the CSS rules in the Code Navigator window and try to locate the rules creating the hover effect. Give up? Code Navigator can't identify the hover effect because it doesn't exist. The effect is generated by JavaScript live in the browser *only* when you interact with the Spry Accordion, otherwise the element is a static piece of HTML code. To help you identify the pertinent rules, Code Navigator will need the help of the Live Code feature and Inspect mode.

Accessing Live Code

Live Code is a feature that permits you to view how the code actually functions in the browser. This is especially helpful for all interactive processes or web applications that can alter the code, such as the Spry Accordion.

1 Click the Live Code button.

The Code view side of the document changes color, indicating that Live Code is active. The HTML code can't be edited when Live Code is active.

▶ Tip: If the pertinent code isn't displayed, you can click the At Home tab to focus the Code view split on the proper section.

2 Position the cursor over the *At Home* Accordion tab. Examine the code display carefully and note any changes. You may need to move the cursor over the tab several times to see the changes.

Note how the class of the `<div>` element containing the text *At Home* is changing interactively from `<div class="AccordionPanelTab">` to `<div class="AccordionPanelTab AccordionPanelTabHover">` and thereby invoking the hover state of the tab. You could write down the pertinent class names to edit them manually later, but there's a better way.

3 Position the cursor over the *At Home* tab. When the tab displays the hover effect, right-click the tab and choose Freeze JavaScript from the context menu.

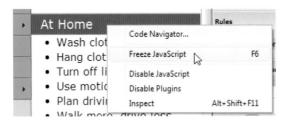

The hover effect freezes in state. A notice appears at the top of the document window indicating that JavaScript is frozen.

4 In the Code or Design view split, right-click the *At Home* text and choose Code Navigator from the context menu.

The Code Navigator window appears. This time it displays the rules that format the hover effect, as well as the ones that govern the PanelOpen behavior. By freezing the JavaScript while you were activating the hover effect, you were able to identify the pertinent CSS styling.

5 Press the F6 key or click the *Resume* link in the notice at the top of the screen to unfreeze JavaScript.

Using Inspect mode

A new tool has been added to Dreamweaver CS5 to help you to identify specific HTML elements and their associated CSS formatting: Inspect mode.

Inspect mode is a new feature in Dreamweaver CS5 that works together with Live view to survey your page content and connect HTML elements to the pertinent CSS styling, visually. Inspect mode can work with Live view alone, or combined with Live view and Live Code.

1 If necessary, open **tips.html**, switch to Split view, and select View > Split Vertically.

2 If necessary, open the CSS Styles panel. Click the Current button.

The CSS Styles panel will display styling for any selected element.

3 If necessary, select Live view and Live Code.

4 Click the Inspect button.

A notice appears at the top of the document window reporting that Inspect mode is most useful with certain workspace settings and offers to make the changes for you.

5 Click the *Switch Now* link to make the workspace modifications.

When Inspect mode is invoked, Dreamweaver highlights elements in color within Design view as the cursor passes over them. At the same time, the selected element is highlighted in Code view and the CSS Styles panel displays the pertinent styling information.

6 Pass the cursor over the text items within the bulleted list.

Dreamweaver highlights the <li> element in Code view and displays the appropriate formatting in the CSS Styles panel.

▶ **Tip:** If you click an element in the document window, Inspect mode is disengaged automatically.

7 Position the cursor over any of the bullets in the list.

Dreamweaver now highlights the `<ul>` element and its formatting. Once the element or formatting is identified, you can also use Code view to edit the HTML or any of the files.

Working in related files

The Related Files interface is practically black magic for coders and developers. It provides access to most of the attached files without having to look for them on the hard drive or server, or even to open them. Each of the related files is displayed at the top of the document window and is basically only a click away. For example, you can use the Related Files interface to access the CSS formatting right inside Code view.

1 Click **mygreen_styles.css** in the Related Files display.

The **mygreen_styles.css** file appears in the Code view split. You can edit the CSS rules directly in this window. Code Navigator can also help to locate specific rules. For instance, the rule that formats the `<h1>` element is stored in **mygreen_styles.css**. Using Code Navigator, you can locate the appropriate rule with a single click.

> **Tip:** Changes made in any related file are not saved when you save the HTML document itself. When you close the document, Dreamweaver will prompt you to save these files. Be sure to click Yes. Or, select File > Save All at regular intervals to prevent the loss of any changes in a crash.

2 Right-click the *Green Tips* heading and choose Code Navigator from the context menu. Select `.content h1` from the Code Navigator window.

The Split view Code window focuses on the `.content h1` rule in **mygreen_styles.css**. Code Navigator will focus on the pertinent rule no matter what file it is stored within.

3 Right-click the *At Home* heading. Using Code Navigator, select the `.AccordionPanelTab` rule.

Dreamweaver loads the **SpryAccordion.css** style sheet and focuses on the `.AccordionPanelTab` rule automatically. If desired, you can access CSS formatting *and* work on the source code in Code view simultaneously.

Accessing Split Code view

Why should coders be denied the ability to work in two windows at the same time? Split Code view enables you to work in two different documents or two different sections of the same document at once. Take your pick.

1   Select View > Split Code.

The interface displays two Code view windows: one focusing on the source code and the other on the CSS style sheet. You can use Code Navigator in Code view to access CSS formatting as you did in Design view.

2   Right-click one of the `<ul>` elements in the Spry Accordion. Choose Code Navigator and select the `.content ul, .content ol` rule.

The window displaying the CSS file focuses on the selected rule. You can even use Split Code view to display two views of the source code.

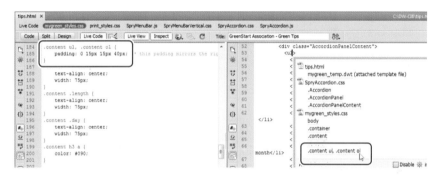

3   Exit Live Code view. Insert the cursor in the window displaying the CSS code. In the Related Files interface, select Source Code. Scroll to the bottom of the source code.

The window loads a second version of the source code. Both windows are editable and both can make changes to the selected document, if desired.

Commenting your code

Comments allow you to leave notes within the code—that won't render in the browser—that can provide important information, say to describe the purpose of certain markup, for example. Dreamweaver has a built-in feature for adding comments.

1   Open **tips.html** and switch to Code view, if necessary.

2   Insert the cursor before
    `<div id="Accordion1" class="Accordion" tabindex="0">`.

3 Choose Insert > Comment.

An HTML comment block appears with the cursor positioned in the center, where you will type a comment.

4 Type **Formatting for the Spry Accordion is applied by SpryAccordion.css located in the SpryAssets folder.**

5 Insert a new paragraph after the comment.

```
48   <h1>Green Tips</h1>
49   <!--Formatting for the Accordion widget is applied by SpryAccordion.css located in the SpryAssets folder.-->
50   <div id="Accordion1" class="Accordion" tabindex="0">
```

6 Switch to Design view and examine the page content at the top of the Spry Accordion.

7 Preview the page in Live view. Examine the page content at the top of the Spry Accordion.

8 Preview the page in the default browser. Examine the page content at the top of the Spry Accordion.

The HTML comment is visible in Code view, but it doesn't appear in Design view, Live view, or the browser.

9 Save all files.

You have used a number of techniques to make working with code easier and more efficient. You have learned how to select code and collapse/expand code; used the Code Navigator, Live Code, and Inspect mode to locate and edit CSS formatting; and added an HTML comment. Overall, you have learned that whether you are a visual designer or a hands-on coder you can rely on Dreamweaver to offer vital features and power to create and edit HTML code without compromises.

Review questions

1 What could cause code and the related tag selectors to appear grayed out?

2 True or False: Collapsed code will not appear in Design view or the browser until it is expanded.

3 How does Dreamweaver assist you in creating new code?

4 How can you check what CSS styling is being applied interactively by a dynamic JavaScript action?

5 What Dreamweaver feature provides instant access to most attached files?

Review answers

1 Code that is locked and uneditable—like that supplied by a Dreamweaver template—appears in gray.

2 False. Collapsing code has no effect on the display or operation of the code.

3 Dreamweaver provides code hinting for HTML tags, attributes, and CSS styling as you type, along with support for ColdFusion, JavaScript, and PHP, among other languages.

4 Switch to Split view and activate Live Code. Position the cursor to invoke the dynamic behavior. Right-click the item and choose Freeze JavaScript from the context menu. The behavior will be frozen temporarily so you can use Code Navigator to identify the applicable styling.

5 The Related Files interface appears at the top of the document window and allows users to instantly access and edit CSS, JavaScript, and other compatible file types.

17 PUBLISHING TO THE WEB

Lesson Overview

In this lesson, you'll publish your website to the Internet and do the following:

- Define a remote site

- Put files on the web

- Cloak files and folders

- Update out-of-date links sitewide

- Get pages from the web

 This lesson will take about 60 minutes to complete. Before beginning, make sure you have copied the files for Lesson 17 to your hard drive as described in the "Getting Started" section at the beginning of the book. If you are starting from scratch in this lesson, use the method described in the "Jumpstart" section of "Getting Started."

The goal of all the preceding lessons is to design, develop, and build pages for a remote website. But Dreamweaver doesn't abandon you there. It also provides powerful tools to upload and maintain any size website over time.

Defining a remote site

Dreamweaver is based on a two-site system. One site is in a folder on your computer's hard drive and is known as the *local site*. All work in the previous lessons has been performed on your local site. The second site, called the *remote site*, is established in a folder on a web server, typically running on another computer, and is connected to the Internet and publicly available. In large companies, the remote site is often only available to employees via a network-based *intranet*. Such sites provide information and applications to support corporate programs and products.

Dreamweaver supports several methods for connecting to a remote site:

- FTP (File Transfer Protocol)—The standard method for connecting to hosted websites.

- SFTP (Secure File Transfer Protocol)—A new protocol that provides a method to connect to hosted websites in a more secure manner to preclude unauthorized access or interception of online content.

- Local/Network—A local or network connection is most frequently used with an intermediate web server, called a *staging server*. Files from the staging server are eventually published to an Internet-connected web server.

- WebDav (Web Distributed Authoring and Versioning)—A web-based system also known to Windows users as Web Folders and to Mac users as iDisk.

- RDS (Remote Development Services)—Developed by Adobe for ColdFusion and primarily used when working with ColdFusion-based sites.

- Microsoft Visual SourceSafe—A version-control system that features check-in/check-out management and rollback capabilities.

In the next exercises, you'll set up a remote site using the two most common methods: FTP and Local/Network.

Setting up a remote FTP site

The vast majority of web developers rely on FTP to publish and maintain their sites. FTP is a well-established protocol, and many variations of the protocol are used on the web, most of which are supported by Dreamweaver.

1 Launch Adobe Dreamweaver CS5.

2 Choose Site > Manage Sites.

3 When the Manage Sites dialog box appears, you will see a list of all the sites that you may have defined. If more than one is displayed, make sure that the current site, DW-CIB, is chosen. Choose Edit.

4 In the Site Setup For DW-CIB dialog box, click the Servers category.

> **Warning:** To complete the following exercise, you must have a remote server already established. Remote servers can be hosted by your own company or contracted from a third-party web-hosting service.

> **Note:** If you are starting from scratch in this lesson, use the "Jumpstart" instructions in the "Getting Started" section at the beginning of the book.

The Site Setup dialog box has been redesigned in CS5 to provide more options. For example, the new Servers category now allows you to set up multiple servers, so you can test several types of installations, if desired.

5 Click the Add New Server icon.
   In the Server Name field, enter **GreenStart Server**.

6 From the Connect Using pop-up menu, choose FTP.

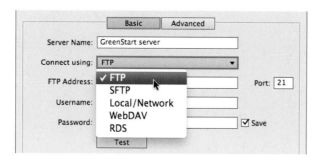

7 In the FTP Address field, type the URL or IP (Internet Protocol) address of your FTP server.

   If you contract a third-party service as a web host, you will be assigned an FTP address. This address may come in the form of an IP address, such as **192.168.1.000**. Enter this number into the field exactly as it was sent to you. Frequently, the FTP address will be the name of your site, such as **ftp.green-start.org**. Dreamweaver doesn't require you to enter the "ftp" into the field.

8 In the Username field, enter your FTP user name.
   In the Password field, enter your FTP password.

   Both fields may be case-sensitive, so be sure you enter them correctly.

9 In the Root Directory field, type the name of the folder that contains documents publicly accessible to the web, if any.

   Some web hosts provide FTP access to a root-level folder that might contain non-public folders—such as cgi-bin, which is used to store CGI (Common Gateway Interface) or binary scripts—as well as a public folder. In these cases, type the public folder name—such as *public*, *public_html*, *www*, or *wwwroot*—in the Root Directory field. In many web host configurations, the FTP address is the same as the public folder, and the Root Directory field should be left blank.

   ▶ **Tip:** Check with your web hosting service or IS/IT manager to obtain the root directory name, if any.

10 Select the Save option if you don't want to re-enter your user name and password every time Dreamweaver connects to your site.

11 Click Test to verify that your FTP connection works properly.

Dreamweaver displays an alert to notify you that the connection was successful or unsuccessful.

Adobe Dreamweaver CS5 connected to your Web server successfully.

OK

12 Click OK to dismiss the alert.

If you received an error message, your web server may require additional configuration options.

13 Click the More Options icon to reveal additional server options.

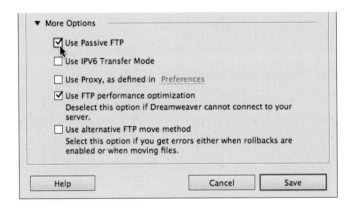

▼ More Options
☑ Use Passive FTP
☐ Use IPV6 Transfer Mode
☐ Use Proxy, as defined in Preferences
☑ Use FTP performance optimization
Deselect this option if Dreamweaver cannot connect to your server.
☐ Use alternative FTP move method
Select this option if you get errors either when rollbacks are enabled or when moving files.

Help   Cancel   Save

Consult the instructions from your hosting company to select the appropriate options for your specific FTP server. The options are:

- Use Passive FTP—Allows your computer to connect to the host computer and bypass a firewall restraint.

- Use IPV6 Transfer Mode—Enables connection to IPV6-based servers, which utilize the most recent version of the Internet transfer protocol.

- Use Proxy—Identifies a secondary proxy host connection as defined in your Dreamweaver preferences.

- Use FTP Performance Optimization—Optimizes the FTP connection. Deselect if Dreamweaver can't connect to your server.

- Use Alternative FTP Move Method—Provides an additional method to resolve FTP conflicts, especially when rollbacks are enabled or when moving files.

Troubleshooting your FTP connection

Connecting to your remote site can be frustrating the first time you attempt it. There are numerous pitfalls you can experience, many of which are out of your control. Here are a few steps you can take if you run into this problem:

- If you can't connect to your FTP server, first double-check your user name and password and re-enter them carefully. (This is the most common error.)

- Then, select Use Passive FTP and test the connection again.

- If you still can't connect to your FTP server, deselect the Use FTP Performance Optimization option, click OK, and click Test Again.

- If none of these steps enable you to connect to your remote site, check with your IS/IT manager or your remote site administrator.

    Once you establish a working connection, you may need to configure some advanced options.

14 Click the Advanced button. Select among the following options for working with your remote site:

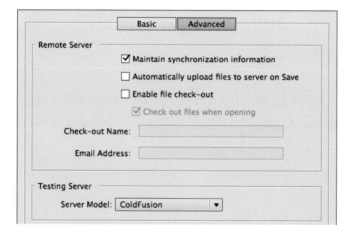

Maintain Synchronization Information—Automatically notes which files have been changed on the local and remote sites so that they can be easily synchronized. This feature helps you keep track of your changes and can be helpful if you change multiple pages before you upload. You may want to use cloaking with this feature. You'll learn about cloaking in an upcoming exercise. This feature is usually selected by default.

Automatically Upload Files To Server On Save—Transfers files from the local to the remote site when they are saved. This option can become annoying if you save often and aren't yet ready for a page to go public.

Enable File Check-Out—Starts the check-in/check-out system for collaborative website building in a workgroup environment. If you choose this option, you'll need to enter a user name for check-out purposes and, optionally, an e-mail address. If you're working by yourself, you do not need to select file check-out.

It is acceptable to leave any or all of these options deselected, but for the purposes of this lesson, enable the Maintain Synchronization Information option.

15 Click to save the settings in all open dialog boxes.

A dialog box appears, informing you that the cache will be re-created because you changed the site settings.

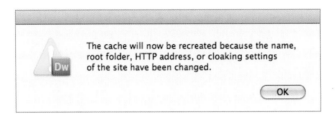

> The cache will now be recreated because the name, root folder, HTTP address, or cloaking settings of the site have been changed.
>
> OK

16 Click OK to build the cache. When Dreamweaver finishes updating the cache, click Done to close the Manage Sites dialog box.

You have established a connection to your remote server. If you don't currently have a remote server, you can substitute a local testing server instead as your remote server.

Establishing a remote site on a local or network web server

Warning: To complete the following exercise, you must have already have installed and configured a local web server.

Note: If you are starting from scratch in this lesson, use the "Jumpstart" instructions in the "Getting Started" section at the begin-ning of the book.

If your company or organization uses a staging server as a "middleman" between web designers and the live website, it's likely that you'll need to connect to your remote site through a local or network web server. You can also use this type of connection to connect to the testing server you installed and configured for Lesson 14, "Working with Online Data."

1 Launch Adobe Dreamweaver CS5.

2 Choose Site > Manage Sites.

3 When the Manage Sites dialog box appears, make sure that the current site, DW-CIB, is chosen. Click Edit.

4 In the Site Setup For DW-CIB dialog box, select the Servers category.

If you installed and configured a testing server in Lesson 14, it will be displayed in the server list. A check mark will appear under the Testing column. To use this server as the remote server, you simply select the Remote option.

> Here you'll select the server that will host your pages on the web. The settings for this dialog box come from your Internet Service Provider (ISP) or your web administrator.
>
> *Note: You do not need to complete this step to begin working on your Dreamweaver site. You only need to define a remote server when you want to connect to the web and post your pages.*

Name	Address	Connection	Remote	Testing
GreenStart Testing Server	Beta Drive/Applications...	Local/Net...	☑	☑

5 If you have a testing server already set up in the dialog box, select the Remote option.

If you haven't set up a testing server yet, you will need to first install and configure a local web server. In Windows, you may want to install Internet Information Services (IIS). Windows and Mac users can choose to install an Apache or ColdFusion server.

For detailed information about installing and configuring a local web server, see Lesson 14 or check out the following links:

- Apache/ColdFusion — tinyurl.com/2h8hey
- Apache/PHP — tinyurl.com/39p3gh
- IIS/ASP — tinyurl.com/2yx46y or tinyurl.com/ybhfaef

Once you set up the local web server, you can use it to upload the completed files and test your remote site. In most cases, your local web server will not be accessible from the Internet or be able to host the actual website.

6 Click the Add New Server (✚) icon.
In the Server Name field, enter **GreenStart Local**.

7 From the Connect Using pop-up menu, choose Local/Network.

8 In the Server Folder field, click the Browse (📁) icon. Select the local web server's HTML folder, such as **Applications/ColdFusion9/wwwroot/DW-CIB**.

9 In the Web URL field, enter the appropriate URL for your local web server, such as **http://localhost:8500/DW-CIB**.

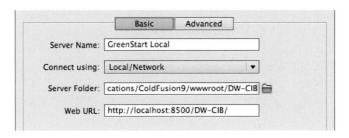

⬤ **Note:** The paths you enter here are contingent on how you installed your local web server and may not be the same as the ones displayed.

10 Click the Advanced button and, as with the actual web server, select the appropriate options for working with your remote site: Maintain Synchronization Information, Automatically Upload Files To Server On Save, and/or Enable File Check-Out.

Although it is acceptable to leave all three of these options deselected, for the purposes of this lesson select the Maintain Synchronization Information option.

11 If you'd like to use the local web server as the testing server too, select the server model in the Advanced section of the dialog box.

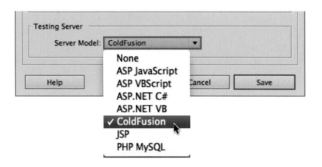

12 Click Save to complete the remote server setup.

13 In the Site Setup For DW-CIB dialog box, select Remote.
If you desire to use the local server as a testing server too, select Testing.
Click Save.

14 In the Manage Sites dialog box, click Done.
If necessary, click OK to rebuild the cache.

Only one remote and one testing server can be active at one time. One server can be used for both roles, if desired. Before you upload files for the remote site, you may need to *cloak* certain folders and files in the local site.

Cloaking folders and files

Not all the files in your site root folder may need to be transferred to the remote server. For example, there's no point in filling the remote site with files that won't be accessed or will remain inaccessible to the website user. If you selected Maintain Synchronization Information for a remote site using FTP or a network server, you may want to *cloak* some of your local materials. Cloaking is a feature of Dreamweaver that allows you to designate certain folders and files that will not be uploaded to or synchronized with the remote site.

Folders you don't want to upload include Template and Library folders. Some Photoshop (.psd), Flash (.fla), or other non-web compatible file types used to create your site also don't need to be on the remote server. Although cloaked files will not upload or synchronize automatically, you may still upload them manually, if desired.

Note: If you are starting from scratch in this lesson, use the "Jumpstart" instructions in the "Getting Started" section at the beginning of the book.

The cloaking process begins in the Site Setup dialog box.

1   Choose Site > Manage Sites.

2   Select DW-CIB in the site list and click Edit.

3   Expand the Advanced Settings category.
    In the Cloaking category, select the Enable Cloaking and Cloak Files Ending With options.

    The field below the check boxes should display the extensions .fla and .psd.

4   Insert the cursor after .psd and insert a space.
    Type **.doc .txt .rtf**.

Be sure to insert a space between each extension. Because these file types don't contain any desired web content, adding their extensions here will prevent Dreamweaver from uploading and synchronizing these file types automatically.

5   Click Save. Dreamweaver may prompt you to update the cache. Click OK to update the cache. Then, click Done to close the Manage Sites dialog box.

    You can also cloak specific files or folders manually.

6 Open the Files panel and click the Expand button to fill the workspace. If you are using the jumpstart method, skip steps 7 and 8. You should not have any lesson folders in your workflow.

Note all the lesson folders. These folders contain a great deal of duplicative content that is unnecessary on the remote site.

7 Right-click the lesson01 folder.
From the context menu, select Cloaking > Cloak.

8 Repeat step 7 for each of the remaining lesson folders.

Template and Library folders are not needed on the remote site because your web pages do not reference these assets in any way. But if you work in a team environment, it may be handy to upload and synchronize these folders so that each team member has up-to-date versions of each on their own computers. For this exercise, let's assume you work alone.

9 Apply cloaking to the Template folder.

A dialog box appears, warning that "Cloaking template or library files will only affect put or get commands, not any batch site operation."

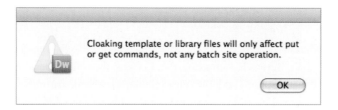

10 Click OK.

11 Repeat steps 9 and 10 to cloak the Library folder.

Using the Site Setup dialog box and the Cloaking context menu, you cloaked file types, folders, and files. The synchronization process will ignore cloaked items.

Wrapping things up

Over the last 16 lessons you have built an entire website from scratch, including dynamic applications and interactive content. But there are a few loose strings you need to tie up. Before you publish your site, you'll need to create one important file and make some crucial updates to your site navigation.

Creating a home page

The file you need to create is one that is essential to every site: a home page. The home page is the first page that most users will see on your site. It is the page that loads automatically when a user enters the domain name for your site into the browser window. Since the page loads automatically, there are a few restrictions on the name and extension you can use.

Basically, the name and extension depend on the hosting server and the type of applications running on the home page, if any. In many cases, the home page will simply be named *index*. But *default*, *start*, and *iisstart* are also frequently used.

As you learned earlier, extensions identify the specific types of programming languages used within a page. A normal HTML home page will use an extension of .htm or .html. Extensions like .asp, .cfm, and .php, among others, are required if the home page contains any dynamic applications specific to that server model. You may still use one of these extensions—if they are compatible with your server model—even if the page contains no dynamic applications or content. Be careful— in some instances, using the wrong extension may prevent the page from loading altogether.

The specific home page name, or names, honored by the server are normally configured by the server administrator and can be changed, if desired. Most servers are configured to honor several names and a variety of extensions. Check with your IS/IT manager or web server support team to ascertain the recommended name and extension for your home page.

1 Create a new file from the site template. Save the file as **index.html**.
   Or, use a filename and extension compatible with your server model.

2 Open lesson17 > resources > home.html.

3 Copy all the content and paste it into the MainContent region of the home page you created in step 1.

4 In the sidebar, replace the image placeholder with **bike2work.jpg**.

5 Replace the caption placeholder with **GreenStart has launched a new program to encourage Meridien residents to leave their cars at home and bike to work next month. Sign up and tell a friend.**

6 Edit the page title to read **GreenStart Association – Welcome to Meridien GreenStart**.

Note the hyperlink placeholders in the MainContent region.

7 Insert the cursor in the *News* link.
In the Property inspector, browse and connect the link to **news.html**.

8 Repeat step 7 with each link. Connect the links to the appropriate pages in your site root folder.

9 Save and close all files.

The home page is complete. Let's assume you want to upload the site at its current state of completion even though some pages have yet to be created. This happens in the course of any site development. Pages are added and deleted over time; missing pages will be completed and uploaded at a later date.

In this scenario, you have created pages for all but two links in your current navigation system: *Green Club* and *Member Login*. Development on the membership and login pages has been postponed for a short time, and the links must be removed. Additionally, a few of the existing links in the vertical menu are currently targeting pages that have been renamed, specifically the Products and Events pages. Before you can upload the site to a live server, you should update the out-of-date links and remove the dead ones.

Updating links

> **Warning:** There are several versions of this item in the lesson folders, be sure to open the correct one for your workflow.

All the out-of-date links are contained in the vertical menu, which is currently generated by a Library item. You can update the entire site by opening the Library item and updating the links.

1 Open the Assets panel and select the Library category.

2 Open the Library item that creates the vertical menu.

This Library item should be a component of all your current site pages.

3 Insert the cursor in the *Green Products* link.

In the Property inspector Link field, browse to the site root folder and select the dynamic Products file you created in Lesson 15, "Building Dynamic Pages with Data."

4 Insert the cursor in the *Green Events* link.

Link to the new dynamic Events page you created in Lesson 15.

Update the links for *2010 Events Calendar* and *2010 Class Schedule.*

5 Insert the cursor in the *Green Club* link.

Click the `<li>` tag selector and press Delete.

By deleting the parent element, both the *Green Club* and *Member Login* links are removed. You can re-create these links at a later date, if and when these pages are developed.

▶ **Tip:** Instead of rebuilding the entire link for the calendar and class schedule, simply change the extension of the filename **events.html** to match your current version.

6 Save **vertical-nav**. Dreamweaver will prompt you to update the site. Click Update.

The Update Pages dialog box appears, reporting what pages were and were not updated. If you do not see the report, click the Show Log option.

7 Click the Close button. Close **vertical-nav**.

The vertical navigation menu has been updated throughout the site, and your pages are now ready to upload, almost.

Prelaunch checklist

Take this opportunity to review all your site pages before publishing them to see if they are ready for prime time. In an actual workflow, you should perform most or all of the following actions, which you learned in previous lessons, before uploading a single page:

- Site-wide browser-compatibility check (Lesson 5, "Creating a Page Layout")
- Site-wide spell check (Lesson 8, "Working with Text, Lists, and Tables")
- Site-wide link check (Lesson 10, "Working with Navigation")

Fix any problems you find, and then proceed to the next exercise.

Putting your site online

For the most part, the local site and the remote site are mirror images, containing the same HTML files, images, and assets in identical folder structures. When you transfer a web page from your local site to your remote site, you are publishing, or *putting*, that page. If you *put* a file stored in a folder on your local site, Dreamweaver transfers the file to the equivalent folder on the remote site. It will even automatically create the remote folder, if necessary.

Using Dreamweaver, you can publish anything from one file to a complete site in a single operation. When you publish a web page, by default Dreamweaver asks if you would also like to put the dependent files, too. Dependent files are the images, CSS, Flash movies, JavaScript files, server-side includes, and all other files necessary to complete the page. Dreamweaver also automatically puts all the dependent files in the proper remote folders, matching their locations on your local site. If a folder doesn't exist on the remote server, Dreamweaver will create it.

You can upload one file at a time or the entire site at once.

1   Open the Files panel and click the Expand (⊟) icon, if necessary.

2   Click the Connects To Remote Host (⏣) icon to connect to the remote site.

If your remote site is properly configured, the Files panel will connect to the site and display its contents on the left half of the Files panel. The remote site should be empty or mostly empty. If you're using your testing server for your remote site, you may see the Connections folder and perhaps one or more files that were tested in Lesson 15. If you are connecting to your Internet host, specific files and folders may appear that were created by the hosting company. Do not delete these items unless you check to see whether they are essential to the operation of the server or your site.

3   In the local file list, select **index.html**.
On the Document toolbar, click the Put (⬆) icon.

Note:
If Dreamweaver doesn't prompt you to upload dependent files, this option may be turned off. To turn this feature on, access the option in the Site category in Dreamweaver preferences.

By default, Dreamweaver will prompt you to upload dependent files. If a file already exists on the server and you're only making minor changes to it, you can click No. Otherwise, for new files or files that have had extensive changes you should click Yes. Dreamweaver will then upload images, CSS, JavaScript, server-side includes (SSIs), and other dependent files needed to properly render the selected HTML file.

You can also upload multiple files or the entire site.

4   Right-click the site root folder for the local site.
From the context menu, choose Put.

A dialog box appears, asking you to confirm that you want to upload the entire site.

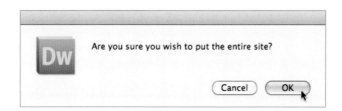

5   Click OK.

Dreamweaver re-creates your local site structure on the remote server. Note how none of the cloaked lesson folders were uploaded. Dreamweaver will ignore all cloaked items when putting a folder or an entire site. If desired, you can manually select and upload individually cloaked items.

▶ **Warning:** Among the pages you are uploading are several that incorporate dynamic content using ASP, ColdFusion, or PHP. The database and support files that are required for these applications but that are not stored within your site structure may not be uploaded during this operation. You will probably have to locate and upload these files and folders manually. In any case, be aware that additional configuration on the remote server will be required before these dynamic applications will function properly.

6 Right-click the Templates folder and choose Put.

Dreamweaver prompts you to upload dependent files for the Templates folder.

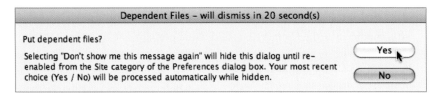

Note: A file that is uploaded or downloaded will automatically overwrite the file at the destination.

7 Click Yes to upload dependent files.

The Templates folder is uploaded to the remote server. Note how the remote Templates folder displays a red slash indicating that it is cloaked, too. At times, you will want to cloak local and remote folders to prevent these files from being replaced or accidentally overwritten. A file that is cloaked will not be uploaded or downloaded automatically. You will have to select any specific files and perform the action manually.

Note: When accessing Put and Get, it doesn't matter whether you use the Local or Remote pane of the Files panel.

The opposite of the Put command is *Get*. The Get command downloads any selected file or folder to the local site. You can *get* any file from the remote site by selecting it in the Remote or Local pane and clicking the Get 🔽 icon. Alternatively, you can drag the file from the Remote pane to the Local pane.

8 Use a browser to connect to the remote site on your network server or the Internet. Type the appropriate address in the URL field—depending on whether you are connecting to the local web server or the actual Internet site—such as **http://localhost/DW-CIB** or **http://www.green-start.org**.

Note: Dynamic pages created earlier may not display properly to a remote site until the database connections are configured properly. Be sure your configuration is complete before testing these pages.

The GreenStart site should appear in the browser. Click to test the hyperlinks to view each of the completed pages for the site. Once the site is uploaded, it is an easy task to keep it up to date. As files change, you can upload them one at a time or synchronize the whole site with the remote server. Synchronization is especially important in workgroup environments where files are changed and uploaded by several individuals.

Synchronizing local and remote sites

Synchronization in Dreamweaver is used to keep the files on your server and your local computer up to date. It's an essential tool when you work from multiple locations or with one or more co-workers. Used properly, it can prevent you from accidentally uploading or working on out-of-date files.

At the moment, the local and remote sites are identical. To better illustrate the capabilities of synchronization, let's make a change to one of the site pages.

1 Open **about_us.html**.

2 In the main heading, select the text *Green* in the name GreenStart.
Apply the CSS class `.green` to this text.

3 Apply the CSS class `.green` to each occurrence of the word green anywhere on the page.

4 Save and close the page.

5 Open and expand the Files panel. Click the Synchronize (⊛) icon in the Document toolbar.

The Synchronize Files dialog box appears.

6 From the Synchronize menu, choose the option Entire 'DW-CIB' Site.
From the Direction menu, choose the Get And Put Newer Files option.

Choose specific options in this dialog box that meet your needs and workflow.

> **Note:** Jumpstart users will see the name of the current site folder in the field menu.

7 Click Preview.

The Synchronize dialog box appears, reporting what files have changed and whether you need to get or put them. Since you just uploaded the entire site, only the file **about_us.html** should appear in the list, which indicates that Dreamweaver wants to put it to the remote site.

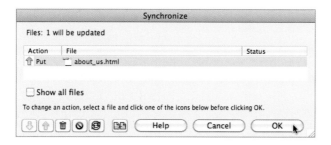

Synchronization options

During synchronization, you can choose to accept the suggested action or override it by selecting one of the other options in the dialog box. Options can be applied to one or more files at a time.

Get—Downloads the selected file(s) from remote site.

Put—Uploads the selected file(s) to remote site.

Delete—Deletes the selected file(s).

Ignore—Ignores the selected file(s) during synchronization.

Synchronized—Identifies the selected file(s) as already synchronized.

Compare—Uses a third-party utility to compare the local and remote versions of a selected file.

8 Click OK to put the file.

If other people access and update files on your site, remember to run synchronization *before* you work on any files to be certain you are working on only the most current versions of each file in your site.

In this lesson, you set up your site to connect to a remote server and uploaded files to that remote site. You also cloaked files and folders and then synchronized the local and remote sites.

Congratulations! You've designed, developed, and built an entire website and uploaded it to your remote server. By finishing all the exercises in this book, you have gained experience in all aspects of website design and development. Now you are ready to build and publish a site of your own. Good luck!

Review questions

1 What is a remote site?

2 Name two types of file transfer protocols supported in Dreamweaver.

3 How can you configure Dreamweaver so that it does not synchronize certain files in your site root folder with the server?

4 True or false? You have to manually publish every file and associated image, JavaScript file, and server-side include.

5 What service does synchronization perform?

Review answers

1 A remote site is a mirror image of your local site; the remote site is stored on a web server connected to the Internet.

2 FTP (File Transfer Protocol) and Local/Network are the two most commonly used file transfer methods. Other file transfer methods supported in Dreamweaver include WebDav, Visual SourceSafe, and RDS.

3 Cloak the files or folders for which you do not want to maintain synchronization.

4 False. Dreamweaver will automatically transfer dependent files, if desired, including embedded or referenced images, CSS style sheets, and other attached content.

5 Synchronization automatically scans local and remote sites, comparing files on both to identify the most current version of each. It creates a report window to suggest which files to get or put to bring both sites up to date, and then it will perform the update.

INDEX

for remote site on local/network web
server, 404
a:visited
hyperlink pseudoclass, 116
modifying hyperlink behavior and,
118–119
predefined rule function, 109

B

background colors
changing with CSS Styles panel, 68–69
for creating faux columns, 121–123
customizing Spry Accordion, 272
of menu items, 99–100
modifying, 96–97
removing for printing, 128–129
styling Spry tables and, 333–334
background, HTML default item, 42, 49
background images
adding to header, 91–92
customizing Spry Accordion, 272
inserting into footer, 69–70
removing for printing, 128–129
banner
adding as background image, 91–92
Flash, adding to web pages, 279–283
modifying page width to match, 96–97
behaviors. see also *specific behaviors*
Dreamweaver. see Dreamweaver
behaviors
hyperlink, 118–121
Berners-Lee, Tim, 22–23
Bindings panel
creating a recordset and, 355–358
creating detail pages and, 375–377
creating master page sets and, 363–365
bit depth, 194
block elements
defined, 26, 31
formatting size of, 48–49
Blockquote button, 240
<blockquote> elements
HTML tag functions, 32
for text indents, 167
Blur option, 299
<body> element
HTML tag functions, 32
in web page structure, 27
writing HTML code and, 23
body rule
changing background colors and, 68–69
changing page width and, 67
defining structural elements, 109
body text, HTML default item, 42
books
on CSS formatting, 52
on HTML, 31
border-collapse property, 175
borders
in CSS box model, 41
customizing Spry Accordion, 272–273
deleting Spry menu bar, 244–245

for images formatted with links, 226
object formatting of, 49
removing for printing, 129
styling table cells and, 176–177
styling tables and, 174–175
for text indents, 169–170
box model, CSS, 41

HTML tag functions, 32
inserting text and, 62
Brightness and Contrast, graphic tool, 214
Browse For File icon
for creating image-based links, 225–226
for creating internal links, 223–224
browser
checking compatibility of, 102
creating external links and, 226–227
graphics resolution for, 193
HTML elements and, 42–43
previewing behaviors in, 261–262
previewing Flash elements in, 278–279
previewing forms in, 290–291
previewing graphics in, 196–197
previewing links in, 219–222
previewing page text in, 160–162
previewing template-based page in,
134–135
previewing web pages in, 76–77, 88, 106
putting site online and, 412
browser-compatability check, 409
Browser Compatibility report panel, 255
Browser Navigation toolbar, 4
Bulletproof Web Design (Cederholm), 52
button(s)
Data Sources, 365
HTML element, on online forms, 292
radio, 292, 294, 306–307
submit, 311–312

C

<caption> elements
adding/formatting, 182–183
styling Spry tables and, 334
cascade theory, 44–45
cascading style sheets. see CSS (cascading
style sheets)
case-sensitivity
of FTP user name/password, 399
in Windows/Linux/Unix servers, 341
cell phones, for Internet access/usage, 83–84
cells
adjusting vertical alignment in table,
181–182
controlling column width in table,
178–179
styling table, 174–178
cellspacing attribute, 175
certification, Adobe, xvi
Change option, 299
Char Width field, 309
character entities, HTML, 33
Check Spelling dialog box, 184–185

checkboxes
<input> tag and, 294
inserting, 304–305
for online forms, 292
child pages
<caption> elements as, 182
producing, 138–140
class selectors, 51
classes
creating custom, 111–113
creating dynamic tables for, 362–363
Classic workspace, 11–12
Classroom in a Book
introduction to, ix
recommended lesson order, xi
client-based functionality, 228
cloaked folders/files
putting site online and, 411–412
setting up remote sites and, 405–406
closing tags, 23, 218
code-hints menu, 386–388
Code Navigator
correcting styling difficulties, 112
editing CSS using, 248–249
locating rules with, 392
modifying content/formatting, 98–99
working with, 388–389
Code view
adding/formatting <caption> elements
in, 182
applying/removing classes in, 112–113
creating lists in, 166–167
creating SSI in, 150–151
editing Library items in, 146
enforcing tabbing order in, 313
features of, 5–6
finding/replacing text in, 187–188
location of, 4
modifying formatting in, 98
options, 382–383
code, working with
accessing Live Code, 389–391
accessing Split Code view, 393
adding comments to code, 393–394
adding new code, 386–388
collapsing code, 384–385
expanding code, 385–386
overview, 380–381
review, 395
selecting code elements, 383–384
tools for, 382–383
using Code Navigator, 388–389
using Inspect mode, 391–392
working in related files, 392
Coder workspace, 12
Coding toolbar
expanding code and, 396
location of, 4, 13–14
selecting code and, 384–385
ColdFusion scripting language
adding repeat regions using, 361–362
creating a recordset using, 354–358

copying/pasting images and, 209
  inserting incompatible file types and, 206
Scalable Vector Graphics (SVG), 192
screen-media style sheet, 126–127
`<script>` elements
  Flash Player and, 282
  HTML tag functions, 33
  inserting Spry elements and, 252
  inserting Spry menus as Library items
    and, 252
scripting languages. see also specific
    scripting languages
  displaying data changes, 328
  supporting, 318
Secure File Transfer Protocol (SFTP), 398
select effects
  Ajax scripting and, 327
  styling Spry tables and, 333
  working with XML-based Spry table,
    337–338
Select External Editor dialog box, 210
Select File dialog box
  adding Flash animation and, 280
  creating internal links and, 223
  inserting go-to-detail-page behavior
    and, 374
Select Image Source dialog box
  inserting dynamic images and, 365–367
  inserting images and, 197–198
  working with Insert panel and, 201
Select Parent Tag icon, 384
Selector Name field, 111
selectors
  creating class and id, 51
  creating descendant, 110–111
  in CSS rule construction, 44
seminars, dynamic tables for, 362–363
server-based databases, vs. stand-alone
    databases, 343
server-based e-mail, 315–318
Server Behaviors panel
  adding repeat regions and, 361–362
  displaying multiple items and, 367–368
server models, 338–339
server-side functionality, 228
server-side includes (SSIs)
  creating, 150–151
  implementing menus as, 254
  inserting, 151–153
  updating, 153–155
  uploading, 411
  using, 149–150
SFTP (Secure File Transfer Protocol), 398
shading, 49
Sharpen, graphic tool, 214
Show Log option
  for updating links, 409
  for updating templates, 142
Show Region behaviors, 370
`.shtml` extension, 151, 153
`.sidebar1` rule
  for creating faux columns, 122–123

defining structural elements, 109
Site Name field, 57
Site Setup dialog box
  configuring testing servers in, 340
  creating sites for lessons, xi
  setting up Dreamweaver site and, 56–57
  setting up jumpstart site, xii
  setting up jumpstart site and, xi
  setting up remote FTP site and, 398–399
SiteCatalyst NetAverages, xvii
16-bit color space, 195
size
  altering text, 72–73
  of heading tags, 165
  of image, matching container, 94
  of image, optimizing with Property
    inspector, 212–213
  object formatting of, 48–49
  in raster graphics, 194
  of Spry menu bar, 242–246
Smart Objects (Photoshop), 207–208
smart phones, 195
software installation, Dreamweaver, x
Source (Bardzell and Flynn), 340
specificity theory, 47
spell-checking, 184–185, 409
Split Code view, 393
Split view
  creating field sets in, 300
  creating lists in, 166
  editing CSS in, 248
  features of, 6–7
  HTML vs. CSS formatting and, 39–40
  inserting checkboxes in, 305
  using Code Navigator in, 388
  working with CSS Styles panel in, 109
  writing HTML code in, 28
spreadsheets, 343
Spry Accordion widgets
  adding additional panels to, 271
  Code Navigator and, 388–389
  customizing, 272–274
  inserting, 269–271
  overview, 269
Spry Data, 233
Spry data placeholders, 360
Spry Data Set dialog box
  working with HTML data and, 329–331
  working with XML data, 336–338
Spry Data Set-Insert Table dialog box,
    331–332
Spry data tables
  discarding, 358–359
  rebuilding, 362–363
  styling, 333–334
Spry data types, 330
Spry Effects, 233
Spry Form widgets, 233
Spry framework
  creating detail pages using, 374–377
  creating master page sets using, 363–365

creating record paging behavior using,
    368–369
displaying images dynamically using,
    365–367
displaying multiple items using, 367–368
displaying record counts using, 371
features/tools of, 233
harnessing Ajax's power, 326
hiding paging controls using, 369–370
inserting go-to-detail-page behavior
    using, 374
styling dynamic data using, 371–374
working with HTML data, 328–332
Spry Layout widgets, 233
Spry menus
  customizing appearance of, 241–247
  editing CSS using Code Navigator,
    248–249
  inserting, 234–239
  inserting as Library items, 250–254
  modifying directly, 239–241
Spry Textarea
  incorporating text areas and, 307–309
  inserting menu elements and, 309–311
Spry Validation Radio Group, 306–307
Spry Validation Text Fields, 298–300
SSIs. see server-side includes (SSIs)
staging server, 398, 402
stand-alone databases, vs. server-based
    databases, 343
standard panel grouping, 7
Standard toolbar, 13–14
statistics, on website access/usage, 83
status bar, 220
streaming, of FLV files, 283
string Spry data type, 330
`<style>` elements
  CSS rules contained in, 106–107
  in CSS Styles panel, 106–107
  HTML tag functions, 33
Style Rendering toolbar
  displaying, 125–126
  location of, 13–14
style sheets. see CSS style sheets
Stylin' with CSS: A Designer's Guide (Wyke-
    Smith), 52
submit buttons, 311–313
Submit option, 299
SVG (Scalable Vector Graphics), 192
Swap Image behavior
  adding to hyperlinks, 268–269
  applying, 265–266
  removing, 267–268
Swap Image Restore behavior
  applying, 266–267
  removing, 267–268
synchronization, of local/remote sites,
    413–414
Syntax Coloring, 383
Syntax Error Alerts In Info Bar, 383

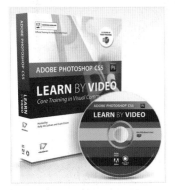

Learn Adobe Photoshop CS5 by Video:
Core Training in Visual Communication
(ISBN 9780321719805)

Learn Adobe Flash Professional CS5 by Video:
Core Training in Rich Media Communication
(ISBN 9780321719829)

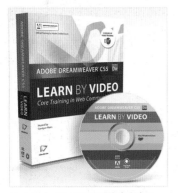

Learn Adobe Dreamweaver CS5 by Video:
Core Training in Web Communication
(ISBN 9780321719812)

The **Learn by Video** series from video2brain and Adobe Press is the only Adobe-approved video courseware for the Adobe Certified Associate Level certification, and has quickly established itself as one of the most critically-acclaimed training products available on the fundamentals of Adobe software.

Learn by Video offers up to 19 hours of high-quality HD video training presented by experienced trainers, as well as lesson files, assessment quizzes and review materials. The DVD is bundled with a full-color printed book that provides supplemental information as well as a guide to the video topics.

Up to 19 hours of high-quality video training

Tutorials-to-Go! Transfer selected movies to your iPhone, iPod, or compatible cell phone

Table of Contents never more than a click away

Watch-and-Work mode shrinks the video into a small window while you work in the software

Video player remembers which movie you watched last

Lesson files are included on the DVD

Additional Titles

- **Learn Adobe Photoshop Elements 8 and Adobe Premiere Elements 8 by Video** (ISBN 9780321685773)
- **Learn Photography Techniques for Adobe Photoshop CS5 by Video** (ISBN 9780321734839)
- **Learn Adobe After Effects CS5 by Video** (ISBN 9780321734860)
- **Learn Adobe Flash Catalyst CS5 by Video** (ISBN 9780321734853)
- **Learn Adobe Illustrator CS5 by Video** (ISBN 9780321734815)
- **Learn Adobe InDesign CS5 by Video** (ISBN 9780321734808)
- **Learn Adobe Premiere Pro CS5 by Video** (ISBN 9780321734846)

For more information go to **www.adobepress.com/learnbyvideo**

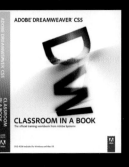

Meet Creative Edge.

A new resource of unlimited books, videos and tutorials for creatives from the world's leading experts.

Creative Edge is your one stop for inspiration, answers to technical questions and ways to stay at the top of your game so you can focus on what you do best—being creative.

All for only $24.99 per month for access—any day any time you need it.

creativeedge.com